FIVE

FOR

FREEDOM

FIVE

FOR

FREEDOM

THE AFRICAN AMERICAN SOLDIERS IN JOHN BROWN'S ARMY

EUGENE L. MEYER

Lawrence Hill Books
Chicago

Published by Lawrence Hill Books
An imprint of Chicago Review Press Incorporated
814 North Franklin Street
Chicago, Illinois 60610
ISBN 978-1-61373-571-8

Library of Congress Cataloging-in-Publication Data

Names: Meyer, Eugene L., author.
Title: Five for freedom : the African American soldiers in John Brown's army
/ Eugene L. Meyer.
Description: Chicago, Illinois : Lawrence Hill Books, [2018] | Includes
bibliographical references and index.
Identifiers: LCCN 2017045333 (print) | LCCN 2017046652 (ebook) | ISBN
9781613735725 (pdf) | ISBN 9781613735749 (epub) | ISBN 9781613735732
(kindle) | ISBN 9781613735718 (cloth : alk. paper)
Subjects: LCSH: Harpers Ferry (W. Va.)—History—John Brown's Raid, 1859. |
African American abolitionists—History—19th century. | Newby,
Dangerfield. | Anderson, Osborne P. (Osborne Perry), 1830–1872. |
Copeland, John A. (John Anthony) | Leary, Lewis Sheridan, 1835–1859. |
Green, Shields. | Brown, John, 1800–1859.
Classification: LCC E451 (ebook) | LCC E451 .M49 2018 (print) | DDC
973.7/116—dc23
LC record available at https://lccn.loc.gov/2017045333

Typesetting: Nord Compo

Printed in the United States of America
5 4 3 2 1

For James P. Shenton

Contents

Cast of Characters

Osborne Perry Anderson (1830–1872) was the sole survivor of the raid and in 1860 published the only insider account, *A Voice from Harpers Ferry*. Born in West Fallowfield, Chester County, Pennsylvania, he immigrated in 1851 to Chatham, Canada West, after passage of the 1850 Fugitive Slave Act. There he worked for Mary Ann Shadd Cary's *Provincial Freeman* newspaper and participated in John Brown's conference to adopt a provisional constitution for the future free state to be created in the Appalachian Mountains.

Fontaine Beckham (1796–1859) was a native of Culpeper County, Virginia, and serving his first term as mayor of Harpers Ferry when the raid occurred. He was also the stationmaster for the Baltimore and Ohio Railroad there. He was closely associated with Haywood Shepherd, a free man of color who also worked for the railroad and was the first fatality of the raid. The following day, Brown's men fatally shot Beckham on the streets of the town.

John Brown (1800–1859) was born in Torrington, Connecticut, and moved to Hudson, in northeastern Ohio, at the age of five. His father, Owen, a deeply religious man, instilled in him a strong sense of morality that included opposition to slavery. Brown lived in several states and had twenty children with two wives. Nine of his children did not survive to adulthood; three sons died in antislavery campaigns, one in Kansas and two at Harpers Ferry.

Brown was captured at Harpers Ferry, then convicted and hanged in Charlestown, Virginia (now Charles Town, West Virginia) on December 2, 1859. He is buried in North Elba, North York.

Mary Ann Shadd Cary (1823–1893), born in Wilmington, Delaware, and raised in West Chester, Pennsylvania, was the mixed-race daughter of a prominent abolitionist. An educated woman of strong feelings and fiery temperament, she taught school in Pennsylvania, New Jersey, and New York before immigrating in 1851 to Canada, where she became the first black female newspaper editor in North America, employing Osborne Anderson as a printer. After recruiting black men to join the Union Army, she moved to Washington, DC, where she was a schoolteacher and principal, obtained a law degree from Howard University, and was active in the suffragist movement.

John Anthony Copeland (1834–1859) attended Oberlin College in 1854 and participated in the Oberlin-Wellington rescue of escaped slave John Price. From his jail cell in Charlestown, Virginia, he wrote several poignant letters to friends and family prior to his execution on December 16, 1859.

Shields Green (1836–1859) was a fugitive slave from Charleston, South Carolina, who escaped on a ship after his wife died, leaving a young son. He eventually reached Rochester, New York, where he stayed for a time with Frederick Douglass, met John Brown, and advertised his services as a clothes cleaner. He was also known as "the Emperor," for his alleged descent from an African king, and as Esau Brown. Accompanying Douglass to a meeting with Brown at a quarry in Chambersburg, Pennsylvania, in August 1859, Green chose to "go with the old man."

Andrew H. Hunter (1804–1888), the prosecutor in the Harpers Ferry cases, later had high praise for John Anthony Copeland, saying he was the defendant who most impressed him with his demeanor and dignity. Hunter served two years in the Confederate Virginia House of Delegates and was an advisor to Gen. Robert E. Lee on civil and military matters.

Lewis Sheridan Leary (1835–1859) was a saddle and harness maker from Oberlin and related by marriage to Copeland. Leary left his wife and child to join John Brown's raid on Harpers Ferry and was fatally wounded while trying to escape across the Shenandoah River.

Dangerfield Newby (c.1820–1859) was the son of a white father and an enslaved mother (with a different owner). He was an enslaved skilled blacksmith who met and wed Harriet, a slave. Together, they had as many as seven children. Newby, freed when his father moved his family to Ohio in 1858, attempted to purchase the freedom of his wife and children. After that failed, he joined Brown in hopes of liberating his family.

Richard Parker (1810–1893) was the judge who presided over the trials of John Brown and associates John Copeland, Shields Green, John Cook, and Edwin Coppoc. He imposed the death sentence on all. Years later, he praised Copeland. Parker represented his district in the US House of Representatives from 1849 to 1851.

Haywood Shepherd (1815–1859), a free man of color from Winchester, Virginia, owned property and had a wife and children. He worked for the Winchester and Potomac Railroad, which ran daily trains to Harpers Ferry, where he assisted with luggage. The night of the raid, John Brown's men ordered Shepherd to halt and fatally shot him when he ignored them. He died the next day and was buried in Winchester. After his death, his wife and children moved to Washington, DC.

Henry A. Wise (1806–1876), a former diplomat and congressman, served as governor of Virginia from 1857 to 1861 and asserted state sovereignty in the prosecutions arising from John Brown's raid. He signed the death warrants for the convicted conspirators. A slaveholder in Accomack County on Virginia's Eastern Shore, Wise initially opposed the doctrine of secession but changed his position and served as a high-ranking officer in the Confederate Army.

Author's Note

Over time, place names change, sometimes completely, other times in subtle but discernible ways—the dropping of an apostrophe, the division of one word into two. Both changes have applied over time to Harpers Ferry, formerly Harper's Ferry, and Charles Town, formerly Charlestown. It is not entirely clear how, why, or when these changes occurred. In writing a book that refers both in quotations and in text to both towns, I have taken special care not to modernize or change the spelling as it appears within quotes from the period.

E.L.M.

Introduction

It was a weekday and the streets were deserted. Harpers Ferry looked very much like a ghost town, and indeed it was haunted, if not by ghosts then by history. Only sixty miles from Washington, DC, and yet seemingly more distant, Harpers Ferry was my introduction to a storied world so removed from the City of New York and its Long Island suburbs from which I'd sprung.

It was January 1965. On my way, I drove down a narrow winding road lined with ramshackle homes through the little hamlet of Knoxville, Maryland. I sensed that I had crossed some invisible threshold into Appalachia, that sad, poverty-stricken swath of rural America that most of the nation, through the Great Society programs of Lyndon Baines Johnson and Michael Harrington's bestselling book, *The Other America*, had then only recently rediscovered.

I drove across the Potomac and Shenandoah Rivers and made a sharp right turn onto Shenandoah Street, the main drag in Harpers Ferry. Beyond the beauty of the setting, at the confluence of two fabled rivers and with a hilltop view Thomas Jefferson once pronounced "worth a voyage across the Atlantic," is the town itself. Set between two limestone cliffs, Maryland Heights across the Potomac and Loudoun Heights across the Shenandoah, Harpers Ferry rises steeply from Shenandoah Street. Narrow, winding lanes ascend above the lower town to the heights where people lived and still live in mostly modest homes.

For more than half a century, Harpers Ferry was a factory town where federal workers made armaments for the US military. It gained fame—or infamy—for its central role in John Brown's raid: the catalytic event that was a prelude to a fratricidal, four-year civil war. During the war, the town changed hands eleven times, and the embers of that conflagration continue to smolder more than 150 years later. The town had been battered not only by humans but also by natural causes, and I was there for the Potomac River flood of 1996, which inundated the lower town, as also happened in 1972, 1936, 1924, and 1889.

Through the decades, another constant presence was the train that disappeared into and emerged from a mountain tunnel across the Potomac, eventually carrying commuters, many of them federal workers, to and from Washington's Union Station, or travelers to points much farther west. This view of trains crossing the Potomac bridge would become iconic for rail buffs, who park themselves and their cameras on the town's station platform to snap pictures.

As I write this, "Black Lives Matter" has entered the lexicon. They mattered back then, too, though not so much in the Southern slave states, except as commodities, as human chattel assessed for the purposes of sales, taxes, and inheritance, along with real estate, livestock, linens, dining room furniture, china, and other family heirlooms. They mattered, too, but in quite a different way, to abolitionist John Brown and the twenty-one raiders who gathered with him to attack Harpers Ferry and seize its federal arsenal in order to foment and arm a slave insurrection.

For five of the raiders, the cause was especially personal. They were African Americans, five for freedom who came together at this time and in this place on a sacred if ill-fated mission. Their names were Osborne Perry Anderson, John Anthony Copeland, Shields Green, Lewis Sheridan Leary, and Dangerfield Newby, and they have been largely forgotten.

My first visit to Harpers Ferry had come just a little more than five years after the centennial of the 1859 raid, which would not so much be "celebrated" as "observed" by a whites-only committee that generally regarded the martyred abolitionist not as a hero but as a fanatic, if not also downright insane. But these were nuances that would escape a young

Shafts of sunlight illuminate Jefferson Rock, situated above the lower town of Harpers Ferry. From this vantage point, the future president noted the view "worth a voyage across the Atlantic." *Eugene L. Meyer*

visitor from north of the Mason-Dixon Line in the still-somnolent but soon-to-be-stirring 1960s.

One sign did not go unnoticed. In one of the few restored buildings, my Northern sensibilities were jarred by the following message: "This is a facility operated in an area under the jurisdiction of the United States Department of the Interior. No discrimination by segregation or other means in the furnishing of accommodations, facilities, services, or privileges on the basis of race, creed, color, ancestry, or national origin is permitted in the use of this facility. Violations of this prohibition are punishable by fine, imprisonment, or both." This legal notice did not address the past I had come to glimpse but the still-uneasy present in the mid-1960s.

Entering the town then, I knew nothing of the African American soldiers in John Brown's little army. But as I glimpsed Brown's story during that brief visit, I became aware of Storer College, an institution seeded by a white Maine patron for the education of those newly freed after the Civil War. The college, on Camp Hill four hundred feet above the town, had a unique history, much of it tied to the raid and its legacy. Frederick Douglass had delivered a memorable speech there in 1881, extolling Brown but also singling out for praise Shields Green. In 1906, W. E. B. DuBois's Niagara Movement assembled there for its second and last meeting, with Henrietta Leary Evans, Lewis Leary's older sister, in attendance and addressing the group.

By the time of my visit, the school had only recently closed, a collateral casualty of the US Supreme Court's decision outlawing school segregation. West Virginia had used the ruling as an excuse to cut off state funding, and the alumni, many of them educated upper-middle-class African Americans residing in the District of Columbia, were fighting over the school's remains.

What I did not learn during my brief initial visit, and was not to know for another thirty-five years, was the story of the five African Americans with John Brown, men who had nobly committed their lives to free their enslaved brethren. Nor did I learn about Haywood Shepherd, the hapless black railroad baggage handler—a free man of color—who was the first to fall in the raid, fatally shot by one of the raiders, and how his death would make him an unlikely martyr to the Lost Cause of the Confederacy soon afterward and even on up to present times.

Such complexities were not widely known then. Moreover, so towering a figure was Brown that the five black Americans with him were consigned to the status of footnotes, if that, in the heroic narrative put forth even by those writers and historians sympathetic to the man.

Drawn by both its history and its beauty, I would return again and again over the years to Harpers Ferry, as the National Park Service renovated its rundown old buildings to period pristine condition. For many years, the black raiders were not part of its accompanying script.

Indeed, it wasn't until 2000 that I learned of the black raiders. On assignment for the *Washington Post*, I wrote about Osborne Perry Anderson, the Brown army's sole survivor, who had also written the only insider account of the raid. Born free in Pennsylvania, he met Brown in Chatham, Ontario, where, in 1858, the abolitionist convened a constitutional convention for his future republic of freed men and women. Several years after the raid, Anderson moved to Washington, DC, where he died in 1872 at the age of forty-two. He was buried in a black cemetery that would become a Metrorail parking lot, and his remains were among fifty-five thousand moved to another cemetery in the Maryland suburbs. A descendant, a man of military bearing named Dennis Howard, would be there to help dedicate a bronze plaque in Anderson's memory at the turn of the century. I would be there, too, to report on the event.

My curiosity was piqued, but in the newspaper business you write one story, and then you move on to other stories, with little time for reflection or follow-up. In the internet age, with constant deadlines, that is even truer today. But I knew there was more to this story, and when I accepted a buyout proposal from the paper four years later—the first of many subsequent buyouts—Osborne Perry Anderson was still on my mind.

My longer article, "Sole Survivor," appeared in the *Washington Post Magazine* in December 2004. I wondered why Anderson's version of events had for so long been discounted and dismissed, even by seemingly reputable historians. Stephen B. Oates, whose 1970 *To Purge This Land with Blood* was the first major John Brown biography in sixty-one years, told me, "Obviously for years racism played a part. He's been overlooked in the main because he's black. Second, turning up stuff on him has been real difficult. It's time this gentleman got his due." I agreed, and I took that as a challenge.

Throughout much of his life, Anderson's biography coincided in many places and at many times with that of Mary Ann Shadd Cary, who like Anderson was of mixed race. Born free in Delaware, she had migrated north to Canada in 1851, following passage of the noxious Fugitive Slave Law. In Chatham, she published the *Provincial Freeman*, an abolitionist newspaper, making her the first black female publisher in North America. Anderson, a printer by trade, soon joined her. After his escape from Harpers Ferry, he wrote his account of the raid, reportedly with her help. During the war, she was a recruiter for the US Colored Troops, hastily organized after the Emancipation Proclamation, and so, apparently, was Anderson. After the war, Shadd Cary moved to the District of Columbia, where she became Howard University's second female law school graduate and an elementary school principal. Anderson was in Washington, too, working as a messenger, according to a city directory. When he died a virtual pauper, Shadd Cary raised money for his funeral. Upon her death, she was buried at Harmony Cemetery, as was Anderson.

Maybe there's more there, I thought. Maybe not.

I could only speculate that, though Mary Ann Shadd Cary was married (and then widowed), the two had a romantic relationship. Some of her papers are housed in Howard University's Moorland-Spingarn Research Center, located in the basement of the school's iconic Founders Hall. In 2007, acting on my suspicions, I went there to examine her papers. I could find nothing about Anderson. If there had been a closer relationship, there was no evidence in the slim files. What I did find were two letters she'd reprinted in the *Provincial Freeman*. They were from John Copeland, another African American raider who had been captured at Harpers Ferry and hanged. The letters were dated shortly before his execution. They were addressed to his brother and to his family back in Oberlin, Ohio, and they were heartbreaking to read.

I had an epiphany. Yes, I realized, there was more to write, perhaps even a book's worth. But it could not be about Osborne Perry Anderson alone. It had to be about all five of the African Americans who went with Brown on the rainy evening of October 16, 1859—two killed during the raid, two later hanged, one escaped. Four of the five would be described as "mulatto," with white antecedents, including one who was the issue of a Caucasian father and an enslaved black mother. America's original sin of slavery, in all its messy complexity, would be manifest in their stories. Thus was born the idea for this book.

Yet it is not just about these five brave men. It is about the times and the country in which they were born, grew up, and died. It is about what came after, their forgotten legacies, their descendants, and the issues their lives and deaths raised then that still resonate today. As Dennis Frye, a National Park Service historian at Harpers Ferry once told me, "This is not a story of the past. This is a story from the past that's relevant to the present."

For me, it's also a personal milestone in a long journey. When I was a Columbia College senior trying to decide on a career, I was considering academia. But Jim Shenton, whose American history courses and Civil War seminar I eagerly devoured, had another idea. "You are more interested in history as it affects the present," he said. "You should be a journalist." Throughout, history has informed my work in journalism—and vice versa. So, too, has it been here.

1

Beginnings

From the nation's capital, Interstate 66 follows a southeasterly path through northern Virginia, from the plush DC suburbs of Fairfax and Loudoun Counties, among the nation's richest, into the horse country of Prince William, and Fauquier, with their still-rural settings, quaint small towns, commercial strips, and large-lot subdivisions—creeping suburbia.

This is also a route into the heart of what was once slave country, not something readily apparent to the casual visitor or even to most who live here. Of course there are road signs for Manassas Battlefield and Manassas Historic District. (Why historic? The signs give no hint.) Other signs signal Dulles Airport North, SplashDown Waterpark, Jiffy Lube Live amphitheater, and Freedom Aquatic and Fitness Center. Traffic streams by at 10 AM as you pause at the Virginia Welcome Center (sponsored by GEICO), which offers information about everything Virginian, with the notable exceptions of slavery and African Americans in the region's hidden history.

The exit 47 sign promises food but makes no mention of my reason for leaving the interstate, the Afro-American Historical Association, tucked away off the main street in The Plains (a town that promotes itself as "The Gateway to Hunt Country!"). It is here where past and present meet, as researchers pore over old court dockets and other records that track, to borrow Hannah Arendt's phrase, the banality of evil,

1

meticulously and shamelessly recorded in official documents reflecting the codification—indeed the normalization—of slavery.

The dry documentation of the South's "peculiar institution," such a striking euphemism for slavery, is manifest in the court dockets: A Free Negro charged with being found "without attested copy of his Register of Freedom, Fees paid to Jailor, discharged, September 23, 1850"; "Benjamin Berry, charged with permitting unlawful assemblage of Negroes, guilty by jury verdict, fined $25 plus costs, November 26, 1835"; another slave, charged with "being permitted to go at large + hire himself out," fine paid to court by his owner, Isham Keith, December 23, 1845. So it goes, page after page.

It could have been different, if only . . .

———————

The success of the American Revolution did not bode well for the new nation's then seven hundred thousand enslaved men, women, and children.

The British had played a major role in the trans-Atlantic slave trade, transporting an estimated 3.4 million slaves from Africa to North America before Parliament abolished the practice throughout the British Empire in 1807.

John Murray, the Earl of Dunmore and the colonial governor of Virginia in 1775, had issued a proclamation freeing runaway slaves willing to fight the revolutionaries. From the British warship HMS *Fowey*, he issued the invitation on November 14, sending ripples of alarm throughout Tidewater, a bastion of revolutionary fervor. The patriots responded by stressing that the British slave trade was an ongoing concern, and who knew what the fate of the renegade slaves would be should the Crown prevail. "Be not then, ye negroes, tempted by this proclamation to ruin yourselves," declared a letter published in Alexander Purdie's *Virginia Gazette* on November 17.

Soon after the proclamation, some three hundred slaves rallied to the British cause. They were called Lord Dunmore's Ethiopian Regiment.

As many as eight hundred men joined up. Then smallpox struck, and by June 1776, the month before the Declaration of Independence, the force was down to 150.

Of course, Great Britain lost the war, and a new nation was formed that made slavery as much a part of its founding documents as the contrasting Bill of Rights: for purposes of "representative" government, slaves would be counted as three-fifths of a person, an implicit recognition that an individual could be both chattel property and count in the Census.

The British would go on to abolish slavery in 1834. Yet, as American slaveholders would protest to critics, they had inherited a system that many claimed to despise and that was foisted upon them by the British slave trade between Africa and the colonies.

Southern ambivalence toward the "peculiar institution" was manifested in various ways. There were so-called emancipationists, presumably slaveholders who would gradually free their slaves, if only in their wills. There were also abolitionists, though not many. Further, there was sentiment to send slaves, whether born in this country or not, "back" to Africa.

In 1808, the US Congress banned the importation of more slaves into the United States. Some states, notably Virginia, also sought to restrict the importation of slaves by nonresidents. Such measures were certainly of no benefit to the slaves, who did not all suffer in silence.

The record shows that some Virginia slaves resorted to violence. From 1800 to 1833, the governor reviewed eighty-eight cases of slaves charged with murder or attempted murder of whites, twenty-seven of attempted poisoning, and fifteen cases of arson.

Gabriel, an enslaved blacksmith later known by his master's surname, Prosser, and who lived six miles outside of Richmond, planned a large slave revolt for the summer of 1800. The plan was discovered, resulting in the execution by hanging of Gabriel and twenty-five other slaves. As was typical following failed slave rebellions, the commonwealth and other Southern states adopted laws prohibiting slaves from becoming educated, assembling, or even being hired out. Other laws further restricted free persons of color. The growth of the free black population in Virginia was especially threatening to slaveholders, who saw them as potentially subversive agents who could embolden their slaves to revolt.

As white fears of living among such a large and potentially mutinous population heightened, efforts arose to reduce the black population through a movement seen as charitable and high-minded, one that would end slavery but also end the black presence. "Colonization," it was called, and some of the most progressive white citizens, impelled by their sense of morality and their opposition in principle to slavery, joined the effort to transport the slaves to Africa. It was a movement that was, ironically, inspired in part by the founding of Liberia on the west coast of Africa in 1819 by free persons of color; even into the 1850s, and later, it was a course of action black abolitionists seriously considered.

"Our own country is blackened with the victims of slavery, already amounting to nearly two millions of souls," the Auxiliary Society of Frederick County for the Colonization of the Free People of Colour in the United States wrote in its annual report, published in Winchester in 1820. The auxiliary had been formed three years earlier as a branch of the American Colonization Society, which a Presbyterian minister from New Jersey established in 1816. The society, an odd coalition of abolitionists and Chesapeake planters who owned slaves, had been instrumental in helping to found Liberia in 1821 for freeborn American blacks. While deploring the evils of slavery, the Virginia auxiliary at least was ready to cast blame elsewhere:

> While we deprecate the horrors of slavery, it is consoling to reflect that our country is originally guiltless of the crime, which was legalized by G. Britain under our colonial government, and consummated by commercial avarice, at a time when our powerless legislatures vainly implored the mother country to abolish a trade so impious in its character and dreadful in its consequences. In the year 1772, Virginia discouraged the importation of slaves by the imposition of duties, and supplicated the throne to remove the evil; and in 1778, having broken the fetters of British tyranny, she passed a law prohibiting the further importation of slaves.

The issue of slavery was front and center at a Virginia constitutional convention in 1829. Delegates from the mountainous western sections who owned few slaves generally supported abolition but also wanted the franchise rules rewritten so that slaves would not count in the Census, which determined representation. Antislavery advocate Alexander Campbell, a representative from the west, reported on one caucus he attended in Richmond "on the question of general emancipation" at which he "heard several gentlemen of Eastern Virginia, men owning hundreds of slaves say that, if Virginia would agree to fix upon some agreeable time, after which all should be free, they would cheerfully not only vote for it, but would set all their slaves free, for they believed slavery to be the greatest curse . . . a burden from which neither they nor their fathers could rid themselves, but which they could not and would not longer endure." In the end, though, a new state constitution was narrowly approved that maintained the status quo.

Such high-minded discussions, however, were soon overshadowed by other events. In 1830, there were 469,000 slaves in Virginia. In a six-month period from May through October, owners posted thirty-eight ads for runaways. Between 1820 and 1830, 265 slaves had gone missing.

In August 1831, Nat Turner, a slave born October 2, 1800, just five months before John Brown entered the world in Torrington, Connecticut, led an insurrection that resulted in the murders of fifty-one whites in Southampton County, in Southside Virginia. Turner was a preacher who believed himself to be a prophet, which infused the revolt with religious fervor. Turner had seen a vision as early as 1825 that seemed to propel him toward a destiny of bloody rebellion. His vision was even more apocalyptic on May 12, 1828, when, as he explained, "I heard a loud noise in the heavens, and the Spirit instantly appeared to me and said the serpent was loosened, and Christ had laid down the yoke he had borne for the sins of men, and that I should take it on and fight against the serpent, for the time was fast approaching when the first should be last and the last should be first."

Turner's first victims were his owner Joseph Travis, Travis's wife and nine-year-old son, and a hired hand, murdered as they slept. Two

"Horrid Massacre in Virginia," from the *Atlantic*, woodcut depicting the Southampton, Virginia, insurrection led by Nat Turner. *Library of Congress, LC-USZ62-33451*

other slaves killed an infant asleep in a cradle, then tossed it into the fireplace. It was August 31, 1831. Turner's hatchet-wielding posse grew as it freed more slaves, and the carnage continued over two days. The uprising was then quickly quelled, but its leader avoided capture for two months, until October 30, when a farmer found him, weak and emaciated and ready to surrender.

Twenty judges, all slaveholders, tried and convicted more than fifty slaves for participating in the rebellion, and the slaves were then executed. Outside the law, outraged whites responded with their own rampage, lynching blacks indiscriminately. Turner was hanged on November 11 in the county seat of Jerusalem, having been convicted of "conspiring to rebel and making insurrection."

Religion, many whites were convinced, could lead to no good when enslaved blacks were fair game for agitating preachers. "The case of Nat

Turner warns us," a writer in the Richmond *Enquirer* opined. "No black man ought to be permitted to turn a preacher through the country. The law must be enforced—or the tragedy of Southampton appeals to us in vain."

As was common following such rebellions, Nat Turner's led to laws across Southern states prohibiting African Americans to preach, or even to learn to read or write. In Mississippi, legislators declared it "'unlawful for any slave, free Negro, or mulatto to preach the gospel' under pain of receiving 39 lashes upon the naked back of the . . . preacher." North Carolina, Georgia, and Maryland passed similar laws. Virginia enacted a law prohibiting both slaves and free blacks from preaching or attending nighttime religious meetings without permission. The penalty: a public whipping of thirty-nine lashes.

The Nat Turner rebellion brought into sharp focus the awful dilemma—moral as well as physical, even perhaps existential—that faced white Southerners of conscience. "We may shut our eyes and avert our faces, if we please," wrote one anguished South Carolinian quoted in the Richmond *Enquirer*, "but there it is, dark and evil at our doors; and meet the question we must, at no distant day. . . . What is to be done? Oh! My God, I do not know, but something must be done."

Slaveholders and even whites who didn't have slaves were terrified by these events, fearful that they presaged more violent rebellions. As the South Carolinian had said, almost despairingly, something had to be done about slavery. That seemingly intractable issue would be put before the Virginia legislature when it convened on December 5.

The 1831–1832 session of the Virginia General Assembly would be the stage for an unprecedented sweeping debate over slavery, with opposing resolutions introduced to either abolish slavery or affirm it in perpetuity. As it convened, the legislature received some forty petitions from all corners of the commonwealth and signed by two thousand citizens variously urging emancipation (gradual or immediate), colonization, or the expulsion of free blacks, who might inspire further subversion or outright rebellion.

A petition for outright abolition came from the Virginia Society of Friends (Quakers) after their yearly meeting, held in Charles City

County, a plantation-rich rural area on the James River east of Richmond. The petition, dated December 14, 1831, urged the Senate and House of Delegates to declare slavery "an evil in our Country an evil which has been of long continuance, and is now of increasing magnitude. We allude to the condition of the African race in our land." Slavery, the petition said, was a "system repugnant to the laws of God, and subversive of the rights, and destructive to the happiness of man."

The petition asked for the emancipation of and granting of "the inalienable rights of men" to all enslaved African Americans in the commonwealth. "We, therefore, solemnly believe that some efficient system for the abolition of slavery in the Commonwealth and restoration of the African race to the inalienable rights of man is imperiously demanded by the laws of God, and inseparably connected with the best interests of the Commonwealth at large."

Another petition, this one from Buckingham County, in the central Piedmont south of the James, on December 16, also sought gradual emancipation but for less noble reasons. The petitioners feared the black population was growing too fast compared to the stagnant growth of the white populace. At current growth rates, the petitioners projected a black population by 1867 of 1,186,000 and by 1894 of 2,372,000, resulting in "four colored to one white person," which it deemed "a menace." Loudoun County petitioners for gradual emancipation also wanted all free blacks expelled from the commonwealth. Petitioners from Northampton County, at the southern tip of Virginia's Eastern Shore, suspecting free blacks of "dangerous intrigues with our slaves," wanted them all shipped to Liberia. Similarly, on December 9, Fauquier County residents sought state funding "to transport free persons of Color to the coast of Africa, and also, the power to purchase slaves and transport them likewise." In neighboring Culpepper, petitioners worried that slaves and free blacks were taking jobs away from white workers and urged that no blacks—free or enslaved—be "placed as an apprentice in any manner whatsoever to learn a trade or art under severe and onerous penalty."

In the midst of this outpouring of citizen sentiment, Governor John Floyd delivered his annual message to the Virginia General Assembly on December 6, 1831. In calling for stricter measures controlling slaves, coupled with colonization, he evoked the horrors of the Turner rebellion:

> Whilst we were enjoying the abundance of last season, reposing in the peace and quiet of domestic comfort and safety, we were suddenly aroused from that security by receiving information, that a portion of our fellow-citizens had fallen victims to the relentless fury of assassins and murderers, even whilst wrapped in profound sleep, and that those bloody deeds had been perpetrated in a spirit of wantonness and cruelty, unknown to savage warfare, even in their most revolting form.
>
> In August last, a banditti of slaves, consisting of but few at first, and not at any time exceeding a greater number than seventy, rose upon some of the unsuspecting and defenceless inhabitants of Southampton, and under circumstances of the most shocking and horrid barbarity, put to death sixty-one persons, of whom the greater number were women and helpless children.

To crush the rebellion, Floyd had called on infantry regiments, augmented by naval forces. With slaves stirred up by black preachers like Turner and by free persons of color, Floyd warned, "all communities are liable to suffer from the dagger of the murderer and midnight assassin."

Without a hint of irony, the governor praised Virginians for "resisting the usurpations of England" in the Revolutionary War in order "to guard against oppression, that her citizens might enjoy the liberty which belonged to them, and appropriate to their own use that which their labor had earned." That Virginians of color should enjoy the same liberty and compensation for their own labor did not enter the equation. Of course, he was referring to tariffs and the unfairness of the federal government's imposition of them—an appeal to states' rights. As to slavery, he recommended the "revision of all the laws, intended to preserve in due subordination the slave population of our state."

The House of Delegates proceeded to appoint a thirteen-member panel to consider citizen petitions and the governor's recommendations, along with the possibility of deporting the commonwealth's free black population. The 133 delegates owned a total of 1,131 slaves, with the smallest number, 36, in the western part of the state, which was dominated by small farmers who weren't slaveholders, and the largest, 574, in Piedmont, Virginia.

Advocating gradual emancipation was no less than Thomas Jefferson Randolph, the third president's oldest grandson. Randolph, a delegate from Albemarle County, had managed Monticello during his grandfather's later years and, as his executor, sold his assets, including 130 slaves. He would go on to serve as chancellor of the University of Virginia and as a colonel in the Confederate Army. Offered as a substitute amendment, his plan would apply to children born into slavery on or after July 4, 1840. They would become the property of the state and serve an apprenticeship to pay for their freedom and after reaching a certain age—females at eighteen, males at twenty-one—be "removed beyond the limits of the United States."

On January 21, 1832, less than six years after the death of his grandfather, the author of the Declaration of Independence whose personal defense of slavery contrasted sharply with the noble principles he had espoused, Randolph addressed the House of Delegates. It was an extraordinary declaration, grappling with the inherent contradictions of slavery in a land of liberty and reflecting the speaker's utter dislike of the system he'd inherited and would three decades later be called to defend as a commissioned colonel in the Confederate Army.

Seeking to soften the impact of his plan on the current slaveholding generation, Randolph said, "It in fact operates upon posterity, and not upon the present generation. . . . Eighty years will be necessary to work their entire extinction [of slavery]; a period sufficiently long for their removal, and the introduction of free labour. If in 1920, the law is found irremediable, a repeal of the law will place us where we now stand." He envisioned the plan to be put to a referendum, in which all Virginians, whether slaveholders or not, would be permitted to vote.

In reaching for what he considered a middle ground, Randolph said he "cannot concur with the hopeless, ultra absolutism of the South." The legislative debate, he noted, had variously "construed slaves as exclusively persons, as exclusively property, or partaking of jointly of both." Under the Constitution he added, slaves "are deemed persons, degraded it is true, into two fifths, but nevertheless as persons, and representation is claimed for them as such."

His plan, introduced into the House of Delegates, was not well received.

Finally, legislators offered dueling resolutions in January 1832, one rejecting emancipation outright, the other calling for a statewide referendum on the subject.

The legislature deadlocked on the issue, the lawmakers opting to await further public responses. In almost inverse proportion, the votes on the resolutions fell clearly within geographical lines: antislavery sentiment was strongest in the west; anti-abolition strongest in Piedmont and Tidewater, whose plantation economies depended on slave labor. Ultimately, none of the resolutions was adopted.

In 1941, historian Joseph Clarke Robert would describe the debate preceding the votes as the "final and most brilliant of the Southern attempts to abolish slavery," and "the line of demarcation between a public willing to hear the faults of slavery and one intolerant of criticism."

Henceforth, instead of liberalizing their policies toward slaves and slavery, the Southern states began to institute even more draconian "black laws" that severely punished slaves adjudged guilty of even the most minor infractions and also greatly restricted the rights of free persons of color.

In Virginia, the General Assembly declared that any slave or free person of color who wrote or printed material that encouraged slave insurrection or rebellion was to be whipped, as was anyone convicted of rioting, assembling unlawfully, trespassing, or making speeches deemed seditious.

Meanwhile, fervid if futile deportation efforts continued. Proponents included Henry A. Wise, the future governor who would among his last executive acts sign the death warrant of John Brown. Wise, then a member of the US Congress, addressed the Virginia Colonization Society on January 10, 1838. In his remarks, he staunchly defended slavery in America as divine in its origin but also advocated the colonization cause. Should it succeed, he suggested, it could be said, "Africa gave to Virginia a *savage* and a *slave*; Virginia gives back to Africa a *citizen* and a *Christian*."

Between a diplomatic assignment to Brazil and his 1856 election to governor, Wise corresponded with a Reverend Nehemiah of Boston, who was writing a book on "The South Side View of Slavery." Wise was then living on the Virginia Eastern Shore of the Chesapeake Bay in his home county of Accomack, whose population included 3,295 free persons of color and 4,987 enslaved. Wise wrote that he had emancipated only one of his slaves but would never free another. Wise's grandson Barton H. Wise wrote in his 1899 biography of Henry that his grandfather "considered the race fit only for the patriarchal state of a Southern plantation." He did not consider emancipation "desirable for either the negroes or the whites, as long as the blacks were to remain here, and that the amalgamation of the races was against the laws of nature."

Yet this leading Southern politician could also write, to another correspondent, that with white officers in command he "would fight a regiment of them against any foreign troops who could land on our shores. They are faithful, they are brave. . . . [The slave] owners love their race and its qualities better than their pseudo-friends the abolitionists do."

In 1860, Virginia had more slaves than any other Southern state: 490,865. And Virginia slaves were valued at $375 million, one-eighth of the $3 billion valuation for the South's entire enslaved population.

Into this strange and complicated world of paradox and perdition were born the five African Americans who would accompany John Brown to Harpers Ferry decades later: Dangerfield Newby, the oldest, born in 1820 in Virginia; Osborne Perry Anderson in 1830 in Pennsylvania; John Anthony Copeland in 1834 and Lewis Sheridan Leary in 1835, both in North Carolina; and Shields Green in 1836. They were destined to enact a raid that led to a war in which 750,000 perished and whose ghosts still inhabit the land.

2

One Bright Hope

From 1822 to 1894 the old courthouse in Brentsville, Virginia, was the political, social, economic and judicial center of Prince William County, an antebellum world cast literally in black and white and now an ethnically diverse suburb of Washington, DC. After the railroad bypassed Brentsville and went through Manassas instead, the county seat moved 8.4 miles north. Brentsville lost its prominent position, the old courthouse fell into disuse and disrepair, the town withered and faded into obscurity.

Today's Brentsville, northwest of Marine Corps Base Quantico, is a quaint relic of that bygone era. There are two churches and a handful of houses lining Bristow Road. The courthouse along with the adjacent jail—"Mobile Tour Stop #5" on a Virginia Civil War trail—have been restored. Taken together, this could be a pristine Norman Rockwell image of pastoral, small-town America, one to be remembered fondly, if at all. But terrible things happened here.

The three-acre "Public Lot" adjoins the courthouse. This "was a lively place," a sign says, "especially when the Court was in session. Then, the atmosphere was festive. Farmers and tradesmen sold their wares while citizens visited, gossiped, and discussed cases." Several yards from the courthouse steps, in front of a one-room schoolhouse built in 1928 for whites only, the sign also tells visitors that "property and estate auctions occurred in front of the Courthouse." And it mentions, almost

Brentsville courthouse today. Slaves were bought and sold here on days when the court was in session. *Eugene L. Meyer*

incidentally, in passing, "Some auctions included slaves." Indeed. Thus, one broker advertised in the November 30, 1844, *Enquirer* newspaper:

> SALE OF NEGROES AND LAND. By virtue of a deed of trust executed to the subscriber by Charles Thomas, I will on the first Monday in February next, that being Prince William Court Day, if fair, if not the next fair day, offer for sale at BRENTSVILLE, in the County of Prince William, the tract of land in said deed mentioned; also eight slaves, consisting of one man, one woman, and the residue boys and girls, they constitute a lot of valuable Slaves.

On January 12, 1846, another broker advertised a trustee's auction to be held at Brentsville. Up for sale was the estate of the late John Hooe Jr., including four hundred acres adjoining Occoquan Run and "ALSO the following Slaves to wit: REUBEN, NANCY, LUCINDA, THORNTON,

PARIS, MARY ANN, BILL, SALLY, LAURINDA, BETSY, HORACE, DAVY, and RICHARD, and the increase of the females since the date of the deed."

In other words, newborn babies.

In the changing economy of Piedmont, Virginia, some slaveholders valued cash more than their human property, and they took advantage of the robust market demand where more enslaved workers were needed—on the growing cotton plantations farther south. Thus, broker W. R. Millam announced he was willing to travel the circuit to neighboring counties in search of buyers. His June 19, 1853, ad, with key words highlighted in capital letters, read:

> NEGROES WANTED—The Subscriber wishes to purchase for the New Orleans market 200 LIKELY YOUNG NEGROES, for which he is prepared at all times to pay the highest cash price. He will attend regularly the Courts of Culpeper, Rappahannock and Prince William. All communications addressed to me at Warrenton, Fauquier County, Va. will be promptly attended to. Liberal commissions paid for information leading to purchase.

It was, of course, all legal, routine, normal—yet also immoral, disruptive, inhumane. This was simply how business and life were conducted in the Commonwealth of Virginia and throughout the slave states of the American South. What mattered most was that the laws, however horrible their impact on the slaves themselves, were adhered to, with proper procedures followed and assessed values taken into account.

Here even supporting abolition could invite public recrimination, or worse. Consider the case of New York–born Solomon Brill, a Prince William constable whose antislavery views brought him before the court of public opinion. At a citizens' meeting in Brentsville to investigate his "soundness or unsoundness . . . upon the subject of slavery," the erstwhile critic recanted. Brill "fully and freely stated his opinions . . . , saying that he recognized the right of property in slaves, and that he considered Slavery neither a social, more nor political evil." Brill was then "declared exonorated [*sic*] from all suspicions as to his unsoundness upon the subject of slavery."

In another case, in 1857, a man identified as Crawford was jailed and charged with declaring "that he was an Abolitionist that he believed a Negro as good as he was if he behaved himself; and maintaining by speaking that persons have not the right of property in slaves under the law." His fine was $312.50, the equivalent of $8,436.52 in 2017 dollars.

That same year, a grand jury indicted John C. Underwood. Commented the *Baltimore Sun*, "The fact that Mr. Underwood is a justice of the peace for this county has tended in no small degree to add to the excitement and has called forth violent expressions of feeling in regard to the matter." In November, Underwood was convicted of "uttering and maintaining that owners have no rights of property in their slaves." His punishment was also a fine of $312.50. The court denied his motion for a new trial and his argument on appeal that the law was unconstitutional. Underwood was a New Yorker who had railed against slavery at the 1856 Republican convention in Philadelphia. Upon his return from the convention, outraged citizens demanded that he leave the state. Noted a British publication, the *Quarterly Review*, "It appears that even in Virginia, once the most civilised in the Union, to speak against slavery, though in another state, is punishable by exile."

It was here in Brentsville, in 1860, that Harriet Newby and her children—all enslaved—were "sold south" by their owner, a newly widowed woman with two small children in pecuniary need. The Newby family saga is a long and tragic love story. It neither began nor ended here. Rather, it was part of a national drama—and trauma—that echoes still today.

It is a complex story, illuminating the darker corners of the already dark side of slavery, in which owners could be cruel or kind and could father children with slaves and then abandon, deny, or somehow support and provide for their mixed-race offspring. The Newby story is particularly poignant, reflecting a mixture of courage, conviction, and desperation.

Theirs was not the mythical and storied land of large plantations, of acres upon acres of cotton or tobacco worked by legions of enslaved field hands. Rather, this was Piedmont, a land of claylike soil and mostly small farms where the cash crops were wheat and corn, with dairy cows, hogs, and sheep. While some worked the fields, many of the enslaved men were tradesmen hired out to do work for others, providing another source of income for their owners.

As a slaveholder, John Fox, a Fauquier County landowner who leased out slaves in Fauquier and at least three other counties, was an exception to the small-lot slaveholders typical of the time and place: he would ultimately own 193 slaves. They included the biracial children of a white man, Henry Newby, and Elsey, his common-law enslaved wife.

The oldest of Henry and Elsey's eleven children in this literally blended family was Dangerfield Newby. He would grow to be six feet two inches tall, a man with light skin and angular features. In the only known photograph of him, taken perhaps in 1859 when he was thirty-nine, he is sporting a mustache and goatee and has deep bags under both eyes. His visage is grim and he appears to be well into middle age.

What happened to the Newby clan is well documented in the public record, plumbed by descendants and by at least one academic, Philip J. Schwarz, a professor emeritus of history at Virginia Commonwealth University. "This is my *Diary of Anne Frank*," he has said. "Whenever I feel I might be complacent or detached from my studies of slavery, I touch base with Dangerfield Newby. It is a sacred obligation for us to follow through on our studies of human beings, especially if their history is hidden."

The complicated and tangled legal and family relationships between owners and their slaves are documented in often confusing and some-times contradictory court records. Beyond the public files are the stories of the people themselves, and the physical setting in which the economic system of slavery endured and defined attitudes toward human chattel.

The adjoining counties of Fauquier and Culpeper and nearby Prince William all depended on slave labor. There were free blacks but far fewer than enslaved. Prince William's 1860 population of 8,213 comprised 5,690 whites, 2,356 slaves, and 167 "other" free persons. In 1860, Culpeper's population of 12,063 was 59 percent black, including 6,675 slaves and 429 free blacks. Fauquier County, with a total population in 1860 of 21,706, counted 10,455 slaves—the largest number of any county in the Piedmont—and 821 free persons of color.

It was not uncommon for owners to free their slaves in their wills and to provide funds for them to travel to a free state, most often Ohio. The move was virtually required, because an 1806 law required manumitted persons to leave the state after a year, unless granted special court dispensation. In some instances, court records revealed, at least by implication, the mixed-race children of owner and slave. Richard McCartney Chichester, born in Fauquier on February 27, 1769, recorded his will on September 16, 1818, and it was probated on March 24, 1830. He left nothing to three of his four "lawful children" and bequeathed 10 percent of his estate to his "natural daughter" Sarah and the rest to the seven sons of Peggy Moran, whom he had purchased around 1810 and freed prior to 1815. Under the terms of the will, some of the inherited money was to support Peggy. The seven sons were each described in the Virginia *Free Register* as "bright mulatto." Their father's name was not recorded. Readers could draw their own conclusions. The Morans used the inheritance in 1833 to buy 117 acres from Chichester's estate for $485.55. The area, four miles southeast of Warrenton, is today a country crossroads known as Auburn Corner.

John Fox, described as an eccentric bachelor, was one of the area's largest slaveholders (and is said to have had children with one of his slaves).

Fox died in April 1859 with a large "inventory" of slaves, but not without providing for them. Under his last will, dated November 15, 1839, all his enslaved workers were to be freed, his personal and real estate property sold, and all debts collected and paid. Of the $30,000 he estimated would be left over, $10,000 was to be used to buy his emancipated slaves land "of good quality" in Ohio and the rest divided among them so they could travel there, build homes, and purchase horses, livestock, household and kitchen furniture, and "plantation utensils and a supply of such clothing and provisions as may be necessary to enable them to live comfortably."

Fox named his sister Elizabeth P. Blackwell as the executor, but she was unable to carry out the task—she died only months after he did. Lengthy litigation ensued. The case dragged on until 1871. Ultimately,

Fox's 335-acre Great Run Tract in Fauquier was divided into thirty-three equal lots for his former slaves. Separately, his 401-acre March Farm was sold in five lots. Measured in 2017 dollars, Fox's 1859 estate was substantial: $30,000 would be the equivalent of $844,000; and $10,000, of $281,500.

Among Fox's slaves was Elsey Pollard, born in 1799 in Fauquier County. Said to be of Native American, African, and European descent, she would bear the children of a white farmer, Henry Newby, born in 1783 in adjoining Culpeper County. Newby, who was acquainted with Fox, owned 248 acres in Culpeper near the Rappahannock River. By local standards, he was not a large slaveholder or plantation owner. His crops—wheat, corn, cattle, pigs, sheep, dairy—did not require as much labor as, say, tobacco, formerly a major cash crop in Piedmont.

Together, Henry and Elsey would have eleven children, all of whom were Fox's property. Dangerfield, born about 1820 in Fauquier County, was the oldest. He would become a skilled blacksmith, and Fox hired him out to work on the fourteen-mile Rappahannock River Canal, built from 1829 to 1849 with forty-four locks and twenty dams and intended to eventually link Waterloo and Fredericksburg. Court records indicate several instances in which Fox sued for payment from individuals who had agreed to retain the services of "slave Dangerfield." In 1844, Fox leased Dangerfield to Henry S. Halley for sixty dollars. When Halley didn't pay up, Fox sued. The two men settled the suit when Halley agreed to compensate Fox "with a hat and blanket—a winter and summer suit of clothes."

Henry Newby would acknowledge Elsey as "a colored woman who resides with me" and as "the mother" of his children, leaving almost all his estate and a horse to her and their son William. Though it was never official, Elsey recorded their marriage date as December 1, 1818, in a widow's pension application she would later file. In the 1840 and 1850 Census, Henry's black family members were listed with him, an unusual accounting for enslaved persons. It is noteworthy that though they lived with Newby, they still belonged to John Fox, their apparently benign owner.

In September 1858, with Fox's permission, Henry took Elsey and several of their children—including Dangerfield—to Ohio. Just living there made them free. In 1856, the Ohio Supreme Court had decided a case, *Anderson v. Poindexter*, in which an enslaved worker from Kentucky, by establishing residence in Ohio, even though hired out by his owner, had become a free man. The court declared the chains of slavery must be broken "and crumble to dust, when he who has worn them obtains the liberty from his oppressor, and is afforded the opportunity of placing his feet upon our shore," referring to the Ohio River that separated the slave and free states.

On September 17, 1858, further cutting his ties to Virginia, Henry sold his land in Culpeper. Six days later, he freed four slaves: his twenty-six-year-old daughter Evaline and three of her children, all of whom moved to Shenandoah County, closer to the Blue Ridge Mountains and to the area's strong Quaker presence. The other Newbys settled in Bridgeport, Ohio, in Belmont County, directly across the Ohio River from Wheeling, and then as now overwhelmingly white. In 1860, the town's population was 641. Bridgeport today, still small with only about 1,800 people, sits in the shadow of the I-70 bridge connecting Ohio and West Virginia. To reach their destination the Newbys followed the valleys and mountain passes, likely passing through Harpers Ferry, then traveling north to Wheeling.

By then, Dangerfield Newby had established a relationship with Harriet, a slave born in 1825 who belonged to the Jennings family in Brentsville. Together, Dangerfield and Harriet had several children—the exact number is uncertain, but several sources put their offspring at seven.

Among their children was a daughter, Elmira, who had her first child in 1859 with an Edward M. Groves, an eighteen-year-old white youth from an adjoining farm. To further confuse the picture, she lived on land belonging to a John Dodd, who died in 1860, bequeathing her to a son, Richard Dodd. Within a year or two, she would marry Eli Tackett, by then a free man, with whom she had more children. After his death, she married another black man, George Jefferson Brown. She hid her Newby origins, perhaps due to Dangerfield's notoriety. It was

Dangerfield Newby joined John Brown to free his enslaved wife and children.
Library of Congress, LC-USZ62-7817

revealed only much later on the death certificates of her children Agnes Pinn, Carrie Brown, and Washington A. Tackett. To further befuddle genealogists and family historians of the extensively intertwined branches of the family tree, Dangerfield had a sister also named Elmira, who went to Ohio with Henry and Elsey.

Dangerfield had been negotiating with Lewis Jennings to purchase his wife and children. According to some accounts, Jennings wanted

$1,000—more than $28,000 in today's dollars. In Ohio, Dangerfield was a man on a mission, determined to obtain sufficient funds. Reportedly, he used his trade and skills as a blacksmith to earn the money. An unsympathetic local newspaper later called it "his begging expedition through this region," but noted he carried a letter of recommendation from Thomas C. Theaker, a machinist and wheelwright in Bridgeport who became a US congressman and commissioner of the US Patent Office.

Accounts vary on Dangerfield's negotiations with the physician Jennings in Brentsville, but it seems clear that he did not have enough money to meet the asking price for his wife and one child. By one account, money was paid and kept without their manumission. By another, the doctor agreed to a price and then reneged on it. Dangerfield had nearly $742 (almost $21,000 in 2017 dollars) in three certificates of deposits, plus interest, in the Bridgeport branch of the Bank of Ohio—$327 deposited in December 1858, $242 in March 1859, and $149 undated but likely that summer.

Bridgeport, the Newby family's base, served as an important station on the Underground Railroad and, owing to its location on the Ohio River, was a port of entry in a free state for fugitive slaves en route to Canada after the Fugitive Slave Act. Though details are lacking, Dangerfield was said to have been actively involved in their efforts. His travels within the state took him to another abolitionist stronghold in June 1859, to Ashtabula County in northeastern Ohio.

There he stayed with T. Smith Edwards, a key figure in the Underground Railroad in the town of Dorset, and worked as a blacksmith for Edwards's older brother Lawrence at his shop across the street. The Edwards home was a haven for traveling abolitionists. In the spring of 1859, the travelers bunking there came to include John Brown, who stayed for two weeks. Others who sojourned in Edwards's home were John Brown Jr. and other raiders: Osborne Anderson, Aaron Dwight Stevens, and Quaker brothers Barclay and Edwin Coppoc.

Newby's feelings and loyalty to his family were strong and immutable. Years after the raid, his brother Gabriel would describe Dangerfield as "a quiet man upright, quick tempered and devoted to his family." Alfred Hawkes, a Brown associate in Pennsylvania who also stayed at the Edwards home, described him as a "light mulatto," six feet two inches tall "in his stockings." Hawkes, in a 1909 interview, recalled learning of another pivotal event in Newby's earlier life in Virginia: "He had a son, 16 or 17 years old, who used to work with him in a shop. One day they took him out and sold him. Dangerfield made a row, ran away, and so got his own freedom. Then he earned money and sent it south to redeem his wife, but they kept the money and the woman, too."

Enter the charismatic Brown, who offered Dangerfield yet another way to liberate his family. Given the otherwise dim outlook, Dangerfield was susceptible to his pitch. It was Hawkes, who in Ashtabula taught Newby how to load and shoot a gun, who introduced Brown to Dangerfield as a potential recruit for the cause. "We aren't buying men," Brown said, suspicious of his motives. But Dangerfield wasn't looking to be "bought" or paid. He had another motive for joining Brown. Brown, in turn, wanted able and willing soldiers who would not waiver when the time came.

If Dangerfield would join Brown's band in seizing the federal arsenal at Harpers Ferry and inciting a slave insurrection, he could in this way accomplish the goal of freeing his wife and family, or so he thought. The situation in Brentsville was not promising, which seemed to make the radical option of joining Brown seem more appealing. The sale of his children and Harriet, a house servant to her owner's wife, seemed increasingly likely. Their probable fate would be to be sold "down the river" to the dreaded plantations in Louisiana, where slavery was said to be far harsher than in the upper South.

While in Ashtabula County, Dangerfield would receive three letters from Harriet, each one sounding more desperate than the last. The letters came from Brentsville and were dated April 11, April 22, and August 16. Each was addressed to "Dear Husband" and signed "Your affectionate wife." According to John Brown historian Jean Libby, "The last letter was delivered to the Lindsey farm in Ashtabula County, where Oliver Brown and others were working and getting ready to go Harpers Ferry."

In the first, Harriet reported that "Mrs. gennings," her master's wife, had been sick after giving birth to a baby girl. Harriet had to stay with her "day and night," so there was no time to write. Their children were all well, she reported. "I want to see you very much. . . . Oh, Dear Dangerfield, come this fall without fail, money or no money. I want to see you so much. That is one bright hope I have before me." In a postscript, she urged, "Write soon if you please."

Harriet received a letter back on April 22 and responded the same day. She had written him several weeks before at "Bridge Port," but said, "I fear you did not receive it, as you said nothing about it in yours. . . . I wrote in my last letter that Miss Virginia had a baby—a little girl. I had to narse her day and night. Dear Dangerfield, you cannot imagine how much I want to see you. Com as soon as you can, for nothing would give more pleasure than to see you. It is the grates Comfort I have is thinking of the promist time when you will be here. Oh, that bless hour when I shall see you once more." And then she added this encouraging tidbit of family news: "My baby commenced to Crall to-day." P.S. "Write soon."

Finally, on August 16, Harriet wrote again, right after hearing from Dangerfield: "It is said Master is in want of money. If so, I know what time he may sell me an then all my bright hops of the futer are blasted for their has ben one bright hope to cheer me in all my troubles, that is to be with you, for if I thought I should never see you this earth would have no charms for me. Do all you Can for me, witch I have no doubt you will. I want to see you so much."

And with added urgency, she wrote, "I want you to buy me as soon as possible for if you do not get me some body else will . . . their has ben one bright hope to cheer me in all my troubles that is to be with you."

Dangerfield would carry these letters with him to the Kennedy farm in Maryland, five miles from Harpers Ferry, where Brown's raiders would assemble and prepare for their futile assault. Dangerfield could not have foreseen that he would be the first fatality among the raiders, that Harriet and their children would indeed be sold south. He could still hope, but only misery lay ahead.

"You know you're in Fauquier County when the air changes," boasts the Fauquier County Department of Economic Development. "Whether you're here for a day or for a while, be prepared to take a step back to a simpler time—and take a deep breath."

Sherrie's Stuff on Main Street in Warrenton, the Fauquier County seat, sells Sherrie Carter's folk art and a variety of small gifts. While her husband manages a Costco store, she runs the shop and creates her pieces in the back. Descended from Dangerfield and Harriet Newby, she has been researching her family's history for years and seems alternately protective of and overwhelmed by it. She says she has boxes of files, including notes given her by Philip J. Schwarz, the now retired historian whose book *Migrants Against Slavery* includes a Newby chapter.

Her great-great-grandfather, she says, was Eli Tackett, John Fox's slave who filed a lawsuit to obtain the land Fox had promised in his will. Tackett's wife, Elmira, Harriet's daughter with Dangerfield, would be Sherrie's great-great-grandmother.

I want to see where the family lived as slaves, and Sherrie provides directions. It's just seven miles south on US Route 15/29 (James Madison Highway), past the Clark Brothers Guns Shooting Range and the sign for Granite Vineyards to Fauquier Motel at Covingtons Corner Road, then a right to the T intersection with Botha Road, the site of Foxville Farm Estates and Doddsville.

The backroads in Fauquier, Rappahannock, and Culpepper Counties have names that are, to the knowing, historic: Foxville Road, Newbys Shop Road, Newby's Crossroads. But there are no historic markers. In what passes for Foxville, Foxville Farm Road leads to Foxville Turn, with several 1980s homes on large lots. On the road going in, a sign declares that a Neighborhood Watch is in effect and urges citizens to "report suspicious activity" to the county sheriff.

Just west lies Doddsville, a smaller subdivision named for the other slaveholder tied to the Fox and Newby clans. Hidden in the woods behind the homes is a small Fox family grave. Just east is St. James

Baptist Church, founded in 1866 as Foxville Baptist Church by those formerly enslaved by John Fox, on land he left them. Directly across Botha Road is the farm where Elmira lived. Except for a smattering of mid-twentieth-century houses, it remains what it was: sparsely settled country.

Before Lewis Jennings moved to Brentsville, taking her with him, Harriet lived in Fauquier, on the Merry Run plantation, named for the stream that flows south into the Rappahannock River. Today's Merry Run Lane, a private gravel road, is south of Foxville off Freemen's Ford Road.

Sherrie's great-great-grandfather Tackett was running the Fox plantation when John Fox died, freeing Tackett. In 1860, the lawyers officially made him the manager. Less than a mile from Foxville, I turn left onto St. Paul's Road and then make an unauthorized left turn onto Tackett Lane, marked "private." The entrance sign says, "Speed limit 15 mph. Slow—children playing—residents and guests only." There are eleven homes, most built in the early 1990s, on large lots. Ninety-four percent of the residents are Caucasian, according to a Spokeo analysis.

Tackett Lane intersects at a T with another street that ends in a cul-de-sac and has six more homes on up to nine acres, each built from 2001 to 2003, with 2017 estimated market values of from $450,000 to $680,000. It is appropriately called Fox Plantation Lane.

3

The Oberlin Connection

Oberlin, Ohio, is now much as it was in 1859, "an oasis surrounded by corn," as my bed-and-breakfast host described it, though the surrounding crops may have been more wheat, hay, and cows than the corn and soybeans that now blanket the countryside. During my visit, Oberlin College was hosting the city's second annual Weekend of Action, focusing on a variety of liberal causes. Then came the 2016 presidential election. In stark contrast to most of Ohio, Oberlin voted overwhelmingly for Hillary Clinton over Donald Trump: 4,724 to 425. When it became clear that Trump had won, many shocked students chose to skip classes to ruminate, mourn, and attend a panel on the "the day after."

Both currently and historically, Oberlin is unarguably the progressive heart of the Buckeye State and home to a college that was the first to admit female and black students.

Inspired by the Second Great Awakening, a Protestant religious revival movement akin to the civil rights ministries of the 1950s and 1960s, Oberlin stood as a bright beacon on the Underground Railroad, a safe haven for escaped slaves.

Nine miles south of Oberlin, straight down the road that is today Ohio State Route 58, lies the village of Wellington, as blue collar and country as Oberlin is educated, white collar, and worldly. In September 1858, it would play a dramatic part in the lives of John Anthony

Copeland and Lewis Sheridan Leary, and a key role in the roiling rebellion that would culminate in the raid at Harpers Ferry.

Copeland and Leary were related through marriage: two Leary sisters had married two Copeland uncles. Leary was a harness maker, a year younger than Copeland. John Anthony, briefly a student in the preparatory division of Oberlin College, had gone to work with his father as a carpenter and lived in a house on Morgan Street—which turned out to be right around the corner from the bed-and-breakfast I stayed in while doing my research in Oberlin.

Both men would be described as "mulatto." Indeed, Leary's father was a white Irishman. Copeland had straight black hair, a thin mustache, and high-boned facial features. Both were free persons of color and had immigrated, several years apart, to Oberlin from their native North Carolina. And there begins their story, with deep—and deeply entangled—roots in America's past.

––––––––––––

John Anthony's father, John C. Copeland, was born in 1808 near Raleigh, North Carolina, the son of his white master and a slave. John C.'s owner-father died when he was eight. The will freed him but left him no inheritance. On his own, he became a skilled and sought-after carpenter, working from 1835 to 1840 on the reconstruction of the statehouse in Raleigh after an 1833 fire. On August 15, 1831, he married Delilah Evans, a light-skinned domestic worker born free in Hillsborough in 1809 and educated in schools for free persons of color. Her family claimed descent from Revolutionary War general Nathanael Greene. The Copelands would have eight children, of whom John Anthony, born August 15, 1834, in Raleigh, was the oldest.

The Copelands were free, but their freedom was restricted and anything but secure.

Following the Nat Turner slave rebellion in Southside Virginia in 1831, North Carolina was among several Southern states to adopt laws restricting the movement and liberties of free blacks. Whites viewed them suspiciously as potentially subversive, able to inspire slave escapes or, worse, murderous insurrections like Turner's. The new laws required them to carry papers attesting to their free status and to present them if asked when traveling from county to county. There was always the threat, too, that when away from their homes, they would be taken for fugitive slaves and sold into bondage, their families torn asunder, their freedoms wrenched away.

In North Carolina, free blacks, previously allowed to vote, were disenfranchised under the state's new 1835 constitution. John C. Copeland, a Democrat, had proudly exercised his franchise, voting for Andrew Jackson in presidential elections. But now he had no electoral voice.

Determined to see their children educated and grow to adulthood in a land of liberty, John and Delilah Copeland made plans to immigrate with their four sons and three daughters to a free state. Their publicly stated destination: Cincinnati.

But due to legal restrictions and threats, the Copelands needed to carry papers from white patrons in North Carolina attesting to their good character. These letters of transit would ease or at least improve their chances of a safe, unfettered trip to the North.

Frances Devereaux, a relatively benevolent slaveholder, wrote in Raleigh on March 3, 1843, that Delilah Copeland, "about to remove to the city of Cincinnati, Ohio with her husband and family," was "an intelligent, discreet and sober-minded woman . . . for many years an acceptable and pious member of the Presbyterian Church . . . and has . . . uniformly conducted herself with the utmost propriety." To add to this glowing testimonial, she said, "I devoutly pray that Divine Providence may abundantly bless her, her husband and children, wherever they may find a home."

John Copeland received a similarly favorable recommendation from some twenty-five prominent white citizens, including merchants, an attorney, a newspaper editor, and county and state officials. Having long known Copeland, they wrote, they took

> pleasure in saying that he has uniformly sustained a fair, honest and industrious character in this community. He is a house carpenter by profession, and esteemed by those who best know him to be a

very good one, and could when work was to be obtained, always find employment in this city, but the recent hard times, together with the years increase of his family, have wisely, in our opinion, induced him to look out for a new home in a more plenteous and populous country; and we doubt not that John, wherever he may locate himself, will prove to be a highly useful and valuable citizen.

Unlike his Presbyterian wife, John Copeland was a Methodist, conducting "himself in a quiet, humble and Christian-like manner. Therefore, as a testimonial of our respect and confidence," his endorsers wrote, "we cheerfully tender to him this recommendation; and devoutly pray that the multiplied blessing of a kind Providence may accompany him whithersoever he may find a home upon the bosom of this green earth."

The Copelands did not go it alone. Allen and Temperance Jones and their children joined them. Among the seven Jones children were Elias Toussaint Jones, born in 1833 and a lifelong friend of John Anthony, and James Monroe Jones, who would graduate from Oberlin College in 1849 and immigrate to Chatham, Ontario, where his skill as a gunsmith earned him the nickname "Gunsmith" Jones. Also along was John Lane, a twenty-eight-year-old blacksmith born free in Fayettevillle. In March 1843, they set out in a wagon train, fourteen travelers in search of a safe haven. In Tennessee, they added one more, an orphaned baby boy named Reuben Turner, whom Delilah found and the Copelands would informally adopt and take with them to Oberlin. Their route next took them through Kentucky and into Ohio.

In planning their trip, they had looked for locales where their families would be not only free but also safe from rogue slave catchers who did not distinguish between free persons of color and escaped slaves. On a friend's recommendation, they headed for New Richmond, Ohio, on the banks of the Ohio River. They crossed the river from Kentucky to the town of Ripley, home to several prominent abolitionists and a key stop on the Underground Railroad, thirty-two miles upriver from New Richmond. Approaching their destination, they met a white farmer named Tibbitts, who offered them food and overnight lodging at his house. He also invited them to an antislavery meeting in the Presbyterian church that evening. They attended, but still fearful of unscrupulous slave catchers, they took their seats in back in case they had to make a quick exit.

At the meeting, they met the Rev. Amos Dresser, who that year had helped draft a strong antislavery statement for the church. Dresser had earned his abolitionist bona fides when he was arrested and whipped in Nashville for belonging to an Ohio antislavery society and distributing antislavery literature. Undaunted, he returned to Ohio to lecture against slavery and study at the Oberlin Collegiate Institute (renamed Oberlin College in 1850), graduating in 1839.

Acutely aware of the dangers facing even free blacks in the waterfront border town, he advised the Copeland party to consider settling instead far inland, in Oberlin, thirty-three miles west of Cleveland and where five routes converged, making it a major station on the Underground Railroad.

Leaving the families behind and following Dresser's directions, John C. Copeland, Allen Jones, and John Lane embarked on the 232-mile scouting expedition. Twenty miles from Oberlin, they stopped for further directions at a tannery, whose hostile workers told them flippantly that Oberlin no longer existed, that it had "sunk." Well then, Copeland said, he would "go on and look into the chasm."

They reached Oberlin on a Sunday, the Sabbath, not normally a day of travel. What they found shocked them. People of both races walked together, prayed together, went to school together. They were even buried together—a degree of closeness in death that was then uncommon in the North and continues to be exceptional in many parts of the country. Further, there was no smoking in public, and the citizens eschewed any Fourth of July celebration because the Declaration of Independence excluded blacks. Instead, the big day in Oberlin was August 1, the date on which slavery was abolished in the British colony of Jamaica in 1834. "Oberlin is peculiar in that it is good," noted John Jay Shipherd, Oberlin College's founder. The town was unlike anything the newcomers had ever seen or even imagined. Allen Jones notified his family back in New Richmond that he "had found paradise and was going to stay." Soon the scouting party returned with their families to make Oberlin their permanent home.

Even in a free state like Ohio, Oberlin was a rarity. It was truly integrated, to the chagrin of slave catchers, one of whom likened the town to an "old buzzard's nest where the negroes who arrive over the underground railroad are regarded as dear children."

Given the origins of many of the town's residents, the prevailing sentiments were not surprising. Yankees flocked to the flat, fertile land in north central Ohio. They brought with them a Puritan ethic and strong moral convictions, including fierce opposition to slavery. Most of Oberlin's early residents were New Englanders. During the first decade of the nineteenth century, the land they immigrated to was known as the Connecticut Western Reserve.

They chose the wooded tract for what they first called the Oberlin Colony specifically as a site for the Oberlin Collegiate Institute. Their purpose was to establish an ascetic Christian community and educational institution to promote the glory "of God in the salvation of men" and to inspire students to join the ministry. They named the school—and the town—after a French pastor, Johann Friedric Oberlin, whose efforts to better the education and living standards of his parishioners won wide praise.

The school opened its doors in 1834 with forty-four students and a year later declared that admission would be "irrespective of color," a change approved by a one-vote majority of the trustees, who declared that "the education of people of color should be encouraged and sustained." By 1856, the school counted forty "colored students" out of a total enrollment of eight hundred. Uniquely, Oberlin had become the first college in America to admit African Americans.

The stories of John Brown and, ultimately, his raid on the federal arsenal at Harpers Ferry are inextricably linked to Oberlin. Owen Brown, John Brown's father, had moved his family from Connecticut to the Western Reserve in 1805 when John was five. Owen, a tanner and farmer, settled in Hudson, south of Cleveland, and there John Brown grew to manhood. The senior Brown was an Oberlin trustee from 1835 to 1844, casting his vote in favor of racially integrating the school. But the progressive policies of town and gown were not universally applauded, even in Ohio. On four occasions, the state legislature tried, unsuccessfully, to repeal the college's charter.

John Anthony Copeland was a boy of eight when the family settled in this accepting environment. His father put his carpentry and cabinet-making skills to good use building several homes, while also championing the abolitionist cause. John Anthony attended school but took time off to work with his father, enabling him to become a skilled carpenter and joiner. He grew into an intense and purposeful teenager and young man. He was, abolitionist William Cooper Nell would write, "determined and unyielding in all that he considered right and just." He was, too, "affable, friendly . . . sarcastic, but not sportive. He was reflective and serious, yet cheerful and easy to please." He was "never sullen or fretful. . . . He was punctual, positive, and self-reliant." He didn't seek "wealth or glory," nor did he "buy anything he didn't need."

In 1854, he enrolled in Oberlin College's preparatory department, completing one year but going no further. His old chum Elias Toussaint Jones also enrolled but completed his studies. During this period, John Anthony also taught school in Logan County, 133 miles southwest of Oberlin.

He frequently attended antislavery meetings held nights at the "Liberty School," where escaped slaves learned to read and write. While there he always paid "sympathetic attention" to the stories of the fugitive bondsmen. "To knock off the shackles which find four millions of men, women, and children, was the sole object of his life," Nell wrote. In debate, when others were unruly, he would solemnly rise, his hands in his pockets, "and with that sarcasm . . . would do much in assisting the Chair to restore order." Even when he did not speak out, he showed his emotions, recalled John Mercer Langston, a native Virginian who would later represent his home state in Congress during the Reconstruction Era. He did so, Langston, wrote, "often by the deep scowl of his countenance, the moist condition of his eyes and the quivering of his lips."

But Copeland could also be vocal. Addressing audiences, he would denounce the "lamentable fact that in the American nation, under its flag of liberty and independence, four and a half millions of human beings are today crushed under iron-shod oppression. We are all regarded . . . as mere things." Given this, he said, referring to Ohio laws restricting the rights of free blacks, "how can we appreciate immunities conferred upon us by a partial public sentiment?" And beyond words, he advocated action. Invoking a hero of Greek liberation killed in 1823, he reminded listeners that "Bozzaris died, but Greece became independent." Likewise, referring to the African American who was the first killed in the 1770 Boston Massacre, he added, "Attucks fell early in the struggle, but the American Revolution stopped not then."

––––––––––––

Though John Anthony Copeland's and Lewis Sheridan Leary's backgrounds were in some ways similar—both born free and of racially mixed parentage—their lives would take divergent paths before they converged in Oberlin and then together went on to Harpers Ferry.

While the Copelands were from Raleigh, the state capital, the Learys lived in Fayetteville, also in the Piedmont but sixty-five miles south. Matthew Nathaniel Leary, the patriarch, was a free man and the son of Jeremiah O'Leary, of mixed Irish and Croatan Indian blood, and Sarah Jane Revels, a triracial woman from Robeson County whose father had been a Revolutionary War soldier.

Matthew Leary learned the trade of harness and saddle making from a young slave apprenticed to William Warden, who owned a wholesale business. Leary and the slave, whose freedom Leary eventually purchased, bought out Warden. Together, they were successful, and Leary became a rich man, wealthy enough to purchase a large white frame house for his family, and, incidentally, become an African American slaveholder. Yet he also gave money to his slaves so they could buy their freedom. In

1825, he married French-born Juliette Anna Meimoriel, whose mother had brought her at the age of six to Fayetteville from the French West Indies. Matthew and Juliette, identified as "mulatto," had three girls and three boys. Most went on to become accomplished professionals.

Their daughter Henrietta was as much of a debutante as a mixed-race girl could be in antebellum Fayetteville. Many years later, she would tell an interviewer about an incident that revealed both the family's station in society and perhaps its attitude toward its own slaves. A bridesmaid, she was going to bring flowers in a box to a friend's wedding, but her mother advised it was beneath her to personally carry them. "A box!" Juliette exclaimed "Matthew Leary's daughter walk through the street with a box in her hand? Call one of the niggers."

The Learys had one child, however, who would gain notoriety rather than fame and fortune. Lewis Sheridan Leary, born March 17, 1835, was Matthew and Juliette's fourth child. His niece later said he was given the middle name of Sheridan after a man who had freed his slaves. Befitting the family's status, Lewis had private tutors and went to a school for free blacks. He would be described as hotheaded and rash, not dwelling on the consequences of his actions, to himself or to others close to him. In the only known photograph of him, undated but perhaps taken in Oberlin, he is wearing a broad-brimmed hat, tilted raffishly to one side.

On one occasion, according to family lore, Leary was said to have stopped an owner from whipping his slave and whipped the slave master instead. This prompted his father to advise him to make a swift exit from Fayetteville. Lewis left soon thereafter, in the dark of night, bound for Ohio and Oberlin, where he took up his father's trade as a saddle and harness maker and actively promoted self-help to fellow blacks. "Men must suffer for a good cause," he advised.

Arriving in Oberlin in 1857, Leary not only pursued a vocation, he also pursued the woman he would marry. Her name was Mary Simpson Patterson. She was an Oberlin College student, also from Fayetteville, "an intelligent and interesting young colored lady . . . also of the same more advanced class of his people," John Mercer Langston would write. They married on May 12, 1858. Mary quit school after the birth of their only child, a daughter they named Lois, in March 1859. After Lewis's death, she would marry Charles Langston, brother of John Mercer, and move to Kansas. She would also become the grandmother of noted Harlem Renaissance writer and poet Langston Hughes.

As if the state codes affecting free blacks weren't bad enough, Oberliners soon found themselves at risk of facing federal charges for aiding escaped slaves. Passage in 1850 of the Fugitive Slave Act—an expansion of the federal fugitive slave act of 1793—roiled abolitionist circles in northeastern Ohio. Critics derided it as a federal usurpation of states' rights. The Supreme Court's 1857 Dred Scott decision reinforced the law, dashing any hope that enslaved black people could be regarded under the law as anything other than human chattel. So intense was the reaction that prominent politicians, including Massachusetts-born Benjamin Wade, who rose from prosecuting attorney of Ashtabula County to US senator from Ohio, suggested the state should secede rather than acquiesce to the act's noxious terms. Under the law, not only could slave catchers enter the state to retrieve human property, citizens could be fined and imprisoned for helping the fugitives.

In response, in December 1850, the citizens of Hartsgrove Township in Ashtabula County met and passed fifteen resolutions in which they resolved to "hold the fugitive slave law in utter contempt, as being no law, and pledge ourselves to despise the conduct of the makers of it for their utter destitution of principle, as well as for their reckless violation of the constitution of these States; which they were sworn to support." Secession talk, it seemed, transcended regional boundaries, as they also resolved that "sooner than submit to such odious laws we will see the Union dissolved; sooner than see slavery perpetual we would see war; and sooner than be slaves we will fight!" Further, rather than comply with the law, they added, "We will not aid in catching the fugitive, but will feed and protect him with all the means within our power; and that we pledge our sympathy and property for the relief of any person in our midst who may suffer any penalties for an honorable opposition or a failure to comply with the requirements of this law."

The Kansas-Nebraska Act of 1854 further inflamed feelings: it repealed the 1820 Missouri compromise under which newly admitted states would be slave or free according to their geographical location above or below an east-west line of latitude. Instead, the law called for popular sovereignty, with residents of the territories voting on the status of their new states, should they enter the Union. To influence the outcome, partisans on both sides poured into the territory, leading to a mini–civil war and the nickname Bleeding Kansas. On behalf of the abolitionists, John Brown and several of his sons and followers took up residence on Osawatomie Creek in Kansas. From there they set out to terrorize slaveholders.

On May 24 and 25, 1856, in retaliation for proslavery forces sacking the town of Lawrence, Brown's band, consisting of four of his sons and two others, brutally killed and dismembered five proslavery settlers near Pottawatomie Creek, in what became known as the Pottawatomie Massacre. These events gave rise to a popular portrait of "Osawatomie Brown" as a fanatic who would stop at nothing—even murder—to further the abolitionist cause. In Oberlin and in other abolitionist strongholds, however, he would be viewed as nothing less than heroic.

Of course, not everyone in Ohio was sympathetic to the abolitionist cause. Many Democrats were pro-Southern and willing to work with the slave catchers. Among these was US marshal Matthew Johnson, a Toledo Democrat whose jurisdiction encompassed Oberlin and its vicinity.

Marshall had replaced another Democrat more passive in the pursuit of slaves. So when the alarms sounded for one John Price, who had crossed the Ohio River from Kentucky, Marshall found at least a few willing citizens to assist in locating and capturing him.

Price was eighteen when he and a cousin surreptitiously left their owner's plantation in Mayslick in Mason County, Kentucky. Their nighttime departure was aided by the absence of their owner, John G. Bacon, who, counting on the loyalty of his slaves not to flee, had gone to visit relatives. Crossing the nearby Ohio River, Price headed to Oberlin, arriving in January 1856. There he lived inconspicuously and unimpeded for two years with James Armstrong, a black laborer. Out of complacency or satisfaction with his adopted town, he reportedly rejected offers of money that would have paid for him to travel to Canada.

Word of his whereabouts got out, and a trap was set. Shakespeare Boynton, the thirteen-year-old son of Lewis W. Boynton, a wealthy proslavery farmer, asked Price if he'd like to work for his father as a field hand. The plot was hatched by Anderson D. Jennings, Bacon's neighbor and a slave catcher who went to Oberlin armed with power of attorney and accompanied by a Bacon employee. Around 11 AM on Monday, September 13, while Price was walking three-quarters of a mile north of Oberlin to the farm with young Shakespeare, Jennings and his posse descended, took him captive and whisked him to Wellington to await the train that would take him to Columbus and from there back to bondage in Kentucky. But luck was not with the slavers.

Two Oberlin students saw Price in a buggy with the Kentucky men heading south and quickly got word back to Oberlin. Within hours, hundreds—estimates ranged from two hundred to six hundred—surrounded the Wadsworth House, the hotel owned by a proslavery Democrat where Price was being held in the attic. The crowd demanded that Price be brought out, and Jennings acceded, bringing him onto the balcony, where Price said he "supposed" he'd have to return to Kentucky because Jennings had a lawful warrant for him. The crowd urged Price to jump. From below, Copeland waved a pistol and threatened "to shoot the damn rascal" who interfered.

Charles Langston—one of the first blacks admitted to Oberlin College—tried to negotiate with Price's captors and, when that failed, tried to get a local constable to arrest the slave catchers for kidnapping. He also sought a writ of habeas corpus for Price, to no avail. At that point, Langston declared, "*We* will have him anyhow" or "*They* will have him anyhow." Which pronoun was said, expressing either intent or observation, would be disputed.

While the abolitionist crowd milled outside, two groups of young men stormed the hotel. Three white Oberlin students went through the front door, while Copeland and others used a nearby construction ladder to climb to the second-floor balcony in back. Hotel employees sought to stop the rescuers but retreated when a shot was fired. Then William Lincoln, one of the white rescuers, and Copeland reached the attic. They demanded the release of Price, who was sequestered with Jennings behind a wall. The door to the room was secured, but Lincoln noticed a hole in the wall, through which he punched Jennings in the face. This caused the marshal to loosen his grip on the rope securing the attic door. First Lincoln, then Copeland rushed in. Copeland and a third rescuer grabbed Price and took him downstairs and out of the building to freedom—with nobody injured.

And off they went in a buggy driven by Simeon M. Bushnell, an Oberlin bookstore clerk and printer, away from Wellington back to Oberlin. There Price would be hidden for several days in a second-floor back room in the home of Professor James Fairchild on—where else—Professor Street.

The federal indictment handed down on December 7 found the rescuers in clear violation of the Fugitive Slave Act, in that they had "knowingly and willfully" rescued runaway slave John Price from Marshal Jennings and his deputy. On December 15, arrest warrants were served on fifteen from Oberlin. As for the slave catchers, a county grand jury charged Jennings and three others with violating state kidnapping laws.

Charged with complicity, Copeland was among those indicted but could not be found to be served and was never arrested. Lincoln, while teaching school in Franklin County, was arrested by deputy sheriff Samuel Davis, a well-known slave catcher and part-time jailer in Oberlin (and one of the four indicted by the local grand jury for kidnapping Price). Lincoln was handcuffed, jailed overnight in Columbus, then taken to Cleveland, where he was again jailed, then released on personal bond.

Rescuer Lewis Leary was not among the indicted, and he wondered why. "I have been thinking why it was that I was overlooked by the marshal's vigilant spies," he wrote a friend. The reason, he supposed, was that he would never post the $1,000 bond to be free pending his trial, thereby depriving the government of this money. Whether this made any sense, he seemed to convey a feeling of disappointment that he had been excluded from this noble group.

But he closely followed the case. In January 1859, during what he described as "quite a mild winter," he wrote to a friend in Logan County. "The rescue case continues to agitate the minds of the people."

The Oberlin antislavery society now had more than seventy-five members, he reported, and "things are working as they should be. . . . White men are beginning to feel that Slavery is driving Iron Shafts into their own Souls." As evidence, he wrote that Davis, when arresting Lincoln, asked the accused "if he would Shoot a white man to rescue a negro, his reply was I am a Christian and would avoid shedding the blood of a fellow man to the last . . . but if I could not do it otherwise I should most assuredly shoot any person who would . . . attempt to enslave a fellow man."

The indicted but elusive Copeland was described as single, a "good looking, bright mulatto" with a "bushy head and near straight hair," also with a mustache. Henry E. Peck, another rescuer and a professor at Oberlin, found him to be "a man of incomplete education, and of few words, but brave and energetic" and "favorably known in our community." Making it a family affair, Copeland's uncles Henry and Bruce Evans were also indicted. So was Ralph Plumb, a lawyer and an active abolitionist who had come originally from New York and Connecticut to Oberlin in 1857 and would later figure prominently in the case against Copeland in Harpers Ferry. Of the total indicted, twenty-five were from Oberlin, twelve were from Wellington, and twelve were black. Their home for several months would be the Cuyahoga County jail in Cleveland.

The trial began on April 5, 1859. First to be tried was Simeon Bushnell, the white store clerk who drove the getaway wagon. He was convicted, fined $600 and court costs, and sentenced to sixty days in the county jail. Next was Charles Langston, who told the court, "I felt it my duty to go and do what I could toward liberating him." He was fined $100 and given twenty days in jail, time he'd already served. Fourteen of the rescuers remained in jail. Finally, a deal was struck: Lorain County dropped kidnapping charges against Jennings and three others who had tried to reenslave Price; in return, the US attorney dropped all charges against those still in jail.

While behind bars, the rescuers, with help from their sympathetic jailer, produced a remarkable document. It was a four-page newspaper, the *Rescuer*, five thousand copies of which were printed in the Cuyahoga County jail and distributed to the public for three cents per copy. Though the paper promised publication every other Monday, there was but one edition, dated July 4, 1859.

"THE RESCUER" announced its publication from the jail "by the POLITICAL PRISONERS There confined." Under the nameplate appeared a line from the Book of Jeremiah: "Deliver him that is spoiled out of the hand of the oppressor." The oppressor was certainly not the jailer, who allowed the prisoners access to the facility's printing press and exercised no censorship. "There is so much 'rescuing' to be done," the paper declared, "that we intend to spend our lives at the business." An oligarchy, it asserted, had taken control of the Senate, the White House, and the Supreme Court—"Come to the rescue and join the rescuers."

At the end, the paper offered "a few words about ourselves, The Rescue Company." Three were from North Carolina; four from New York; one each from Ohio, Louisiana, and South Carolina; and three from England. Ten were married, with a total of thirty-seven children. The rescuers were printers, upholsterers, cabinetmakers, a shoemaker, a harness maker, a schoolteacher, a student, a lawyer, a college professor, and a minister. Most were Congregationalists, but there was also one Methodist and an Episcopalian. They prayed morning and evening and twice on the Sabbath. Their third-floor quarters contained a sitting room, two bedrooms, and three cells. "Our food is good and is served with a neatness which challenges our constant gratitude," they wrote. And they declared their "'landlord,' Sheriff Wightman, as noble a man as ever drew breath."

"I'll help you if I can," the sheriff told them. Type was found, pages were laid out, the paper printed. They apologized for a lack of italics. "We must ask our readers to supply the emphasis according to taste."

They returned home late on July 6, 1859, local heroes, the pride of Oberlin. "Out of Jail!" screamed a flier circulated in town. "The

Rescuers Are Coming TO-NIGHT. Let there be a grand gathering." The mayor's office urged "that the citizens en masse turn out to meet them."

And turn out they did. A band greeted their arrival and a large crowd marched to First Church to listen to speeches honoring them and their cause. Following their release after eighty-four days, the rescuers immediately assumed a prominent place in Oberlin's history. One hundred and sixty years later, their exalted status remains secure in the lore and gestalt of the small Ohio college town.

And what of Price? After his days-long stay in Professor Fairchild's home, his movements went unrecorded. Several sources say that Copeland took him to Canada, most likely to Chatham. However, there is no documented evidence of his ever being there. Copeland, of course, had absented himself from Oberlin, thereby avoiding arrest. But the central character in the rescue drama, it seemed, would simply vanish into the haze of history.

―――――――――

John Brown made an appearance in the Western Reserve during the trial. At a Cleveland lecture in March, he spoke alongside John Henry Kagi, a lawyer whom Brown met in Kansas and who became his secretary of war and second in command. Leary heard the charismatic Brown's talk and was mesmerized by his eloquence and passion. As a correspondent for the *New-York Tribune*, Kagi covered the trial. He also visited the prisoners in the Cuyahoga County jail. That August, a month after the triumphant release of the rescuers, Brown's son John Jr. was in Oberlin and in touch with Leary.

"Leary did not believe much in talking," William Cooper Nell would later write, "for he considered the people to be tired of that, but his motto was, action, action!"

On October 13, John Brown Jr., initially under an assumed name, met John Mercer Langston, Charles Langston's older brother. His purpose, he said, was to seek black recruits for his father's mission to free the slaves. In the parlor of Langston's Oberlin home, they were joined

Lewis Sheridan Leary, nattily attired, left a wife and young child to join John Brown's band. *Library of Congress, LC-USZ62-11711*

by John Copeland and Lewis Leary. Copeland, Langston later wrote, as he had "honored himself" with thirty-six others who rescued John Price, now "would honor himself in service to the cause of humanity."

Brown Jr., declared John Mercer Langston, had "secured two of the bravest negroes that this country has produced." Informed of the mission, Leary declared, according to Langston's account, "I am ready to die! I only ask that when I have given my life to free others, my own wife and dear little daughter shall never know want." Leary and his wife were now the parents of a six-month-old daughter. "Let me be assured," he told Langston and Brown Jr., "that they will be cared for, protected; and if my child shall live, be suitably educated and trained to usefulness." They would in fact receive such assistance in the future.

John Anthony Copeland, an Oberlin antislavery activist, was recruited by Leary for John Brown's raid. *Library of Congress, LC-USZ61-748*

But the two new recruits could not join Brown's band without the means to get there. On September 8, Leary wrote Kagi, addressing Kagi by the alias J. Henrie and saying in coded language that he needed money for travel. He had been unhealthy "for quite some time," he wrote, adding that he had "grown quite well" though. He had, he said, a "handy man who is willing and every way competent to dig coal, but, like myself, has not tools. If the company employs him, they will have to furnish him tools. . . . He is an honest man and will do as much labor as the common runoff men." That man was Copeland, and the "tools" were money. Leary approached Ralph Plumb, the lawyer-abolitionist who had helped rescue Price, for funds to be used in "assisting slaves to escape." Plumb came up with $17.50 but later said he hadn't asked for specifics and wouldn't have given money to fund an insurrection.

Copeland, in his defense, would later say he thought the plan was simply to rescue slaves and take them to Canada, certainly not to foment an insurrection or commit murder.

To his family he said he was leaving to teach in a "colored school." Leary wouldn't even give his family that much information. He would leave Oberlin abruptly without informing his wife of his destination or his purpose.

Leary was known to often quote lines from William Smith O'Brien, a nineteenth-century Irish nationalist and member of Parliament, expressing perhaps his own guiding purpose:

> *Whether on the scaffold high,*
> *Or in the battle's van;*
> *The fittest place for man to die,*
> *Is where he dies for man.*

Resolved to liberate slaves, if not to provoke a full-scale rebellion that would devolve into a bloody battle and their own deaths, John Anthony Copeland and Lewis Sheridan Leary began their journey, first by train to Chambersburg, Pennsylvania, and then, virtually on the eve of the raid, to a nondescript farmhouse five miles from Harpers Ferry, and their final rendezvous with destiny.

4

North to Canada

Your national ship is rotten sinking, why not leave
it and why not say so boldly, manfully? Leave that
slavery-cursed republic.

—Mary Ann Shadd Cary

Except for the wind turbines, the Ontario landscape east of Detroit
and the Ambassador Bridge is, by all descriptions, similar to what
fugitive slaves and free blacks encountered in the 1850s when they
crossed the international border into what was then known as Canada
West. Fertile farmland—now in corn and soybeans—as far as the eye
could see, and, invisible but no less tangible, the fresh air of freedom.

This is the country and the peninsula wedged between Lake Ontario
and Lake St. Claire to which Osborne Perry Anderson and other persons of color immigrated to make a better life for themselves and their
families after passage of the Fugitive Slave Act.

The most noxious part of the Great Compromise of 1850, which
also admitted California as a free state, was sponsored by US senator
James Murray Mason. His grandfather was George Mason, a signer of
the Declaration of Independence, slaveholder, and author of the Virginia
Bill of Rights, a document whose principles seemed to contradict the
very system of slavery it also condoned. Backers viewed the compromise as an effort to save the Union, but at what cost? Under its terms,
harboring slaves became a federal crime. Authorities in free states were

legally bound to capture fugitives and return them to their owners. Even free persons of color felt in danger, as the slave catchers also threatened them with kidnapping and slavery.

In Christiana, in Pennsylvania's Lancaster County, slave catchers sought four runaways from the adjoining state of Maryland. Their efforts, led by owner Edward Gorsuch, accompanied by deputy US marshal Henry H. Kline, met with strong resistance from the black community. In September 1851, in what became known as the Christiana rebellion, the posse was confronted by William Parker, a former slave who harbored the fugitives on his farm. Dozens of black neighbors armed with guns, knives, and scythes joined with Parker to prevent their capture. In the ensuing melee, Gorsuch was killed. Parker and his family fled to Canada, where he became a correspondent for Frederick Douglass's newspaper, the *North Star*.

Indeed, three thousand blacks crossed into Canada within three months of the law's passage. The *Pennsylvania Freeman* reported that more than a third of Boston's black population immediately moved to Canada. Most of the new immigrants landed in the southwestern corner of what is now Ontario, and many of them settled in Chatham, a river town dating back to the 1790s as a naval shipyard.

It was, Rev. William M. Mitchell proclaimed, "the head quarters of the Negro race in Canada. It has acquired considerable notoriety, even in the United States, because of the great number that settled there. The better class live in . . . (two story frame [houses], painted white outside)—numbers of their unfortunate brethren live in log houses, with gardens around them well stocked with vegetables. . . . The hearty loyalty of the coloured population in Canada is attested to by all that come in contact with them."

Of the fifteen thousand American-born black residents in Canada in 1860, some two thousand lived in Chatham. A business census that year showed blacks employed in an array of trades and professions: as seamstresses, carpenters, grocers, doctors, lawyers, and barbers, among others. In 1852, the "colored population of Upper Canada," another name for Canada West, was estimated at thirty thousand. Surely that number grew in the wake of the Fugitive Slave Act; although numbers vary, some sources estimate as many as forty thousand.

"Canada was a good country for us," a former slave wrote, "because master was so anxious that we *not* go there."

The British promised freedom in the nascent United States as early as 1775 when Lord Dunmore, the colonial governor of Virginia, made the offer in return for American slaves joining the royal forces against the revolutionaries. The appeal lured African Americans into the loyalist camp, even as some joined the patriotic cause for independence. But the British went on to defeat, and, though Britain formally abolished slavery in 1832, as did Canada a year later, the United States had never confronted the issue as directly, save for a spirited debate in the 1831–1832 Virginia legislature, which ended inconclusively.

Even before the Fugitive Slave Act, runaway slaves had begun to cross the international border. Notable among them was Josiah Henson, a slave on the Riley plantation in Montgomery County, Maryland, who, failing in his efforts to buy his freedom from his master, had fled with his wife Nancy and their four children in 1830, crossing the international border at Niagara Falls. Harriet Beecher Stowe would later immortalize Henson as the fictional slave in *Uncle Tom's Cabin*. But in Canada West, Henson wasn't the mostly passive Uncle Tom of Stowe's book. In reality, he was an activist who founded a settlement and trade school for black émigrés in Dawn Township. At its peak, the Dawn settlement had a population of five hundred.

But financial mismanagement and debt plagued the school, known as the British-American Institute, which the British and Foreign Anti-Slavery Society wrested from black control based on unproven allegations that Henson had misused funds. During these 1857 investigations, Osborne Perry Anderson was appointed secretary of the committee formed to regain control of the settlement for the black émigrés. The effort ultimately failed, and the Dawn settlement and school withered and closed in 1868.

In nearby Buxton in 1849, the Rev. William King, an Irish-born minister from Louisiana who had inherited and then freed his wife's eight slaves, founded a settlement named after Lord Elgin, the British governor-general of Canada. King accomplished this in part by securing an assignment from the Presbyterian Church to do missionary work there. King bought land six miles long by three miles wide and sold farm lots to black settlers, over opposition from three hundred local whites who tried to block the settlement with a petition.

Nonetheless, starting with 150 settlers, by 1861 the settlement had three hundred families. It also had two hotels, a general store, a post office, and three integrated schools. At one time, its population was said to have exceeded two thousand people. Most of today's one hundred residents are descendants of slaves who immigrated there.

Those who immigrated to Canada West came from Kentucky and Texas and from the Carolinas and Virginia. Many of those who were not enslaved came from Ohio and Indiana, where even free persons of color were subject to oppressive laws and sometimes kidnapped and taken to Southern states to be sold into slavery.

Conditions in Canada were far better than even in the free states but far from perfect, according to narratives published by Benjamin Drew, who gathered stories in fourteen localities from Toronto to Windsor.

J. C. Brown, born in Frederick County, Virginia, close to Harpers Ferry, was the son of a white father and an enslaved mixed-race mother. His story was long and complicated. He had purchased his freedom, married, had children, and encouraged others to immigrate to Canada, where he eventually settled. Moving in 1849 to Chatham, he described it as "then a little village of frame buildings and log cabins. There were then no masons, bricklayers, or plasterers among the colored men." But eventually there were four black churches and separate schools.

In addition, he reported, Chatham has many black property owners, most of them immigrants, who were arriving "sometimes 20 in one day," and five charitable organizations to serve "the sick and destitute." The children were growing up "entirely differently from their fathers," "having not fear of any white man, and being taught to read and write." Yet, the legacy of slavery could still be felt among the new arrivals. "I have seen fugitives, brought as witnesses, afraid to testify against a white man. This is a part of the horrid effects of slavery."

The *Richmond Republican* in Virginia scoffed at claims that Canada offered a warm, soft landing for fugitive slaves. "As to the negro paradise in Canada, we dare say that the fugitive slaves have discovered that liberty to freeze and starve to death is not great luxury after all," sniffed the newspaper.

The Richmond newspaper's comment came in response to a statement in Horace Greeley's *New-York Tribune*: "The directors of the Underground Railroad report us to the passage, through our city, last Monday, of *forty-one* human chattels, from the land of the slave-whip and coffle, on a pilgrimage to the North Star. They are now all safely landed in Canada, where they have ceased to be stray cattle, and become men, women, and children, no more to be subjects of the auction block and brand."

But not all immigrants stayed in Canada. Leaving Chatham were sixteen "fugitive slaves," the Southern-sympathizing *Cleveland Democrat* reported. They arrived on the mail boat *Union* from Port Stanley, Ontario. "Becoming weary of Canada freedom, which to many blacks embraces the exalted liberty of going inadequately clothed and of being nearly starved to death, they were about to return to the South, preferring plantation life to the responsibilities attendant on a state of existence for which circumstances have rendered them peculiarly disqualified." One elderly woman, identified as "Old Aunty," reportedly gave her opinion of Canada: "Dey kin all talk about dar freedom over dar (pointing with a can-brake finger across the blue water . . .), but I'd a keep leveyer stay with dem down in old Kentuck."

In 1854, abolitionist Frederick Douglass added his voice to the campaign encouraging black migration north to Canada. From the Chatham courthouse steps on August 3, he proclaimed, "Beneath the pale light of the North Star, where the Lion reposes with his foot on the Virgin's lap fit emblem of England's Queen and nestling in his mane, can the sable sons of Africa find a refuge, free from the bloody beak of the American Eagle."

Canada also beckoned to Osborne Anderson, a free man of color and mixed racial origins. He was born on July 27, 1830, in West Fallowfield, a still-small township in a rural area of Chester County, in southeastern Pennsylvania. The county, adjoining Delaware, is one jurisdiction removed from Philadelphia. Anderson was the oldest of four sons of Vincent Anderson, a free black man born in Virginia, and Sophia Taylor Anderson. Oral tradition is that Anderson's mother was a red-haired white woman from Ireland or Scotland. Census records list both Osborne and Vincent Anderson as *M* for mulatto and indicate that Osborne lived with his father and siblings.

He would grow to be tall, six feet two inches. A man of handsome looks and serious mien, he had a "thoughtful" tan oval face, "sadly-earnest eyes, and an expression of intellectual power that impressed the observer strongly," Richard J. Hinton, a London-born immigrant, abolitionist, and journalist, would later note.

Given his status as a free African American raised in an area actively engaged in aiding fugitive slaves, it is not surprising that Anderson would become a staunch abolitionist and dedicated ally and conspirator in John Brown's scheme to free the slaves. Chester County was a hotbed of abolitionism, heavily influenced by its Quaker population, and it was a safe haven for fugitive slaves, containing many stations on the Underground Railroad. West Chester, the county seat, counted three hundred free blacks among its population in 1850, nearly 14 percent of the town's population.

Growing up in Chester County, Osborne Anderson went to public schools. Some sources say he also attended Oberlin College, although the school has no record of him. During his formative years in Pennsylvania, Anderson became well acquainted with another free black family, the Shadds, who had moved there from nearby Delaware, a less hospitable slave state, though with a mere 4,509 enslaved persons in 1820, compared to nearly 112,000 in adjoining Maryland and the District of Columbia.

If John Brown would become the most influential and defining man in Anderson's life, then Mary Ann Shadd would be the most influential woman. Her paternal grandfather was a Hessian soldier wounded during the French and Indian War who married into the black family that nursed him back to health. Seven years older than Anderson, she was born free in Wilmington on October 9, 1823, to a black mother and a mulatto father, who was a prosperous shoemaker and boot manufacturer.

When Mary Ann was ten, the Shadds moved from Wilmington to nearby West Chester, home to nearly three hundred free blacks by 1850. The oldest of thirteen children, she attended a Quaker boarding school there for six years. Her teacher and the head of the school was Phoebe Darlington, a delegate to the 1838 Anti-Slavery Convention of American Women. West Chester was a key station on the Underground Railroad, and Mary Ann's father, Abraham Doras Shadd, was a conductor there as well as in Wilmington. In 1833, Abraham became president of the National Convention for the Improvement of Free People of Color. He amassed considerable property in Wilmington and West Chester. By 1850, his estate was valued at $3,000, equal to about $90,408 in 2017 dollars. The Shadds' racial identity as mulattos further enhanced their status within the community.

In boarding school, Mary Ann was taught that not only the races but also the genders were equal and should be treated accordingly. Mary Ann then returned to Wilmington to organize a school for young blacks. From 1839 to 1850, she taught there, and then at schools for black students in New York City; Trenton, New Jersey; and West Chester and Norristown, Pennsylvania.

In the fall of 1851, many of the Shadds—including Mary Ann and father Abraham—joined the migration to Canada. After attending an antislavery society meeting in Toronto, on September 16, she wrote to her brother Isaac, still in Pennsylvania, encouraging him to follow, which he did. "I have been here more than a week, and I like Canada," she wrote. "I do not feel prejudice and if you were to come here or go west of this where shoemaking pays well and work at it and buy lands as fast as you made any money, you would do well."

In Windsor, across the Detroit River from Detroit, Michigan, she taught school. (The 1851 Canadian Census identifies her as twenty-seven, a "school mistress," and a Methodist.) To keep the racially integrated school of fifty-six children operating, she accepted a stipend of $125 a year from the American Missionary Association. But, fearing public knowledge would discourage tuition payments, she kept it a secret. The information somehow surfaced, and the association withdrew its funding in January 1853.

Mary Ann also had black benefactors, notably Henry and Mary Bibb, who published the *Voice of the Fugitive* newspaper in Windsor and raised funds to help newly arrived black émigrés adjust to their new country. Philosophically, though she had accepted the church money, she felt that blacks should be self-sufficient and not "beg" for white support. She also accused the Bibbs of using some of the money they collected for themselves. Mary Ann and the Bibbs became bitter antagonists. Their feud may have inspired her to produce her own newspaper.

On March 24, 1853, the first edition of the *Provincial Freeman* appeared in Windsor. Its motto: "Self-Reliance Is the True Road to Independence." Later, Mary Ann and the paper would move to Toronto, and finally, in 1855, to Chatham, where the newspaper was housed in the Charity Block, so-called not because it housed the paper for free but because it was owned by James H. Charity, a black man who operated his Great Western Boot and Shoe Store in the same building. Bowing to the gender prejudice of the times, the paper listed two men as editors, but there was little doubt in the community that it was Mary Ann Shadd's newspaper. She was the first black female editor in North America. Osborne Anderson, who had moved to Canada West to manage her uncle Absalom's farm but didn't take to it, went to work for the newspaper in June 1856, first as a subscription salesman and then as a printer.

During this time, Mary Ann also lectured widely, both in Canada and in the Midwestern states at a time when it was rare for women to be public speakers.

In 1856, Mary Ann married Thomas F. Cary, an older widower with three children who continued to operate his Toronto barber shop

Mary Ann Shadd Cary, North America's first black female editor, published the *Provincial Freeman* in Canada West. *Library and Archives Canada*

during their marriage, while Mary Ann and the children lived in Chatham. Cary died in 1860, leaving his wife with two more children of her own, Sarah Elizabeth and Linton. He bequeathed to her little if any money, but his legacy included his last name. Outspoken in a gender-conscious society, Mary Ann wrote and published often under the name of M. A. S. Cary. Using her married last name, she editorialized against black immigration to Africa and against what she characterized as "begging" for money and white support.

Soon, Anderson was writing for Mary Ann's *Provincial Freeman*, and echoing her views. In the August 8, 1857, edition of the newspaper, he wrote that "begging for refugees in Canada" was among "the greatest wrongs" and that the suggestion "we must be expatriated to the shores of Africa . . . I detest and ever will." He added that "it is a lamentable fact in the opinions of some whites that as a people we are incapable of taking care of ourselves. This has been felt in the United States and Canada, and this monster lurks in the midnight hour, stealing along, degrading us, giving sanction to that doctrine of the proslavery and colonization parties that acclaims we can't live on the continent of America."

In a piece full of literary allusions, reflecting what must have been a classical education, he urged readers to follow the words of Sir Francis Bacon, the English philosopher: "Against the winds, against the tide, now steady, on with upright zeal." To this, he added, "Let us follow the example and test the benefit that 'knowledge is power' here in Canada."

The newspaper, however, was not above seeking funds for its own survival. In February 1857, Mary A. S. Cary and associate H. Ford Douglas, "Editors," asked for funds to "enable us to go on." "The scars of oppression have to be healed," they wrote, "and the responsibilities belonging to men who live under the just and merciful rule of Her Majesty—and the British Government—the only shelter for this people—have to be inculcated." What better instrument to accomplish this, they implied, than the *Provincial Freeman*? Donations, they added, would be acknowledged in print.

Chatham, with its close-knit community of Afro-Canadian expatriates, would be a perfect plotting ground for Brown, who with his followers had infamously murdered slave sympathizers and one of their infants in Bleeding Kansas. The deadly battleground between pro- and antislavery forces followed the 1854 Kansas-Nebraska Act, which called for popular sovereignty, under which residents would decide if Kansas would be admitted to the Union as a slave or free state.

Brown arrived in Chatham in April ahead of his men, who had been spending the winter in Iowa. After taking care of some preliminary business, he went west and brought back a dozen, all white except for a former slave from Missouri he had helped liberate. The purpose of the Chatham meeting was preordained: to draw up and approve a provisional constitution for the free government of liberated slaves he hoped to establish in the Appalachians of Virginia. Indeed, he had already mapped out mountain areas from which he thought the guerrillas could wage war on slaveholders in the valleys below, inspiring more slaves to join them and sending shock waves through the plantation South that would once and for all bring down the hated institution.

He returned to town on April 30. The preliminary meeting to review the proposed constitution met where Brown stayed in Chatham, in the two-story redbrick home of Isaac Holden, a black émigré from Louisiana. John Kagi and Osborne Anderson acted as secretaries. Brown next issued a mail call on May 5 for "a very quiet conference" to be held in Chatham three days later. Prominent among those invited were African American abolitionists Frederick Douglass and Harriet Tubman, who was then living in Ontario's Niagara region and had relatives in Chatham and whom Brown referred to as "the General" for her many successful southern forays to guide runaway slaves to freedom. Neither would attend—Tubman due to illness. Douglass, who'd known Brown for eleven years, would be offered—and decline—the presidency of the free mountain republic Brown hoped to establish. Those who did attend were sworn to secrecy.

Brown was indeed an imposing figure, "a Puritan of the most exalted type," Anderson would recall of his first impression. "His long white beard, thoughtful and reverent brow and physiognomy, his sturdy, measured tread, as he circulated with hands . . . under the pendant coatshirt of plain brown Tweed, with other garments to match." Anderson apparently also impressed Brown, who appointed him to be not only a secretary at preconvention meetings but also a full participant in the conference, which began at 10 AM on Saturday, May 8. The publicly stated purpose was to establish a black Masonic lodge, but that was a ruse.

Those assembling that first day at the British Methodist Episcopal (BME) Church on Princess Street were Brown's closest associates, who were white, and a large contingent of Afro-Canadians, including

Anderson and Shadd Cary's husband and brother. But Shadd Cary, though she had met Brown, was absent. Women (except for Tubman, not attending) were excluded from the conference.

Also present at the convention was Martin R. Delany, born in Charlestown—a mere eight miles from Harpers Ferry—to a slave father and a free mother of color. He had trained as a physician, written for Douglass's *North Star* newspaper, and in 1856 moved to Chatham, where he was a leading citizen and also contributed to the *Provincial Freeman*. At times, he advocated black immigration to Africa, but in 1863 when blacks were allowed to enlist for the Union, he was a recruiting agent with Mary Ann. He then became the first black commissioned officer to lead an all-black unit, as a major in command of the 104th Regiment of the US Colored Troops. While helping Brown organize the meeting, acting as its cochair and signing the provisional constitution, Delany was wary of his plans, thinking them unlikely to succeed.

After meeting, first at the BME church, whose minister was uneasy over its radical nature, the convention moved to the nearby King Street School and, finally, to the First Baptist Church, a wood frame structure that still stands (though sheathed in brick) on King Street. The assembly was solemn and businesslike. "There was scant ceremony at these opening proceedings," one participant noted. "No civic address to this Canadian town; no beat of drums; no firing of guns. . . . The place was rude and unadorned, yet the object of this little parliament was the freedom of four million slaves."

The conference reconvened on Monday at 10 AM. On Brown's motion, John Henry Kagi, Brown's closest advisor, was elected secretary.

A provisional constitution and ordinances for the prospective free republic were adopted, with forty-eight articles. "Whereas slavery . . . is . . . a most barbarous, unprovoked, and unjustifiable war of one portion of its citizens upon another portion . . . in utter disregard and violation of those eternal and self-evident truths set forth in our Declaration of Independence," the preamble began, "Therefore, we, citizens of the United States, and the oppressed people who, by a recent decision of the Supreme Court, are declared to have no right which the white man is bound to respect, together with all other people degraded by the laws thereof, do, for the time being, ordain and establish for ourselves the following Provisional Constitution and Ordinances, the better to protect our persons, property, lives, and liberties, and to govern our actions."

At 6 PM, the convention elected officers: John Brown for commander in chief, by acclamation; Kagi for secretary of war, also by acclamation. After the conference resumed at 9 AM on Monday, Osborne Anderson was elected as one of the first two members of the future free black state's congress. He was also appointed to a fifteen-member committee to fill vacant offices. Sources differ on whether the Harpers Ferry raid was discussed at Chatham. But at least the organizational framework had been laid. The record shows that Anderson voted for the provisional constitution and ordinances put forward by Brown.

James Monroe "Gunsmith" Jones, the African American gunsmith, engraver, and later justice of the peace in Chatham, attended the convention and added his signature to the provisional documents. Born a slave in Raleigh, North Carolina, he had moved as a child with his family and the Copelands to Oberlin, where he went to college, and then moved to Chatham in 1849. He would use his gunsmithing skills to fashion firearms for the Harpers Ferry raid. In 1883, he would recall Brown's many visits to his gun shop and, during the abolitionist's monthlong stay in Chatham, that he "never for once saw a smile light up his countenance. He seemed always in deep, earnest study or thought." It was Brown's belief, Jones reported, that only the death of whites in the cause of abolition would have the necessary impact to stir to action the free whites of the North. "He knew well that the sacrifice of any number of negroes would have no effect."

A signer of Brown's provisional constitution and ordinances, Jones was nonetheless skeptical of his plan, predicting that slaves would not rally to the cause as they had in the Caribbean, because they were "different from the slaves in the French West India Island, San Domingo; the latter imbibed some of the impetuous characteristics of their masters." Brown would not hear it.

Of the thirty-four black men attending the convention, fifteen of the African Americans would later enlist in the US Colored Troops formed after Abraham Lincoln issued his Emancipation Proclamation effective January 1, 1863. But only one—Osborne Perry Anderson—would go with Brown to Harpers Ferry—and that wouldn't be for seventeen months yet. Indeed, there was no crush of volunteers from Chatham. When the time came, the duty fell to Anderson, by lottery.

Four months after the Chatham convention, two remarkably similar events occurred hundreds of miles apart in which two of Brown's black raiders took part. On September 13, citizens of Oberlin, Ohio, including John Copeland and Lewis Leary, rescued fugitive slave John Price from slave catchers who sought to return him to his owner in Kentucky. Copeland then, by several accounts, whisked Price off to Canada West, and freedom.

Price left Oberlin on or about September 16, 1858. The date of his arrival in Canada West is not documented, nor is Copeland's role in spiriting him there, or even whether their trip ended in Chatham, though given his long acquaintance with Gunsmith Jones since their families migrated together to Oberlin in 1843, it seems likely. Just ten days after Price left Oberlin, a similar rescue took place in Chatham in which both Anderson and Copeland almost certainly participated.

W. R. Merwin of New York had claimed to be the owner of a ten-year-old free boy of color, Sylvanus Demarest, originally from New Jersey, who was with him in Canada West. How or why the boy was there remains unclear. Accounts are contradictory and incomplete.

Most agree that Merwin intended to take him back to the United States for sale as a slave. But there were obstacles. Elijah Leonard, the former mayor of London, Ontario, spotted the man and boy on the train platform there and was suspicious. "A recognition of the injustice of slavery was, I suppose, born in me from the first, as it was in all Northerners," he recalled in an 1889 memoir published posthumously five years later.

It was the only blot on the American people as a nation, and I disliked it the more I heard the stories of so many escaped slaves. Canada was then their only safe place of residence. I was at the Great Western Station one noon on the arrival of the train from the Suspension Bridge, when I noticed a dandy sort of a fellow pacing up and down the platform with a bright negro boy at his heels, acting as his body servant, and sending the little innocent to buy his papers and cigars. He was rather communicative, and told in my hearing how much the boy was worth when he got him south.

I had heard stories of this illegal traffic going on in the North but had never come face to face with it. I knew in a moment this creature had been east and had enticed this boy, perhaps from his home. In turning around I saw on the station Anderson Diddrick, the colored man who carried the Union Jack in front of our firemen when in procession. I told him I was afraid that boy was going to slavery and it was too bad to see him dragged off free British soil to work all his life for someone else, and perhaps be badly treated. The train started, the man whistled to the boy, and off they started for Detroit. This brought the tears to Diddrick's eyes. I asked him if he knew anyone in Chatham. "Yes, several." "Would they take the boy away from this man?" "Yes, they would," but he had no money to telegraph. I gave him some, and he immediately wired the state of affairs, which was responded to in great shape.

When Chatham men and women boarded the train "with clubs and staves" and demanded the boy, Leonard wrote,

Mr. Kidnapper was very glad to get off with a whole skin from this departure company[.] The railway company had these people all summoned for disturbing the peace, and quite a fuss was made about it. I was summoned to attend court in Chatham, but the papers miscarried. I believe, when the magistrate learnt the whole truth, he bound over some of the foremost, and the act of trespass was in short time forgotten. I have been given to understand the boy lived for many years afterwards near Chatham.

Who was this kidnapper? An account in the *Detroit Free Press* reprinted in the *Chatham Planet* on October 15 reported W. R. Merwin's version while he was in Detroit awaiting further developments. "He feels as deeply the loss of 'Jack' as though he was his own child," the newspaper reported.

> There are very many Southern Masters, like Mr. Merwin, who would feel such as loss as though it were *his own child*, but whether it was his own child or not, the boy was a slave and notwithstanding Democracy, in these United States has, through its highest Court, declared that every State in the Union is, in fact, slave soil. . . . The boy is to be pitied for, if he really is attached to his Master and is not old enough to feel the iron of bondage entering his soul, his rescue from his master was cruelty to the boy's feelings, but there should be no empathy wasted on the Master for he had no business to take his slave upon English soil.

But the kidnapper was no master. He was a fraud, according to the sworn affidavit of O. J. Wood, Merwin's distant relative, given "from a sense of duty, and as an act of justice" in New York City on October 18 and published in the *Planet* a week later. Merwin had been born in Grange County, Ohio, and "from an early age . . . followed peddling various goods and services for a living." He traveled to California, returning to New York in 1856 for three or four weeks "in the employ of O. J. Wood & Co.," for whom he traveled as a "selling and advertising agent" to the South and then back up north to Rochester but with "no means or money" except a salary for traveling and "certainly with no means while traveling in the South with which to purchase a negro."

Merwin had told Wood that he'd taken the Demarest boy with him to help distribute circulars for the company, which "seemed reasonable" until he'd read the bogus account in the *Free Press* in which he'd also claimed to own the youth's father, mother, brothers, and sisters. The Chatham paper opined that Wood's affidavit "fully settles the question of Merwin being 'a Southern planter,' or the 'boy Jack,' 'his father, mother, brother, and sister' being his property as asserted." In fact, Demarest was the freeborn son of a Sarah Brown by her first marriage.

When the Grand Western train carrying Merwin and the boy stopped for water, the Chatham Vigilance Committee—of which Anderson was a member and "M. A. S. Cary" was assistant secretary—swung into action. An estimated 100 to 150 black men and women intercepted the train, and several armed members boarded it. The railroad pressed charges against seven of the rescuers, two white and five black. Among them was Isaac Shadd, who was given temporary custody of the boy.

Though Anderson was not among those charged nor named in any of the accounts, it's reasonable to assume that he, as an officer of the Vigilance Committee, was among the rescuers. It is likely, too, that Copeland, newly arrived with John Price, was also there to liberate the child.

For a time, it appeared the trial of the Chatham seven would go forward as scheduled on October 18. By then, the financially strapped *Provincial Freeman*, "organ of the fugitives," according to Shadd Cary, had largely suspended publication. But that did not stop her from seeking donations to help pay for the defense of the rescuers. "As an agent appointed by our Vigilance Committee, established here to conduct the case growing out of the release of the slave boy spoken of by the *New-York Tribune*, and an Assistant Secretary of the same, I am authorized, and beg to enlist your pecuniary aid towards defending the suit brought against" seven, including Isaac Shadd. All but two were "colored men and poor men," she noted, and 150 others faced similar charges. "Please assure us of your sympathy by a word of encouragement, and whatever your generosity will prompt you to give or send."

The presiding judge imposed fines—ranging from ten to thirty dollars—rather than jail sentences, and noted "the force of a higher law" than those on the statute books. The *Chatham Planet*, in an editorial, concurred: "If in releasing this boy the laws of our country were slightly overstepped, we feel that Canadians of every class, creed, and colour are not altogether dead to recognition of a higher law than all human laws."

In the extensive newspaper accounts, Demarest was sometimes described as a "slave child," which affected some of the coverage. The *Detroit Free Press* claimed the rescuers were club-, gun-, and knife-wielding "rioters" engaged in "kidnapping." The paper castigated "stout, burly Negroes" for intervening on the youth's behalf. The *Chatham Planet* took a contrary position, accusing the Detroit paper of sensationalism pandering to Southern slaveholders.

After the charges were dropped, Demarest stayed in the home of Isaac and Amelia Shadd for a brief time.

Following the rescue, Osborne Anderson remained in Chatham for nearly another year, while plans hatched at the quiet convention were on hold for further fundraising and concern over a leak. Finally, on September 13, 1859, he left Chatham to rendezvous with Brown a week later and then five days after that to go with him to Harpers Ferry. Anderson, the sole survivor of the five African Americans on the raid, would later return to Chatham a free man of color but a fugitive from federal authorities in the land of his birth.

Chatham today is the seat of the combined Chatham-Kent municipality, with a total population in 2016 of 103,000—of whom 2 percent are black—and it is still largely rural. The city of Chatham, fifty-four miles east of Windsor, is just off Canada's Highway 401, a superhighway that stretches from Windsor, on the Canadian side of the Ambassador Bridge, all the way to the Quebec provincial boundary, 514 miles to the east. By far the municipality's largest community, Chatham boasted nearly forty-five thousand people in 2011. On its outskirts, it resembles any small American city, with its chain hotels and fast-food restaurants. The older city center is notable for its large Victorian homes and the Thames River, which runs through on its way to Lake St. Claire.

Chatham's East End is still the largely black section of town, though since racial barriers have fallen it is more mixed than otherwise. On its residential streets are two black churches and small, detached houses.

Gwendolyn Robinson, a great-great-grandniece of Mary Ann Shadd Cary and founder in 1992 of the Chatham-Kent Black Historical Society, lives here in a modest brick house that was once a school, with an addition her late husband John added where she "did hair." In 2003, she was awarded the coveted Canadian National Griot, a heavy statue that is Oscaresque in appearance. *Griot* is an African word for storyteller, and she is that.

When I visit, Gwen is eighty-five, a gregarious light-skinned widow. She is brimming with stories to tell about Chatham's past and present. "There was a time when [white] people wouldn't cross William Street," she says, referring to a road that runs a few blocks to the west that used to separate white and black Chatham.

Aside from books and documents, she has something else to show me. It's a short, one-block walk to the BME Freedom Park, a small corner space dedicated in 2002 on the former site of the British Methodist Episcopal Church, where Brown's constitutional convention first met. There are five metal benches, and in the center of it all is a striking bust of Mary Ann Shadd Cary created by noted sculptor and Shadd descendant Artis Lane, an American great-great-great-grandniece. Around the corner is First Baptist Church, where Brown ended his meeting, with Osborne Anderson as secretary, and up the street is a newer building at 177 King Street, the W.I.S.H. Centre, which houses a health clinic, a community center, and the Chatham-Kent Black Historical Society. There is a modest museum and a separate room for research and the society's small staff.

Here I meet Terry Shadd, who sat on the society's board of directors. He is one of ten Shadds listed in the Chatham-Kent phone book as of August 2016. Shadd is a great-great-grandnephew of Mary Ann and the great-great-great-grandson of Abraham D. Shadd, Mary Ann's father. This descendant, a board member of the historical society, had retired from the local hospital, where he'd worked as both a nurse and building engineer. He was living on what was left of the original family farm, one hundred acres now planted in soybeans and wheat close to A. D. Shadd Road about eleven miles south of Chatham. The farm

Osborne Perry Anderson, the sole survivor who published the only insider account of the raid. *Library of Congress, LC-USZ62-7821*

is just north of the tiny but historic community of North Buxton and within sight of the MacDonald Cartier Freeway (Highway 401).

"We've always been kind of quiet. Never said too much," Terry Shadd says. "We always knew what we did but kind of stayed in the background."

There is little in either North Buxton or Chatham to remind a visitor of Osborne Perry Anderson. A plaque at the North Buxton museum lists 107 names of Chatham-Kent men who enlisted in the Union Army during the Civil War. Anderson's name is among eight whose regiments are unidentified.

The building where he worked at the *Provincial Freeman*, at King and Adelaide Streets, close to the train tracks in the Chatham East End where the rescue occurred, is long gone. In its place is a small, low-slung building with a convenience store, King Street Variety, and a Laundromat. Easily overlooked on the west side of the building is a small plaque noting the site's historic importance in Canadian and American black history.

5

The Road to Harpers Ferry

The small farmhouse, restored in the 1970s, sits on twelve acres off Harpers Ferry Road in Washington County, Maryland. It is now, as it was in 1859, in a remote location four miles uphill from the Potomac River and another mile from the railroad trestle to Harpers Ferry. Over many years, it had been a piece of historical detritus left to decay. But its significance could not be denied.

A century after it had served as a key staging ground for John Brown's ill-fated raid on Harpers Ferry, the farm became a popular stop on the Chitlin' Circuit, a venue for top African American entertainers like Chubby Checker, Ray Charles, Aretha Franklin, Diana Ross, Little Richard, and James Brown. Hundreds packed into a large hall behind the farmhouse to hear the music, to dance, to socialize in a former slave state that was only then, in the middle of the twentieth century, starting to desegregate. There was a certain incongruity—and also an odd symmetry—here: the property that had housed armed abolitionists became a venue for rhythm-and-blues stars and a peaceful retreat for black audiences during the waning years of legal segregation.

The 2016 book *John Brown to James Brown* recalls that era. Before its restoration, the farmhouse and grounds were owned by the Tri-State Elks Lodge, known as the Black Elks. They intended to turn the house into a museum and memorial to John Brown. After that dream faded, they sold the farm to a white man, a World War II navy veteran and

The restored farmhouse in 2017. *Eugene L. Meyer*

Civil War buff who'd led a Confederate infantry regiment in a 1976 reenactment, belonged to the Sons of Confederate Veterans, and owned Universal Floors in Washington, DC—a man named, ironically, South, whose ancestors had once owned slaves. South T. Lynn had invested in the farmhouse's restoration and secured it a place on the National Historic Register. While largely unknown to the public, the farmhouse had become an essential stop on the John Brown route trod by scholars, students, and acolytes of the martyred abolitionist, if not also of the five African Americans with him. The farmhouse is still visible from the road, but on a spring weekday morning the gate is locked and access is limited—a tourist attraction without tourists but open for tours by appointment through the John Brown Historical Foundation, the property's nonprofit overseers.

Sprigg Lynn, South's son, is nonetheless eager to show the house and share its story. "We love our history and we love our floors," he tells me.

Indeed, wax figures of some of the raiders now occupy the house—Shields Green in the attic, John Brown seated at the kitchen table. The faux tableau has actual historical antecedents. On July 3, 1859, Brown, with sons Owen and Oliver and Jeremiah Anderson, a Brown lieutenant, had arrived by train at Sandy Hook, a mile downriver from Harpers Ferry, on the Maryland side of the Potomac. Sandy Hook was—and is—a tiny town composed of a strip of two-story houses nestled against the steep cliff of South Mountain and fronting on the train tracks, the Chesapeake and Ohio Canal, and the Potomac River. Brown claimed that he and two of his sons (posing as Isaac Smith and Sons) were New York cattlemen searching for a farm where they could raise and feed livestock. A local man directed them to the then vacant farmhouse.

The two-and-a-half-story stone-and-log house had been built and owned by a Dr. Robert Kennedy, who died without a will early in 1859. John Brown would rent it from the executors of his estate for thirty-five dollars in gold for nine months. Throughout the summer and early fall, the two-story farmhouse would be a secret staging ground, harboring his small band of raiders, who hid in the loft during daylight hours. It also housed an arsenal of Sharps rifles, revolvers, and pikes he had had shipped, first to Chambersburg, Pennsylvania, and then to the house for the ultimate assault on the Ferry.

The raid had been long planned and long in preparation, but Brown had delayed it for more than a year after Chatham. The postponement stemmed from concern that an insider, a British-born soldier of fortune named Hugh Forbes, had divulged—and criticized as impractical—his plans to several antislavery politicians and donors. This, in turn, discouraged the donors. To reassure them, Brown needed to demonstrate his ability to act decisively and with military precision on behalf of the abolitionist cause. Thus, he traveled to Kansas and Missouri, where during Christmas week in 1858 he and twenty of his men freed eleven slaves at three farms, killing one of the owners and taking "horses, mules, oxen, bedding, and two old Conestoga wagons." Over the next two months, he took those he freed across Iowa, then by train to Chicago and Detroit, where, amid much publicity, they crossed over into Canada. The donations resumed.

During these months, Brown also traveled to his farm at North Elba, New York, and to key locations in Ohio. At all stops he was busily soliciting money to fund his plan to free and arm slaves who would then wage a guerrilla war against slaveholders from the Appalachian Mountains, to which they could easily retreat after each foray into the valleys. Still, if he had hoped to liberate large numbers of slaves, Harpers Ferry seemed an odd choice. It was in an area of mostly small farms, not the large plantations that had been fertile recruiting grounds for Nat Turner's rebellion. But Harpers Ferry was a potent symbol of federal power in a slave state that had long treated African Americans as chattel property—and it had the federal arsenal, armory, and rifle works that were key to his bold plan. In his mind at least, if he could capture and secure them, anything seemed possible.

Before Brown rented the farm in Harpers Ferry, he leased the upstairs room of a two-story frame boardinghouse in Chambersburg belonging to an abolitionist widow, Mary Ritner, at 225 East King Street, which still stands. Several of the raiders also stayed there.

The town is the seat of Franklin County, which borders Maryland. In 1860, the county had 1,800 black or mixed-race residents, with a large concentration in Chambersburg, which was also an important stop on the Underground Railroad. That meant there would be a welcome mat for the likes of Brown and his followers. The Confederate Army would repeatedly invade and set the town ablaze during the war, but that was yet to come. In the 1860 Census, Chambersburg was a thriving center of 5,255 residents thirteen miles from Maryland and fifty miles from the Kennedy farm. Brown lived there off and on from June to October.

Brown's Chambersburg cover story was a modified version of what he'd been saying in Washington County, Maryland. In Chambersburg, he identified himself as Dr. Isaac Smith, a man interested in iron mining—and this became a metaphor for the arms and other supplies he was buying (including tools from the local Lemnos Edge Tool Works), bringing to town, and storing in the Oak and Cauffman Warehouse as

John Brown, as he appeared in 1859. *Library of Congress, LC-USZ62-2472*

"mining equipment" for eventual transfer to the Kennedy farm. These were to include nearly one thousand pikes forged in Connecticut, which would be affixed to wooden shafts, and two hundred Sharps rifles. Six influential wealthy New England abolitionists, known as the Secret Six, had bankrolled the effort. Though their identities and involvement would later be revealed, all avoided arrest and prosecution.

In hopes of furthering his plan and legitimizing the larger assault against slavery, Brown thought he needed a nationally prominent African American to join him. The obvious candidate was Frederick Douglass.

Traveling in the same abolitionist circles, they had known each other for about a dozen years. Brown had invited Douglass to the Chatham conference, though he did not attend. A few months prior, in January and February 1858, Brown stayed at the Douglass home in Rochester, New York, where the famed abolitionist had established himself as a newspaper publisher and leading antislavery activist.

Another Douglass house guest at the time was a fugitive slave named Shields Green, who claimed to be descended from African royalty and was also known as "the Emperor." From Charleston, South Carolina, Green—who had changed his name from Esau Brown—had fled on a ship after his wife died, leaving behind a six-month-old son. He reportedly worked as a sailor, possibly on a cotton ship making its way up the East Coast. His date of departure, his path from Charleston to Rochester, and how he found his way to Douglass are not well documented, though it has been said that he was also in Canada, where he learned about John Brown. Better documented is his time in Rochester, where he lived with Douglass, worked as a clothes cleaner, and even had his own business card, which advertised:

CLOTHES CLEANING

The undersigned would respectfully announce that he is prepared to do clothes cleaning in a manner to suit the most fastidious, and on cheaper terms than any one else. Orders left at my establishment, No. 2 Spring Street, first door west of Exchange Street, will be promptly attended to. I make no promises that I am unable to perform. All kinds of Cloths, Silks, Satins, &c., can be cleaned at this establishment.

SHEILD [*sic*] EMPEROR

Rochester, July 22, 1858

It was in Douglass's home that Brown revealed to his host and to Green more about his plans to free the slaves.

"Shields Green was not one to shrink from hardships or dangers," Douglass wrote years later. "He was a man of few words, and his speech

Shields Green was an escaped slave who met Brown at Frederick Douglass's home in Rochester, New York. *West Virginia State Archives*

was singularly broken; but his courage and self-respect made him quite a dignified character. John Brown saw at once what 'stuff' Green 'was made of,' and confided to him his plans and purposes. Green easily believed in Brown, and promised to go with him whenever he should be ready to move." William C. Nell, evoking the testimony of others who knew Green, wrote that he was "an uncommonly brave man, knowing no fear but possessed with all the properties of a hero." Of medium build and dark complexion, Green was unable to write, "yet left an indelible mark in Virginia of his eternal hostility to American Slavery," Nell wrote.

In August 1859, Brown wrote to Douglass informing him that "a beginning in his work would soon be made." He requested a meeting at an abandoned quarry on the outskirts of Chambersburg, where, he wrote, his "mining tools" were stored. Douglass was to bring Green with him. Second in command John H. Kagi would also be at the parley.

Douglass and Green were soon on their way, passing through New York City, where they stopped in Brooklyn to see Rev. James Gloucester and his wife, Elizabeth, "and told them where and for what we were going, and that our old friend needed money. Mrs. Glocester gave me ten dollars," Douglass wrote, "and asked me to hand the same to John Brown, with her best wishes."

The meeting with Brown began on Saturday, August 19, and stretched into Sunday as Brown spelled out his plans to take Harpers Ferry and sought to convince Douglass to join in the raid. "Come with me, Douglass; I will defend you with my life," Brown pledged. "I want you for a special purpose. When I strike, the bees will begin to swarm, and I shall want you to help hive them." The "bees" were the slaves Brown expected to flock to his banner.

Douglass argued against the venture, saying that Brown was "going into a perfect steel-trap, and that once in he would never get out alive; that he would be surrounded at once and escape would be impossible." Brown countered that his taking of hostages from among "the best citizens of the neighborhood" would be his bargaining chip out of the trap. "I looked at him with some astonishment," Douglass wrote, "that he could rest upon a reed so weak and broken."

For reasons of discretion or cowardice, as Douglass put it, he declined to go along, though he did, as promised, give Brown the ten dollars from Elizabeth Gloucester. When he was about to leave, Douglass asked Green what he wanted to do "and was surprised by his coolly saying, in his broken way, 'I b'leve I'll go wid de old man.'" So Douglass returned to Rochester, and Green went to the Kennedy farm and to Harpers Ferry, and, ultimately, to his doom.

Owen Brown accompanied Green during his trip from Chambersburg to the farm, and they narrowly escaped detection and capture. As they hid in a cornfield near Hagerstown, three men spied Owen's coat. Thinking they were on the trail of a fugitive slave, the men returned twice to investigate but were temporarily deterred by the sound of Owen's revolver going off. Green and Brown, still pursued by searchers, made it to the mountains and traveled all night, reaching the farm the next morning, exhausted. "Oh, what a poor fool I am," Shields confided to Owen. "I had got away out of slavery, and here I have got back into the eagle's claw again!"

Years later, Owen Brown also recalled other trips by horse and wagon to Chambersburg with his father in early September and into October "to see if any express packages (colored volunteers) had arrived." Beyond the five, none had, nor would they.

The African American soldiers were, in alphabetical order, Osborne Perry Anderson, John A. Copeland, Shields Green, Lewis Sheridan Leary, and Dangerfield Newby. They differed in background and in appearance. Three were born free, one had been freed, and the fifth was a fugitive from slavery. They could be more accurately described as African American than black, because four of the five were of mixed race. Shields Green was the exception.

Even before the Douglass-Brown meeting at Chambersburg, the population at the Kennedy farmhouse had begun to swell. Most of the recruits—all of them white—had been with Brown in Kansas. On August 6, Brown's sons Watson, Owen, and Oliver, and the Thompson brothers William and Dauphin—North Elba neighbors of the Brown family—had taken up residence. Then came the Kansas veterans: Charles Plummer Tidd, then Aaron Dwight Stevens, then Albert Hazlett, the two Coppoc brothers Edwin and Barclay, and William H. Leeman, who would arrive near the end of August. Stewart Taylor, a Canadian by birth who'd met Brown in Iowa, also joined the group. John E. Cook, a well-bred and educated Connecticut native who was also with Brown in Kansas, had preceded all of them, living for more than a year in Harpers Ferry, where he taught school and was a canal lock tender. He had even married a local woman and become acquainted with the area's slave-owning gentry, including Col. Lewis Washington, the great-grandson of George Washington, whose family was well represented in Jefferson County. Dubbed John Brown's spy, Cook had established himself there by design.

During the third week in July, two young women journeyed from John Brown's farm in North Elba to join the men. They were Annie

Brown, John Brown's fifteen-year-old daughter, and Martha Brown, his sixteen-year-old daughter-in-law. Their assigned tasks at the Kennedy farmhouse were purely domestic. Martha would do the cooking; Annie would serve the food, sweep the floor, and in general try to keep the house clean. The men would wash their own clothes, but the women put them outside to dry. Their presence would serve another purpose: to lend an air of domesticity that might ward off neighbors' suspicions.

While there, they would also come to know the men who were largely confined to quarters, and Annie would remember each in great detail. She playfully referred to them as "my invisibles." Invisible, perhaps, but not silent. "Shields Green," she said, "was a perfect rattle-brain in talk; he used to annoy me very much, coming downstairs so often. He came near betraying and upsetting the whole business, by his careless letting a neighbor woman see him, when she came to the house one day. I had to do a great deal of talking and some bribing to shut her up."

Osborne Perry Anderson would be the only Chatham convention member to join Brown. His reputation preceded him by letter from another black conference member, who wrote to Brown announcing Anderson's departure. Anderson, he wrote, would be "found an efficient hand." He would also be described as "brace, modest, reticent." Another black member recalled sixty-four years later that Anderson might not have been there at all had it not been for the drawing of lots among the principals of the *Provincial Freeman* newspaper, which felt obliged to send at least one recruit.

Anderson had emerged the winner, or loser, depending on one's perspective.

Paying his own way, he left Canada on September 13 and arrived by train in Chambersburg three days later, on Friday morning. There, on September 20, he met with John and Watson Brown and John Kagi and learned that boxes of weapons had already been moved to the Kennedy farmhouse. Anderson left Chambersburg on September 24 on foot to meet Brown fifteen miles south at the Mason-Dixon Line.

"I walked alone as far as Middletown, a town on the line between Maryland and Pennsylvania, and it being then dark, I found Captain Brown awaiting with his [one-horse covered] wagon. We set out directly, and drove until nearly day-break, the next morning, when we reached the Farm in safety." As a precaution, Anderson wrote, all "the colored men . . . who went from the North made the journey from the Penn line at night."

Together, Anderson and Brown proceeded south, arriving at the farmhouse at dawn on September 25. There Anderson declared he was ready for war. But the days and nights came and went as Brown waited for more recruits but kept his battle plan to himself. His recruits envisioned a hit-and-run raid, running more slaves off to Canada with the raiders also exiting north. When Brown revealed the full extent of his plan, a majority—including his three sons—lined up against it. The news that they would be going south, not north, roiled the room. "It nearly broke up the camp," Tidd said. Facing a wall of opposition, Brown offered to resign, but Kagi argued that only their leader could lead them, and the men fell in line. Tidd went to Cook's house in Harpers Ferry for three days "to cool off." Throughout, "Chatham Anderson," as they called him, remained steadfast in his devotion to Brown.

Anderson found at his new temporary home an "earnest, fearless, determined company of men. . . . There, as at Chatham, I saw the same evidence of strong and commanding intellect, high-toned morality, and inflexibility on purpose . . . and a profound and holy reverence for God. . . . There was no milk and water sentimentality—no offense contempt for the negro, while working in his cause; the pulsations of each and every heart beat in harmony for the suffering and pleading slave."

At the Kennedy farm, Brown's army hid by day in the loft. But at night, Anderson wrote, "we sallied out for a ramble, or to breathe the fresh air and enjoy the beautiful solitude of the mountain scenery around, by moonlight." Staying inside during the days did not seem to bother Anderson. He was, Annie Brown said, "accustomed to being confined in the house, being a printer by trade, so that he was not so restive as some of the others." He was just grateful for the grapes, chestnuts, pawpaws, and fall flowers that Annie and Martha gathered.

From the outside, the house and its grounds were unremarkable. "Rough, unsightly, and aged," Anderson recalled, "it was only those privileged to enter and tarry for a long time, and to penetrate the mysteries of the two rooms it contained—kitchen, parlor, dining-room below, and the spacious chamber, attic, store-room, a [makeshift] prison, drilling room, comprised in the loft above—who could tell how we lived at Kennedy Farm."

During his three weeks at the Kennedy farm, Osborne Anderson would later write, "no less than four" slaves died in the vicinity. One, Jerry, "living three miles away, hung himself in the late Dr. Kennedy's orchard, because he was to be sold South, his owner having become insolvent." The other three were murdered. "They were punished so that death ensued immediately, or in a short time." Others related variations of these unsettling events. On October 10, Kagi shared the news in a letter to John Brown Jr., in Ohio: "A fine slave man near our headquarters hung himself a few days ago because his master sold his wife away from him." He added, somewhat ambiguously, "This also arouses the slaves." And Watson Brown, in a letter to his wife, Isabell, in North Elba, said the incidents had only solidified support among the men for the mission they were soon to undertake.

Dangerfield Newby, of course, had a very personal reason for joining the group: the imminent sale of his enslaved wife and their children, who lived some sixty miles southeast in Brentsville, Virginia. "Newby seemed a good-natured sensible old man," Annie Brown later recalled. "He had a wife and several children that were slaves, and he was impatient to have operations commenced, for he was anxious to get them." Meanwhile, Newby would intently study John Brown's maps of the planned operations that encompassed the Appalachians.

"Newby was quiet, sensible and very unobtrusive," Annie Brown wrote, describing him physically as a tall (six feet two inches), "splendid, light-skinned specimen."

To *sensible*, she might have added *sensitive*. "Poor man, he used to get very low spirited and impatient at what appeared to him the long delay and preparation," she remembered. "We tried to cheer him up, for we really liked him."

Newby was familiar with the provisional constitution that had been adopted in Chatham, and, Annie Brown recalled, was especially moved by article 42: "The marriage relation shall be at all times respected and families kept together, as far as possible; and broken families encouraged to unite and intelligence offices established for this purpose."

During this pre-raid period, when others remained sequestered at the farmhouse, Newby moved in and out while working on a farm along the Maryland-Pennsylvania border, incidentally also collecting intelligence. He would not be a full-time resident until shortly before the raid.

But he was more than all in. Newby also tried—unsuccessfully—to recruit two of his brothers, Gabriel and James, back in Ohio. He wrote asking them to join him, but he didn't say why, and they didn't come. Gabriel, however, was instrumental in receiving and forwarding letters from Harriet Newby to Dangerfield.

The most restless among the group, Dangerfield showed Harriet's letters to John Brown and to others at the farmhouse. The last, dispiriting letter was dated August 16, two months before the raid, expressing again her "one bright hope" that Dangerfield would liberate her before it was too late. He asked when he could respond. "Soon, soon, Dangerfield," Brown cautiously replied.

Incoming mail, addressed to Isaac Smith and collected at the Harpers Ferry post office, also included the *Baltimore Sun* and a farmers' publication to which Brown had subscribed. In the downstairs rooms were unpacked boxes containing weapons. The men spent most of the days in the loft, venturing downstairs only for dinner and breakfast, when Brown would read to the them from his Bible and offer a special prayer for the oppressed. "I never heard John Brown pray," Anderson said, "that he did not make strong appeals to God for the deliverance of the slave."

But there were other chores and conversations to occupy the time. For one thing, there were near one thousand pike heads to be affixed to wooden shafts. And there was more, as recalled by Osborne Anderson: "We applied a preparation for bronzing our gun barrels—discussed subjects of reform—related our personal history; but when our resources became pretty well exhausted, the ennui from confinement, imposed silence, etc., would make the men almost desperate. At such times, neither slavery nor slaveholders were discussed mincingly."

With the days of reckoning fast approaching, Martha and Annie were to go back to North Elba. The night before, Shields Green, described as "the negro man with Congo face, big, misplaced words, and huge feet," bade the women farewell. "This was the greatest conglomeration of big words that was ever piled up. Some one asked [Osborne] Anderson 'if he understood it,' and he replied, 'No, God Himself could not understand that.'" The next day, September 29, Oliver Brown, Martha's husband, escorted the women to Troy, New York, where he left them to return on their own to North Elba. With the women gone, Anderson wrote, "The men then sobered down and acted like earnest men working hard preparing for the coming raid."

John Anthony Copeland and Lewis Sheridan Leary were the last of the five African Americans to arrive. Both were already battle-tested veterans of the abolitionist cause, having participated in the armed Oberlin-Wellington rescue of a fugitive slave a year before. Leary had heard Brown speak in Cleveland and was immediately inspired by his fiery rhetoric. He was related to Copeland through marriage and, learning of Brown's plans, recruited him to go along. They departed Oberlin on October 10, a Monday, spending that night in Cleveland and boarding a train there the next day. To help pay for the trip, they had received $17.50 from Ralph Plumb, another member of that successful rescue; the donor would later deny any involvement in the plot. By Wednesday, they were in Chambersburg. From there, they proceeded with Kagi and Watson Brown to the Kennedy farm, arriving Saturday morning. The last man, F. J. Merriam, grandson of a prominent Boston abolitionist and suffragist, reached the farm that evening. He had first gone to Baltimore to purchase more supplies.

John Brown had planned to attack the Ferry on October 24. The plan, according to James Redpath, a Scottish-born journalist and sympathetic early biographer, was to seize the arsenal that evening and to take the arms and "a number of the wealthier citizens of the vicinity as hostages, until they should redeem themselves by liberating an equal number of their slaves."

But there was word that his plans had gotten out, and the neighbors were growing increasingly suspicious: two or three days before the raid, slaveholders in Carroll County, which adjoins Washington County, in Maryland, intercepted slaves armed with long knives fashioned from old scythe blades and with their masters' horses. When interrogated, they said they had been "induced to leave their masters and to join the attempt to be made somewhere in Virginia to liberate the slaves." Thus, even though John Brown Jr. had written from Canada that blacks in Ohio and Canada expected to arrive later that month, the self-styled Capt. John Brown decided to move the date up a week. It was one of a number of fateful decisions that would affect the outcome and foreclose the escape from the "steel trap" that Douglass had predicted would doom the enterprise.

Before Sunday morning breakfast on October 16, Brown led the men as usual in worship, reading a Bible passage Anderson deemed "applicable to the condition of the slaves, and our duty as their brethren." It was a solemn day, with military protocols that included roll call. At 10 AM Brown convened a meeting of his provisional army, appointing Anderson to act as the chair. For several of the men, this was the first time they had learned of the plan in any great detail. John Copeland would later claim that it was much more than he'd bargained for; perhaps naively, he'd never entertained the possibility that there would be fatalities on either side. This was to be not the limited rescue of slaves, as in Kansas and Missouri, but a full-scale assault on federal power, both literal and figurative.

Aaron Stevens read aloud the provisional constitution adopted in Chatham. Brown administered to the men an oath of fidelity and secrecy. There were officers and privates. Kagi handed out signed commissions. None of the African American raiders were so anointed, and they would be given not rifles but pikes, a decision from which there was no dissent.

"It has been a matter of inquiry," Anderson later wrote, "why colored men were not commissioned by John Brown to act as captains, lieutenants, &c. . . . John Brown did offer the captaincy, and other military positions, to colored men equally with others, but a want of acquaintance with military tactics was the invariable excuse. . . . I declined a captain's commission tendered by the brave old man, as better suited to those more experienced . . . my excuse was accepted. The same must be said of other colored men . . . who proved their worthiness by their able defense of freedom at the Ferry."

At some point, however, Green was accorded the honor of being elected a member of Brown's provisional government. Copeland was to become a judge on the Supreme Court. That afternoon, Brown presented eleven orders, assigning to each man specific tasks to be performed in the hours and days ahead. Owen Brown, Barclay Coppoc, and F. J. Merriam would stay behind to guard the arms and supplies that would be needed later on, after the initial raid, as well as more items that were stored in a small schoolhouse.

After they had eaten their last meal together, Brown commanded, "Men, get on your arms. We will proceed to the Ferry." It was now 8 PM.

It was a damp, misty night when John Brown, wearing the cap he'd worn in Kansas, climbed onto the horse-drawn wagon, preceded on foot by Cook and Tidd with rifles slung over their shoulders. In all, there were nineteen men, including Brown. It was barely a platoon, much less an army, but their course was set, their destiny determined. Warmed in woolen shawls, they walked silently in double file behind the wagon, "as solemnly as a funeral procession," Anderson wrote, for that in fact is exactly what it was.

6

The Raid

An imposing nineteenth-century manor house welcomes a visitor to Beallair Estates, a twenty-first-century subdivision of large homes, some attached, some not, midway between Harpers Ferry and Charles Town. The development adjoins a golf course and is set back from US Route 340, a divided highway connecting the two historic towns.

Beallair, the antebellum home fronting the development, once belonged to Col. Lewis W. Washington, the grandnephew of the first president. His still-imposing plantation house would play a role in the drama that unfolded on the rainy night of October 16, 1859.

The Washingtons were then, and remain, prominent citizens of Jefferson County. Charlestown, now bifurcated into *Charles Town*, is named for Charles Washington, the first president's youngest brother. Like George Washington, Lewis's family owned slaves and opposed any form of abolition. That meant, during the Harpers Ferry raid, they would be prime hostages.

John Brown had been quite explicit about this. His eleventh and final order to his men at the Kennedy farm was to take Lewis Washington prisoner and to have him turn over his arms to Osborne Anderson: "Anderson being a colored man, and colored men being only *things* in the South, it is proper that the South be taught a lesson upon this point."

Brown dispatched six of his men to Beallair to execute his orders. In a four-horse wagon on the road to Beallair, Anderson wrote, "we met some colored men, to whom we made known our purpose. They said they had long been waiting for an opportunity of the kind." Aaron Stevens urged them to "go around among the colored people and circulate the news."

The men Brown had dispatched arrived at Beallair around midnight, rousing Washington and his family. "You can have my slaves if you will let me remain," Washington pleaded, to no avail. The hostage takers included—in addition to Anderson and Stevens—John Copeland, Shields Green, and John E. Cook. The last man was not a stranger to the planter. He had made Washington's acquaintance during the year he'd lived in the area, working as a canal lock tender and schoolteacher. From his visits to the manor house, Cook knew that Washington had the sword Frederick the Great had given his great-uncle, the prize that Washington would be forced to hand over to Anderson to bring back to John Brown. They would also confiscate two pistols that the Marquis de Lafayette had given the first president.

While the slave-owning gentry would portray the patrician Washington as a brave and heroic man in this situation, Anderson found him "speechless or terrified," writing, "The Colonel cried heartily when he found he must submit" and "stood 'blubbering' like a great calf at supposed danger."

The raiders then hustled Washington and four of his slaves into the colonel's horse-drawn wagon bound for Harpers Ferry, five miles distant.

On the way, they stopped at the farm of John Allstadt, likely another slaveholder Cook had known. They reached his two-story frame house between 1 and 2 AM. The sleeping family was awakened by the sound of a slamming door. Two family members rushed to the window. "Take in your heads, or I'll blow out your brains," a gun-wielding black man shouted at them, eighteen-year-old John Thomas Allstadt recalled. The downstairs room was full of armed men.

"What are you going to do?" John Thomas asked.

"To carry your father and you to Harpers Ferry. John Brown has taken possession of the Government works."

"That isn't much," the younger Allstadt said. "There's only one watchman there."

"You shut your damned mouth, or I'll blow your brains out," Stevens declared, and ordered an unidentified armed black man, possibly Anderson, to keep John Thomas quiet.

The Allstadts were led outside to join Washington, his slaves, and "our six negroes" in Washington's four-horse wagon, John Thomas recalled. The senior Allstadt put the number of his slaves taken at seven.

"We could have his slaves, also, if we would only leave him," the Allstadt patriarch had said, according to Anderson. "This, of course, was contrary to our plans and instructions. . . . At last, seeing no alternative, he got ready, when the slaves were gathered up from about the quarters by their own consent, and all placed in Washington's big wagon."

Their final destination would be the fire engine house inside the armory yard, where Brown and several of his men had established their raid headquarters. The hostages could be bartered for more slaves from the surrounding countryside, Brown reasoned.

On the way, they stopped at the house of "an old colored lady" who "had a good time over the message we took her," Anderson wrote. "This liberating the slaves was the very thing she had longed for, prayed for, and dreamed about, time and again; and her heart was full of rejoicing over the fulfillment of a prophecy which had been her faith for long years."

John Brown's band of brothers reached the train trestle late Sunday evening, October 16. John Henry Kagi and Charles Plummer Tidd, who was accorded the rank of captain, cut the telegraph wires on both sides of the Potomac.

Nestled in a gap in the Blue Ridge, Harpers Ferry was flanked by limestone cliffs—Maryland Heights to the north, Loudoun Heights across the Shenandoah to the south. Shenandoah Street stretched the width of the lower town, from the federal arsenal with its twenty-two buildings and adjacent armory half a mile to Hall's Rifle Works. From the bottom, High Street climbed steeply up to Bolivar, the adjoining town named for the South American liberator where many of the armorers lived. Narrow lanes with some modest homes diverged like tributaries from High Street. Arsenal brass lived on the higher ground in larger homes. But the peninsula on which Harpers Ferry had been built between the two great rivers served to compress the town into a sharply defined area.

The early incursion into Harpers Ferry had gone well. Brown drove the wagon across the covered Potomac River bridge. There were very few guards on duty, and they did not resist, allowing Brown's men to quickly secure their three main objectives: the federal arsenal, the adjacent armory, and the rifle works between Shenandoah Street and the Shenandoah River. The arrival of the hostages appeared to strengthen the hand of the leader for whatever course he chose to pursue.

"I came here from Kansas, and this is a slave state," Brown told his hostages. "I want to free all the Negroes in this state; I seek possession of the U.S. Armory, and if the citizens interfere with me I must only burn the town and have blood."

There was one unexpected disturbance to break the silence and mar the night. A westbound Baltimore and Ohio train came to an unexpected stop on the Maryland side of the bridge. Brown had stationed two sentinels on the covered railroad bridge, and they had detained a night watchman named Patrick Higgins. Hearing a ruckus, Haywood Shepherd, a forty-four-year-old free man of color who was a railroad baggage handler and an occasional ticket seller, went out to investigate. Brown's men ordered him to halt. He either ignored or didn't hear them and turned back. Shots rang out. The second struck him in the back, and the bullet emerged from below his left nipple. It was about 1:30 AM. In great pain, he staggered back to the station office, where he lay on a plank between two chairs. The shooters did not know the race of their target.

John Starry, the thirty-five-year-old town doctor, heard a shot and a cry of distress from the iron railroad trestle. The noise woke him, and he rushed to his window, which faced the bridge. He crossed the street to the railroad office, where he found Shepherd. Starry did what he could to make him comfortable, giving him water, but he was unable to save him, and Shepherd slipped away, twelve hours after being shot.

"Thus," opined the *Winchester Evening Star* some years later, "the first victim of these ruffians who claimed to have the sacred obligation of liberating the negroes was one of the very race they professed to have a desire to save." Alexander Boteler, a Shepherdstown slaveholder and congressman for the district who raced to the scene, called Shepherd "one of the most respectable free negroes in the county."

Shepherd had been in charge of the depot in the absence of Fontaine Beckham, the mayor of Harpers Ferry who also worked as the B&O stationmaster. Shepherd was in essence a rail commuter, living in Winchester and working for the Winchester and Potomac Railroad at Harpers Ferry, where the lines intersected.

"Had he stood when ordered, he would not have been harmed," wrote Osborne Perry Anderson in *A Voice from Harper's Ferry*, his 1861 account of these events. "No one knew at the time whether he was white or colored, but his movements were such as to justify the sentinels in shooting him, as he would not stop when commanded."

In his 1903 eyewitness account, Harpers Ferry resident Joseph Barry surmised that Shepherd's death had dampened any slave uprising and was "in fact the only thing that prevented a general insurrection of the negroes, for some of the farmers of the neighborhood said they noticed an unusual excitement among the slaves on the Sunday before the raid. If it is true that the negroes knew anything of the intended attack, it is probable that they were deterred from taking part in it by seeing one of their own race the first person sacrificed."

It had been a quiet night, until, suddenly, it wasn't.

The town and indeed the entire area was aroused as word spread from those fleeing the invasion. Rumors of the "insurrection" abounded far out of proportion to reality. Insurrectionists numbered in the hundreds. Hundreds of slaves, an armed "gang of negroes," had risen up to join them. Blood flowed in the streets and there was more to come.

Of these reported rumors, the last at least would be true. Near panic ensued among the whites of Jefferson and nearby counties.

Frightened villagers cowered in their homes or sought refuge elsewhere. "Last night a band of ruffians took possession of the town," Mary E. Mauzy wrote to her daughter Eugenia in England, where her husband, formerly a master armorer at Harpers Ferry, was supervising the manufacture of the Enfield rifle. "Every face is so terror stricken. . . . God only knows what will become of us all."

When Anderson returned with the hostages, he and Albert Hazlett were assigned to guard the arsenal gate. Kagi and Copeland were dispatched to the rifle works. Four slaves sent by Brown, and later Lewis Leary, the other black raider from Oberlin, would join them. Inside the engine house, Brown had given the slaves pikes with which to guard what were now eleven fearful white hostages crouched in the watch room at the rear of the brick building. Brown's men, weapons at the ready, stationed themselves in front where there were three heavy oak doors. With only high, arched windows, Allstadt's slave Phil Luckum used masonry tools to dig gun holes in the walls.

As local militia and armed farmers poured into town with guns ablaze, Harpers Ferry turned into a war zone. The ruckus caused another train, this one eastbound, to pause for several hours in Martinsburg, some twenty miles west of Harpers Ferry. Joseph G. Rosengarten, a twenty-four-year-old Philadelphia lawyer traveling east from Chicago, impatiently decided to walk ahead from Martinsburg to Harpers Ferry "to see all the armory workshops and wonders." A country doctor he met on the way said there was a "riotous demonstration by the workmen," nothing more.

Rosengarten learned otherwise when he reached the town, where he saw dead on the streets and was taken into custody on suspicion of being an insurrectionist and transported to the Charlestown jail. On the way, he noted the "odd sight" of "black and white children playing soldiers, led by a chubby black boy, full of a sense of authority, and evidently readily accepted by his white and black comrades in child-like faith." Charlestown, in contrast, was full of drunken white men incensed over the raid. Some of them, he recalled, broke into the jail and "hurried from cell to cell to mine a poor black prisoner, who was forthwith hanged."

Rosengarten, at last, was released, returned to Harpers Ferry, and resumed his journey.

Meanwhile on Monday morning, Brown allowed the eastbound train, full of frightened passengers, to proceed through the town, a tactical mistake. He thought this gesture might reassure the outside world of his benign intentions, but instead it set the stage for his ultimate denouement. When the train reached Monocacy, eighteen miles downriver, the conductor wired top railroad officials of the insurrection. President James Buchanan, Virginia governor Henry A. Wise, and military officials were quickly alerted in turn. The president would soon order US troops to quell the invasion.

Though under fire from local militia and armed citizens, Brown was nothing if not solicitous of his hostages. That morning, he sent out for breakfast from the nearby Wager House hotel. So far, both sides were observing civilities that allowed the transaction to occur. The food was forthcoming, but Brown, thinking it might be poisoned, ate none. He also allowed panicked hostages to visit with their families, under guard, a kindness that further delayed any departure for the hills with seized arms and liberated slaves.

Shortly before noon on Monday, Alexander Boteler arrived to survey the scene. Near Bolivar, he wrote, he encountered "a little old 'darky' coming across a field toward me as fast as a pair of bandy legs, aided by a crooked stick, could carry him. From the frequent glances he cast over his shoulder and his urgent pace, it was evident that the old fellow was fleeing from some apprehended danger, and was fearfully demoralized."

The man said he was fleeing from the insurrectionists at the Ferry. But local "colored people" hadn't joined in, the man told him. Boteler was relieved by "the assurance that the negroes had nothing to do with the trouble."

The Gault House Saloon, adjoining Wager House, was doing a brisk business. Thus, fueled by alcohol as the day wore on, the crowd became drunk with fury, a mob bent on vengeance. Shouts of "Kill them, kill them" resounded through the streets. The Jefferson Guards, a local militia, seized control of both the Potomac and Shenandoah River bridges. At the entrance to the latter, Brown had stationed three of his men, among them Dangerfield Newby. As two men encroached on what Brown's men regarded as a sixty-foot security perimeter, Newby opened fire.

First to fall was Thomas Boerly, an Irish-born grocer. Slaveholder and West Point graduate George Washington Turner took aim at Newby, but Newby fatally shot him first. Increasingly besieged, Newby and the others attempted to retreat to the relative security of the engine house. To get there they had to cross an open area. Then, from an upper window of a brick corner house at High and Shenandoah, a sniper took down Newby, the first of the raiders to die. The sniper was believed to be Richard B. Washington, kin to the hostage Col. Lewis Washington. It was 11 AM Monday.

"Newby was a brave fellow," wrote Anderson, who added that he saw him shot from his post nearby at the arsenal. "He fell at my side, and his death was quickly avenged by Shields Green, the Zouave of the band." By Anderson's account, Green "raised his rifle in an instant, and brought down the cowardly murderer." But Newby's end was neither painless nor pretty.

The rifleman, lacking bullets, had inserted a six-inch iron spike into the barrel of his gun. It sliced across Newby's neck. Newby fell, bleeding and in agony and died quickly. Boteler was also a witness. "I saw his body while it was yet warm as it lay on the pavement in front of the arsenal yard," he recalled, "and I never saw, on any battle-field, a more hideous musket-wound than his. For his throat was cut literally from ear to ear."

Then the mutilation began. The citizens who milled around the dead man began the process of dismembering him, slicing off his ears and cutting them into pieces as souvenirs.

As a correspondent for the proslavery *Frederick Herald* described the scene, "The huge mulatto that shot Mr. Turner was lying in the gutter in front of the Arsenal, with a terrible wound in his neck, and though dead and gory, vengeance was unsatisfied, and many, as they ran sticks into his wound, or beat him with them, wishes that he had a thousand lives, that all of them might be forfeited in expiation and avengement of the foul deed he had committed."

Joseph Barry would recall Newby's "rather pleasant face and address" and what happened after some citizens had dragged him into a nearby alley. "Shortly after Newby's death a hog came up, rooted around the spot where the body lay and, at first appeared to be unconscious that anything extraordinary was in its way," Barry wrote. "After a while the hog paused and looked at the body, then snuffed around it and put its snout to the dead man's face. Suddenly, the brute was apparently seized with a panic and bristles erect and drooping trail it scampered away, as if for dear life. This display of sensibility did not, however, deter others of the same species from crowding around the corpse and almost literally devouring it."

Newby's remains lay in the street for more than a day and a half.

As if the desecration had not been enough, the following evening another citizen, "who had not had a chance to distinguish himself in the skirmish of Monday, fired a shot into what was left of Newby's body, a feat which, it must be supposed, tended to exalt him in his own estimation." Barry wrote that the citizen was "under the influence of whiskey when he fired the superfluous shot," but Barry also saw another man, this one sober, "kick the dead man in the face."

Hog Alley, a short street near the railroad tracks and not far from Shenandoah Street, where Newby fell, remains as a sort of grotesque reminder of Newby's horrific death and dismemberment.

———

"Poor doomed Harpers Ferry," wrote Mary Mauzy to her daughter abroad. "We little dreamed that our quiet peaceful streets should ever be the scene of Battle."

Ultimately, it would amount to much more than a street battle. The specter of another Nat Turner rebellion terrified the South, and Brown's raid further polarized an already badly divided nation. That many Northerners saw Brown in particular as a noble warrior in a just cause further enflamed feelings. Southern politicians had begun calling for secession over slavery even before Harpers Ferry, and the invasion there served to accelerate the dissolution of the Union. On December 1, 1859, the South Carolina General Assembly, citing the Brown raid and the need to defend and secure "African Slavery," given the sentiment in the "so-called free States," resolved that, "should the South's system be endangered, the region should discard said Union at once and forever." Finally, the resolution called on South Carolina's governor to forward a copy to all Southern governors, senators, and congressmen. In truth, as the resolution made clear, slavery was at the heart of it all, and the spark lit at Harpers Ferry would burst into flames before too long.

Forty-four years later, resident Joseph Barry wrote that the raid "may be considered as the commencement of our unhappy civil war. . . . Harper's Ferry enjoys the distinction of having been the scene of the first act in our fearful drama of civil war."

On Monday afternoon, Fontaine Beckham, upset over the death of his close friend and coworker Haywood Shepherd, walked cautiously into the area of conflict and stood watching from behind a water tank. He was tall, sixty-three years old, a widower with two sons and a daughter, and a native of Culpeper County, Virginia. His local ties were strong: his brother was a master armorer, his sister married the armory superintendent, and his niece wed Andrew Hunter, the Charlestown lawyer who would figure so prominently in the forthcoming trials. Beckham then incautiously stepped out into the open and was immediately cut down by one of the raiders firing from inside the engine house. It was 4 PM. This further incensed the already enraged crowd, which now included armory workers who had grabbed weapons from their government employer's stock.

Stationed in the armory yard, raider and former shoemaker William H. Leeman, at twenty the youngest of Brown's men and a veteran of his

Kansas campaign, panicked. He sought to escape by swimming across the Potomac. Perhaps wounded, he crawled from shallow water onto a large boulder and tried to surrender. A pistol-toting citizen waded out and shot away half his head. During the day, his body was further pierced with bullets as townspeople and militia joined in. The next day, others who had missed out on the earlier shooting "showered it with a shower of balls, but the action was one of very questionable taste and propriety," a *Baltimore Sun* reporter wrote.

Sensing his position was increasingly hopeless, Brown sent out William Thompson, with a hostage under a flag of truce, to try negotiating a way out. Thompson instead was taken to the Wager House, where his hands and feet were bound and he was interrogated. He was then dragged to the Potomac River bridge, where his captors, including Andrew Hunter, intended to hang him. Instead, they threw him over the side and repeatedly shot at him. Hit but still alive and clinging to a bridge pier, he was further riddled with bullets.

Inside John Brown's fort at the engine house, Shields Green guarded the hostages, including Lewis Washington, who later described him as "impudent." A National Register nomination for the Allstadt house in 1984 called him "brutal and threatening." Barry, more descriptive, found him to be "a negro of the darkest hue, small in stature and very active in his movements. He seemed to be very officious in the early part of Monday, flitting about from place to place, and he was evidently conscious of his own great importance to the enterprise. . . . He was very insulting to Brown's prisoners, constantly presenting his rifle and threatening to shoot some of them."

On Monday afternoon, two of the five black raiders—Copeland and Leary—remained at their assigned posts at Hall's Rifle Works, under Kagi's command. Also with them were "three colored men from the neighborhood," according to Anderson. Kagi was becoming increasingly impatient with Brown's apparent reluctance to retreat or even to devise any practical plan of escape should the "steel trap" Frederick Douglass had predicted begin to close on them. He sent a message to Brown urging their departure with raider Jeremiah Anderson, who had come to check on the situation at the rifle works. Brown's response was to hold firm a little while longer. By 2 PM, however, the rifle works was all but ringed by armed townspeople, who began shooting. An advance group had even entered the building. The raiders retreated to the building's rear and then hurriedly out the back door facing the Shenandoah River. They quickly realized that only by swimming across the Shenandoah might they save themselves, but even that route was perilous.

They waded in shallow water through rapids to a rock halfway across. There they came under heavy fire from both sides of the river. Only Copeland, "who met his fate like a man," Anderson wrote, survived, to be taken to the guardhouse in town and then to the jail in Charlestown.

In a letter from jail on December 10, Copeland wrote to a friend in Oberlin about the attempted escape: "On entering the river we turned and fired one round at those who had by this time opened fire on us from all sides." Kagi got about two-thirds of the way across the river when he was fatally shot in the head and sank below the water. At least fifty armed men then turned their fire on Copeland and Leary, who managed to climb onto some stones before Leary was struck by several bullets and mortally wounded. He would be taken to the nearby Herr's cooper shop and survive for ten painful hours. Reporters were among those witnessing his slow death. Leary beseeched them to write his wife back in Oberlin, who even now may not have known why her husband had abruptly left home.

"He was a young man," Barry recalled of Leary, "but his personal appearance cannot be described minutely by any person not acquainted with him before the raid, as he was suffering a great deal from wounds when he was captured."

Copeland was still armed, but his rifle was water-soaked and useless. Both he and townsman James H. Holt fired at each other, but the river water had rendered both weapons ineffective. "I was pulled out of the water with the intention of being shot," Copeland wrote, "but some of those that were present not being such cowards as to want to kill a man when disarmed and a prisoner prevented it." Copeland owed this temporary reprieve to Dr. Starry, the town physician, who intervened on his behalf to hold off the angry lynch mob that had already begun to fashion a noose. Instead, Copeland was placed in a wagon and taken to jail in Charlestown.

A slave named Jim, hired out to Lewis Washington, had accepted a pistol and ball cartridges from Brown's men and was sent to guard the rifle works, where he was posted in front. But Jim quickly denied any allegiance to the raiders. As local militia prepared to execute him on the spot, Charles White, a visiting Presbyterian minister who had preached a Sunday sermon in Harpers Ferry, intervened. He informed a would-be executioner that the man was now a prisoner, and possibly innocent. "Stepping between the two, I ordered him not to fire," he wrote later. "So enraged were the multitude that it was with difficulty they were restrained from hanging and shooting . . . on the spot." The slave's life was momentarily spared, but he soon drowned in the canal adjoining the river.

White was no Brown sympathizer, though. Princeton educated and from Fredericksburg, Virginia, he lived in Berryville, seat of adjoining Clarke County. "During the affair," he wrote, "the negroes of H F were terribly alarmed and clung as closely as they could to master & mistress. One negro hid under a water wheel in the armory canal and didn't come out till Tuesday. . . . Not one slave that we can discover was *willingly* with them." This would be a recurring theme in accounts and recollections from contemporary white sources.

By Monday afternoon, militia had taken control of both the Potomac and Shenandoah River bridges, the primary escape routes for Brown and his men. As Brown's redoubt in the engine house was surrounded and taking fire, Anderson and Hazlett were watching from the nearby arsenal. They saw, Anderson wrote, "that we could be of no further avail to our commander, he being a prisoner. . . .We could not aid Captain Brown by remaining." But a small rear guard had remained at the Kennedy farm to bring more arms as needed to the Ferry. "We might, by joining the men at the Farm, devise plans for his succor," he speculated. When Shields Green arrived with a message from the armory, they sought to persuade him to leave with them. Brown seemed "puzzled" on what to do next, Anderson wrote. Doubtless, they told this to Green, but his answer was the same as before, to "go with the old man."

"The charge of deserting our brave old leader and of fleeing from the danger has been circulated to our detriment," Anderson noted, adding that he and Hazlett "never left our positions until we saw, with feelings of intense sadness, that we could be of no further avail to our commander, he being a prisoner in the hands of the Virginians."

Anderson's account did not go unchallenged, even by sympathetic Brown historians. Oswald Garrison Villard, grandson of abolitionist William Lloyd Garrison, in his 1910 Brown biography, inferred from Anderson's statement that their commander was "a prisoner" of the Virginians when they fled. That meant they left on Tuesday, when Brown would indeed be a prisoner. Thus, Villard labeled Anderson's account "incredible . . . misleading and exaggerated. . . . In all probability, they left their posts in the arsenal about nightfall on Monday, when everybody was watching the armory yard and the engine house."

That may, in fact, have been what Anderson meant, if not in so many words. But Anderson muddled the picture by claiming to have seen marines storming the engine house, which occurred Tuesday morning. This section of his account seemed to call into question the timing. Villard concedes, however, "their escape, by whatever means, was miraculous."

According to Anderson, he and Hazlett walked along the river, hiding on a hill outside town for three hours, then returned to town and followed the railroad tracks along the Potomac, briefly taking an armed citizen hostage and then finding a boat to cross. On the Maryland side, they hiked five miles up the C&O Canal towpath to a culvert that took them under the canal. From there they walked the four miles uphill to the farmhouse, looking for food and allies. Finding neither, they headed into the mountains. It was dark and raining. Their destination, Chambersburg, with its Underground Railroad stations, was fifty miles north.

Ten miles south of the Pennsylvania town, Anderson left Hazlett, who had become too weary, hungry, and sore of feet to continue. Anderson kept going and slipped in and out of Chambersburg without detection. From there he traveled to York, Pennsylvania, where William Goodridge, a black man and Underground Railroad stationmaster who also owned a railroad line, put him on a Philadelphia-bound train. On October 22, Hazlett was arrested outside his hometown of Carlisle and extradited to Charlestown, where he was tried, convicted, and hanged on March 16, 1860.

Back at the Kennedy farmhouse, authorities found Harriet Newby's desperate letters to Dangerfield, along with documents implicating several of Brown's New England backers and suggesting that Frederick Douglass was also part of the conspiracy. He wasn't, of course, but, with federal marshals in pursuit, Douglass left Rochester for Canada and then went to England to avoid arrest.

The view that few slaves voluntarily joined or even passively supported the raid soon became the conventional wisdom among most Southerners and many Northern historians. But there are some countervailing facts to challenge this view. In the weeks that followed in the surrounding area, barns were set ablaze. A Richmond paper reported that "the heavens are illuminated almost daily by the lurid glare of burning property." It was more convenient to blame abolitionists than slaves.

Wealthy Virginia planter Edmund Ruffin, a slaveholder and ardent secessionist who visited Harpers Ferry during this period, attributed five barn burnings near Charlestown to "Northern abolitionists." He noted in his diary on November 21 that the barns belonged to farmers who had been jurors in John Brown's trial. Ruffin would become famous for firing the first shot of the coming Civil War at the Battle of Fort Sumter in 1861. Though advanced in years, he served as a Confederate soldier and, when the South lost the war, committed suicide.

Others attribute the failure of a general uprising to confusion over when the raid would occur. Recall that Brown intended for it to commence a week later but moved up the date when he feared word was getting out locally that something suspicious was afoot.

James Redpath—abolitionist, activist, and journalist who had first interviewed Brown in Kansas—would write soon afterward:

> Many, who started to join the Liberators, halted half way; for the blow had already been struck, and their Captain made a captive. Had there been no precipitation [earlier attack], the mountains of Virginia to-day, would have been peopled with free blacks, properly officered and ready for action. . . . The negroes, also in the neighboring counties, who had promised to be ready on the 24th of October, were confused by the precipitate attack; and, before they could act in concert—which they can only do by secret nocturnal meetings—were watched, overpowered, and deprived of every chance to join their heroic liberators.

A *New-York Tribune* reporter writing from Charlestown challenged the notion that area slaves were uninterested or unsympathetic to the Brown raid. "People may say what they please of the indifference of the negroes to the passing events," he wrote. "They burn with anxiety to learn every particular, but they fear to show it."

Osborne Anderson would assert in an 1870 conversation with Richard J. Hinton that there were at least 150 "actively informed" slaves and other blacks "who tilled small areas of land and worked 'round that also could be depended on." Frederick Douglass claimed in 1881 that Brown "rallied fifty slaves to his standard."

For years, historians dismissed Anderson's accounts of sympathetic slaves eager to join in John Brown's raid. It was left largely to Jean Libby, a California community college instructor, to come to Anderson's defense and rediscover him in a serious way. Her *Black Voices from Harpers Ferry*, self-published in 1979, reprints Anderson's original work, annotates it, and, drawing on a variety of sources and Libby's own deductions, refutes or challenges much of the assertions by others who downplay the role of slaves. The quiet change in the planned date of the attack was critical, she suggests, in the failure of alerted slave reinforcements to come to the Ferry. Several slaves—possibly four, perhaps more—went to the Kennedy farm and delivered more arms to the schoolhouse transfer station across the Potomac near the Ferry. Charles Tidd, among the raiders who were never apprehended, reported, "The negroes proved ready enough to follow Brown, but naturally slipped back to their masters when they saw the enterprise was to fail." Other slaves, Libby noted, rather than return to their masters, simply escaped during the chaotic two days. She cites four possible such instances. The Charlestown *Virginia Free Press* reported on January 19, 1860, that "seven fugitives from slavery—one direct from Harper's Ferry—passed through Syracuse on the Underground Railroad last week."

"For slaveholders, minimizing the efforts of slaves to rebel was necessary for safety," Libby wrote. "Relief at the absence of such a massacre [as in Nat Turner's rebellion] when it was possible may have led slaveholders to truly believe their slaves were not in rebellion."

Federal forces, including ninety US marines, arrived Monday night under the command of Col. Robert E. Lee, ordered to Harpers Ferry from Arlington House, his Virginia home on a hill facing the nation's capital across the Potomac, and Lt. J. E. B. Stuart—the future leaders of the Confederate Army. Lee decided to wait until Tuesday morning to put an end to the raid that had begun so auspiciously for Brown late Sunday night.

Brown had twice sought to negotiate his escape in return for the release of the hostages, and twice his offers were declined. This morning, Lee sent Stuart to the engine house with his own demand for unconditional surrender. This time, Brown declined. The marines stood at the ready in front of John Brown's fort. Behind them stood a crowd of about two thousand spectators. When directed by a thumbs-up sign from

Captured raiders Shields Green and Edwin Coppoc under guard at the arsenal engine house. *West Virginia State Archives*

Stuart, the marines attempted to ram their way into the building. As they breeched the entryway, one marine was fatally shot, and Lt. Israel Green thrust a bayonet into Brown, severely wounding but not killing him. Within three minutes, the thirty-six-hour insurrection was over.

It was 11 AM. Inside the engine house, marines found the white hostages, as well as slaves who had been liberated or also held hostage, as some would assert, and several dead—including John Brown's sons Watson and Oliver. Raider Shields Green dropped his rifle and ammunition box and tried to blend in with the slaves, hoping to be taken for one. Lewis Washington thought this cowardly, others smart. In any case, the ruse did not work, and Green was taken into custody to face trial, conviction, and the ultimate penalty two months later.

Governor Wise arrived on the scene around 1 PM with more volunteers. He proceeded to question the wounded Brown as the leader lay on the grass outside the engine house; he would interview Brown more extensively later in jail. Brown, he said, "repelled the idea that his design was to run negro slaves off from their masters. He defiantly avowed that his purpose was to arm them and make them fight by his side in defense of their freedom. . . . He avowed that he expected to be joined by the slaves and by numerous white persons from many of the slave as well as the free States."

In an impromptu address to the Virginia militia on his return to Richmond, Wise described Brown as "a fanatic, vain and garrulous; but firm, faithful and intelligent." He specifically excluded in his remarks "the free negroes with him" from possessing these noble characteristics.

For slaveholders like John Allstadt, the raid had tangible consequences.

On January 9, he filed a claim with the Virginia legislature seeking compensation for two slaves "deceased from fright at their capture at night, by John Brown's party, 16th October 1859." One of the slaves, identified as Ben, age twenty, was taken to be one of the insurgents and sent to jail in Charlestown, where, otherwise healthy, "he was immediately taken sick and died." Allstadt had sent Ben's mother, Ary, to nurse him, and she stayed with him until he succumbed on October 31. Heartbroken, she returned to the Allstadts' and died ten days later.

Allstadt sought compensation of $1,450 for Ben (the equivalent of more than $40,000 in 2017) and $600 (nearly $17,000 in 2017 dollars) for Ary, "on the ground that his property has been sacrificed and destroyed by Civil War and commotion, within the territory of the State wherein he had just reason to suppose his property would be entirely and efficiently protected."

Attesting to the slaves' market values were Capt. John Avis, who jailed Ben, and Joseph L. Eichelberger, an Allstadt neighbor who deemed Ary's worth to be "at the least Six Hundred Dollars, in the common market, and if exposed to public sale without reserve of bidders, she would have sold for a much larger price."

Dead or alive, Ben and his mother were nothing more than chattel.

There is no prominent monument at Harpers Ferry today to John Brown's raiders, and none that singles out the African American soldiers in Brown's revolutionary army. A small bronze plaque, easily overlooked, is affixed to a brick wall on Public Way, a narrow path off High Street.

Half hidden behind a bush, it is dedicated to "a group of men led by John Brown who, at Harpers Ferry on October 17, 1859, struck a blow against slavery." Erected on August 19, 2001, by the Jefferson County branch of the National Association for the Advancement of Colored People, it lists those killed, executed, and escaped, with an asterisk next to each of the five black raiders.

"Nothing has ever been accomplished until white communities or individuals got involved," James L. Taylor, former NAACP president, tells me. "If John Brown had been black, we might all [still] be slaves." This wasn't just James Taylor speaking. He recalled his grandfather passing on what his father had told him at the time of the raid. "At first, they thought it was a Nat Turner type of thing," quickly quashed with no long-term effect, he said. "But when they realized whites were involved, they were elated, they knew this time it would be different."

Midway between Charles Town and Harpers Ferry, the Beallair manor house—where Anderson, Green, and Leary had taken their high-profile hostage—stands at the entrance to a "signature gated community in an exquisite natural oasis." Residents hold garden parties and other community events in Lewis Washington's historic home there. The facility is also available for weddings and anniversary parties. Evoking the planter's more revered great-uncle, the upscale subdivision is called the Mount Vernon Collection at Beallair. The cookie-cutter McMansions and townhomes line streets whose names play on the mystical past even as they mark the present: Lewis Washington Drive, Beallair Mansion Drive, Louisa Beall Lane.

Adjoining this "Historic Master Planned Community" is the Sleepy Hollow Golf and Country Club, established in 1962, and the Sleepy Hollow Estates subdivision, named for no apparent reason after the pre-Revolutionary town north of New York City on the Hudson River and immortalized in Washington Irving's classic short story. One Halloween, the community's Facebook page touted it as "home to stray animals and ghosts." In Irving's fertile imagination, Sleepy Hollow was inhabited by ghosts that haunted residents and visitors. Which, after all, seems fitting for the adjacent former slave plantation, so closely tied to the Harpers Ferry raid. Surely there are also ghosts at Beallair that will never be stilled.

7

Trial and Punishment

A few blocks from Washington Street, which runs through the middle of Charles Town, West Virginia, is a well-mowed plot of land on which sits a water tower. At the curb, a plaque identifies the plot's former use as the "Coloured Grave Yard," dating to 1836, when Andrew Hunter, the future prosecutor of the Harpers Ferry raiders, and his wife sold the lot to the city trustees for fifty dollars. According to the original deed, it was intended "for and always be used as a potters field and burying place for coloured persons."

Directly across the street is the much larger fenced-in white burial ground known as Edge Hill. It is a typical Southern graveyard, segregated, of course, and sprinkled with Confederate crosses, marking the service of the many residents who were in rebellion against the United States.

If the Civil War and the John Brown raid, trial, and execution seem distant, it is not so here, perhaps half a mile from the county courthouse where John Brown, Edwin Coppoc, John Cook, John Copeland, and Shields Green were tried, and an equal distance from where they were executed on December 2 and December 16, 1859. The courthouse, at the corner of Washington and George Streets, looks from the outside much as it did then, although a second story was added after the war.

But instead of hundreds of federal troops providing security, there is one sheriff's deputy and a metal detector. Apprised of the purpose of my visit, the deputy waves me through. It seems that John Brown and Civil War buffs are no threat to the peace and tranquility of current-day Charles Town. The first-floor corridor of the courthouse is a gallery of illustrations and portraits from the trials. As always, John Brown is the leading man, the others mere secondary props.

———————

Charlestown (as it was spelled then) was overwhelmingly Southern in its sympathies. Slavery was seen as an essential element of the agricultural economy of the area. It was the social, political, and economic norm. The county's leading citizens were all slaveholders.

The 1850 Census for Jefferson County recorded a total population of 15,357, of whom 4,341—28 percent—were slaves and 540 were free blacks, most of them employees at the federal armory in Harpers Ferry. In the 1860 presidential election, Abraham Lincoln received no votes. John Bell of Tennessee, candidate of the Constitutional Union Party, which took no position on slavery, won a plurality with 959. A slaveholder, Bell initially opposed secession but later supported the Confederacy. A majority of Jefferson County voters, 813 to 365, supported their state's decision to secede from the Union in the spring of 1861.

For the captured raiders, including Copeland and Green, these demographics did not auger well when it came to selecting jurors inclined to acquittal.

In the jail, cattycorner across Washington Street from the Jefferson County courthouse, Copeland would share a cell first with Coppoc and then later with Green. Their cell had one window, which looked out onto the small courtyard.

Although a federal arsenal was the raid's ostensible target, Virginia governor Henry A. Wise, with the quiet acquiescence of President James Buchanan, a Pennsylvanian sympathetic to the South, successfully asserted state jurisdiction. So, the trials would be held in a court of the commonwealth, prosecuted by a commonwealth's attorney, motions

John Copeland (right) and Shields Green (left) seated in their Charlestown cell, from *Frank Leslie's Illustrated Newspaper.* Kansas State Historical Society

ruled on and sentences handed down by a Jefferson County judge, and verdicts reached by local slave-owning jurors. Southern justice would be swift; it took the grand jury, already in session, only twenty-four hours to hand down indictments.

Accordingly, on October 26, Thomas Rutherford, the Jefferson County grand jury foreman, conveyed to the court indictments against five men: Brown, Cook, Copeland, Coppoc, and Green. "With other confederates to the jurors unknown," they did "feloniously and traitorously make rebellion and levy war against the said commonwealth of Virginia" and "did forcibly capture, make prisoners and detain divers good and loyal citizens."

They were charged with treason, "conspiring with Negroes to produce insurrection," and with murder in the first degree of five men: Harpers Ferry mayor Fontaine Beckham; railroad employee Haywood Shepherd; George W. Turner; Thomas Boerly; and Marine Pvt. Luke Quinn, killed during Brown's last stand at the engine house. All crimes were punishable by death. The weapons employed, the indictment said,

The arraignments of Brown and four others, with Copeland and Green standing behind Brown. Sketch by Porte Crayon (David Hunter Strother), *Harper's Weekly*, November 13, 1859. *West Virginia State Archives*

were Sharps rifles, with which the accused "feloniously, willfully and of their malice aforethought, did strike, penetrate and wound" Boerly "upon the left side," Turner "in and upon the left shoulder and breast," Beckham "in and upon the right breast," and Shepherd "in and upon the back and side," in all cases causing mortal wounds. Copeland had not fired a weapon but was implicated as an accessory to the deaths.

David Hunter Strother, Virginian, journalist, and magazine illustrator who went by the nom de plume of Porte Crayon and covered the trials, was impressed by if unsympathetic toward Copeland, writing that "even though he was literate," he was "a likely mulatto who would have made a very good genteel dining room servant."

On November 26, Wise wrote from Richmond that he was dispatching five hundred troops to the scene to prevent any attempt to rescue Brown or the other prisoners. "You will prepare for the execution of Brown, and notify sheriff that you require to know his arrangements," the governor wrote to Maj. Gen. William B. Taliaferro, in charge of security.

Keep full guards on the line of Martinsburg to Harpers Ferry on the day of 2d Decr: Warn the inhabitants to arm and keep guard and patrol on that day and for days beforehand. These orders are necessary to prevent seizure of hostages. Warn the inhabitants to stay away and especially to keep the women and children at home. Prevent all strangers, and especially all parties of strangers from proceeding to Charlestown on the 2d Decr.

Wise ordered that on Brown's hanging day those in charge should "form two concentric squares around the gallows and have strong guard at the jail and for escort to execution. Let no crowd be near enough to the prisoner to hear any speech he may attempt. Allow no more visitors to be admitted into the jail."

It is fair to say from the extensive coverage, though, that the Harpers Ferry raid and subsequent trials and executions were the top news stories of the day, if not the decade. They aroused and further polarized an already deeply divided nation, more so perhaps than had the 1850 Missouri Compromise, which included the Fugitive Slave Act; or the 1857 Dred Scott decision, which, after all, had the imprimatur of the highest court of the land. Unlike these legislative and judicial acts, with their sheen of constitutional legitimacy, presumably well thought out and considered by educated minds, indeed even codified, the entire Harpers Ferry affair was all raw passion, bringing out into the open what some would consider the most inflammatory, even treasonous statements challenging governmental authority and constitutionally protected ownership of slaves. Given its resonance, its gut-wrenching appeal on both sides of the Mason-Dixon Line, newspaper reporters came en masse to Jefferson County.

The Charlestown *Virginia Free Press* provided the most comprehensive coverage, supplementing its own reports with those from other newspapers north and south. But other papers—notably, the *Baltimore Sun*—were also present.

"The excitement in town is increasing as the time for trial approaches," the *Sun* reported on its front page of October 25. "The town is guarded by a very large body of military."

On November 24, the *Free Press* seemed almost giddy describing the scene. In a story headlined "The Excitement," the paper breathlessly reported the growing "core of southern chivalry" that was assembling to maintain law and order. These included the 175th Virginia Militia from Alexandria, the Mount Vernon Guards, four companies from Richmond, the Continental Guards of Winchester, the Jefferson [County] Guards, two companies from Fauquier County, and the Montgomery Guards. Everyone, it seemed, wanted in on the action.

Fearful of outsiders, the Shepherdstown council even enacted an ordinance prohibiting outsiders from entering the area without express permission or a specific reason to be there.

Governor Wise was deluged with letters seeking Brown's pardon or commutation of his sentence to life in prison. There were some appeals that Cook, with powerful political allies in New York, be spared, and an avalanche of requests to pardon or at least commute Brown's death sentence to life. Notably, the appeals almost always failed to mention Green and Copeland.

There were, an unidentified governor's aide noted, "vulgar letters every day." Some were marked "insulting." Some were death threats. A New Yorker warned of ten persons "sworn to assassinate" Wise. A self-described "colored man" from Detroit had it "on good authority" that several "hear and in Canada have sworn to avenge" Brown's death. "As you are aware the Head Quarters of the colored people of this section is in Chatham Canada West where several secret societies are already formed for the above purpose. There is also one in this city."

James McPherson of Indianapolis wrote threatening letters in "every mail," Wise's secretary noted, "but they are so vulgar that most of them have been burned." One dated December 16, the date of the executions of Copeland, Green, Cook, and Coppoc, began, "*Dear Son-of-Bitch and Southern Dog* today is your day of *wholesale murder*. . . . My poor friends are probably in heaven while I pen these few lines; but you Southern dog's on the way to *Hell!*"

Some of the more respectful pleas were for Cook, John Brown's "spy" who had established himself in the area for a year and was politically well connected. No such entreaties were made specifically on behalf of Copeland or Green, not even from the antislavery societies. There was, however, an appeal from Mary A. Child, a Quaker from Darby, Pennsylvania, requesting leniency toward the other condemned men on December 8, after Brown's execution: "Will not one suffice, will not the blood of John Brown that great and heroic, (tho misguided) martyr to freedom, satisfy the too eager thirst (for the life current) of an excited and terror-stricken community." Apparently not.

Before Brown's execution, Wise also received letters—some anonymous—reporting that hundreds were massing beyond Virginia to liberate Brown, with again no mention of the others by name. Even to abolitionists, they were afterthoughts, if that. He received a petition from New York City with 341 signers on November 25 seeking a reprieve for Brown "and his confederates."

One correspondent who professed no sympathy for Brown nonetheless warned of his "many warm friends," adding, "there is now to my certain knowledge 100,000 men enrolled and sworn by their lives their fortune and their sacred honour (if John Brown or any of his men are harmed in the least—other than in a fair fight) that they will avenge them with a vengeance that will be terrible." The writer, signing as "Simeon Suredeath," asked Wise to "act the part of an honourable man and not a vengeful tyrant."

From the *Weekly Register* publisher in Indiana County, Pennsylvania, came a request for a pair of the pikes—shafted weapons with pointed heads—seized from the Kennedy Farm, John Brown's pre-raid headquarters. Wilson, North Carolina, was happy to receive just one pike "by express" because "our people are very anxious to see one. Ours is a thriving little town and we want a little of every new thing for exhibition." Pulaski, Virginia, requested three of "the old gentleman's pikes . . . for the sake of exhibiting to curious eyes of Western Virginians." Two men from Warrenton, Georgia, requested the rope used to hang Brown, to hang unlicensed peddlers said to be "contaminating Our Colored Population and others."

One letter, dated November 30 but received after Brown's execution, came from a woman in Rock Island, Illinois, warning of suicide bombers. "They number about sixteen and wear large petticoats filled with powder, having slow matches attached," Maria Black wrote. "If caught they intend to set themselves off and (so effective is the inflammable material about them) the consequence will be awful. In fact, Virginia will be blown sky high." Her concern was not remote; two of the children "aforesaid" were hers. "If you find the girls, send them back before they blow up and send some chivalry along." There is no indication the would-be suicide bombers carried out their alleged plans.

The prosecution fell to assistant commonwealth's attorney Andrew H. Hunter, a slaveholder related by marriage to the slain Harpers Ferry mayor Beckham. During the war, he would serve as an advisor to Robert E. Lee.

Two local lawyers—Lawson Botts and Thomas C. Green, who was also the mayor of Charlestown—were appointed to represent the defendants. Brown wrote from the jail requesting outside council, which was forthcoming. Shields Green and John Copeland were soon represented by audacious Boston lawyer George Sennott, an outsized personality ridiculed locally for his girth but who did not hesitate to challenge slavery as "illogical and absurd." Opined the local Charlestown newspaper, "George Sennott has come to us upon a mission of great bigness, and his size, so far as latitude is concerned, shows him fully up to the immortal standard of envoys extraordinary." The Charlestown paper, not mocking Sennott, reported that he was "doing his damndest" on behalf of Green, whom it described as "a regular out-and-out tar-colored darkey."

Green's one-day trial took place on November 3. Sennott made several technical arguments that impressed prosecutor Hunter but not the judge. The next day the jurors deliberated for just an hour before finding Green guilty on three counts. They agreed, however, that he could not be convicted on a count of treason, acceding to Sennott's assertion that, under the Dred Scott decision, a black man was not a citizen and therefore could not commit such an act against the government.

In some abolitionist circles this was no solace but rather cause for outrage, because this conclusion required accepting the logic of the Dred Scott Supreme Court decision. "It was the climax of tyranny to rob us of the paltry privilege of being traitors to this devil-inspired and God-forsaken government," railed William J. Watkins, a black abolitionist from Rochester, New York.

While Shields Green remained something of a cipher, for the most part keeping his own counsel and saying little, John Copeland had not been so circumspect. Matthew Johnson, the Democratic proslavery marshal from Cleveland, still angry at failing to arrest Copeland for his leading role in the 1858 Oberlin-Wellington rescue of slave John Price, traveled to Charlestown. Accompanied by another federal marshal, from Virginia, his purpose was to interview the prisoner in jail. Two days before the trial, he did just that, and Copeland gave quite an account of himself and of events leading up to the raid.

Naively, perhaps, Copeland answered all seventeen questions, laying out in detail how he had come to join Brown and what his own motives were, not to cause the slaves to rebel but simply to run away. He also implicated others in Oberlin, notably Ralph Plumb, another participant in Oberlin-Wellington. Plumb, Copeland said, had provided fifteen dollars in travel money.

The details of their conversation were published in the *National Democrat*, an unsympathetic Cleveland newspaper, and became known as Copeland's "confession," to be used as evidence against him at trial. This published "confession" prompted letters dated October 31 from Plumb brothers Ralph and Samuel to the *Cleveland Morning Leader*. Ralph Plumb categorically denied any suggestion that implicated him in the Harpers Ferry conspiracy. "I never had a word of conversation with Copeland upon the Harper's Ferry insurrection among slaves, nor did I give Copeland money for the purpose named, or for any other purpose." Samuel supported his brother's account and added that Ralph had had only one conversation with Copeland when he'd represented him as an attorney in an assault case involving an Oberlin marshal.

During Copeland's trial, which followed Green's, George Sennott argued that the alleged jail confession had been coerced and was therefore inadmissible. The judge quickly overruled the lawyer's objection. Then, posed Sennott, if the entire confession were admitted, so, too, must Copeland's statement that he had intended only to "run off slaves," which might have made him guilty of slave stealing but not of murder or inciting them to rebel. It was a novel argument that impressed the judge, who paused to ponder the matter before leaving resolution of this technical legal question up to the jury. The verdict was the same as Shields's: guilty.

Like Shields, Copeland was convicted of murder and inciting slaves to rebellion and again invoking the logic of the Dred Scott decision, Sennott was able to get the treason count dismissed. His argument, which even Hunter had to accept, was that Copeland could not possibly be a free man of color convicted of such a charge since, in Virginia, a black man was presumed to be a slave unless proven otherwise—and then there was Dred Scott to buttress his case.

Coppoc and Cook, tried separately from the two black defendants, were convicted on all counts—treason, murder, and inciting slaves.

On November 10, Cook, Copeland, Coppoc, and Green appeared in court to be sentenced by Judge Richard Parker, a slaveholder, as were virtually all of the county's leading and many of its lesser citizens. A former paymaster at the Harpers Ferry armory, Parker invited the four convicted men to address the court. Cook and Coppoc "protested their ignorance of the attack on Harper's Ferry until the Sabbath before the night of the attack," the *Baltimore Sun* reported. Green said he had nothing to say. Copeland simply remained silent, knowing perhaps the futility of any statement.

Intoned Parker, "Your trials, on which we have been so long employed, have at length ended, and all that remains to be done to complete these judicial proceedings, is to pronounce and record the judgments which by law must follow upon the crimes for which you have been tried, and of which you have been found guilty."

During the sentencing, the *Sun* reported, "the utmost silence was observed, and the solemnity was very marked. Many spectators wept, as also did the judge." The local *Virginia Free Press* said the judge was evidently laboring under much feeling" as he pronounced sentence on the four men, "the silence of death almost pervading the Court hall."

Judge Parker preceded the sentencing with his own view from the bench, noting the "predetermined purpose" to incite a "servile insurrection" that included taking "several of our best citizens" hostage and arming slaves with deadly weapons to use against their owners, "whom you denounced to them as their oppressors." Happily, he continued, "Not a slave united himself to your party, but soon as he could get without the range of your rifles . . . made his escape from the men who came to give him freedom, and hurried to place himself once more beneath the care and protection of his owner." That was what Parker chose to believe at least.

So egregious were the crimes, the judge said, that the men must be hanged not inconspicuously in the jail yard but in a more public place for all to see. It would be a field several blocks from the jail and nearby courthouse. On this site in 1891, John Thomas Gibson, commander of the Jefferson Guards, the Virginia militia who led the first armed response to Brown's raid, would build a large Victorian home, at 515 South Samuel Street. Gibson would serve as a Confederate officer and later as mayor of Charlestown, where he is buried in the town's Edge Hill Cemetery.

Years later, Judge Parker and prosecutor Hunter revised their views on Copeland. Parker said, "Copeland was the prisoner who impressed me best. There was a dignity to him that I could not help liking. He was always manly." Concurred Hunter, "From my intercourse with him I regard him as one of the most respectable persons we had. . . . He was a copper-colored Negro, behaved himself with as much firmness as any of them, and with far more dignity. If it had been possible to recommend a pardon for any of them it would have been this man Copeland as I regretted as much if not more, at seeing him executed than any other of the party."

No salvation army showed up to rescue Brown, whom the jury convicted on November 2 after only forty-five minutes of deliberation, and the execution went ahead as scheduled on December 2. Before his hanging, Brown was permitted to visit the other prisoners. He found Green and Copeland confined together in one cell and told "the two faithful colored men" to "stand up like men, and do not betray your friends!" Brown gave each of the prisoners a "small silver coin for remembrance."

"The day opened beautifully," the *Richmond Dispatch* reported. "The heavy clouds that hung along the eastern sky reflected most splendidly the rays of the rising sun. . . . The gallows was erected soon after the rising of the sun." The small hill on which the scaffold was erected afforded a full view of the town. East and south "loomed" the Blue Ridge, and south and west lay the Great Valley of Virginia, on which opposing armies would march and fight and die.

The Richmond reporter's account did not include Brown's foreboding last words, conveyed in a written note to a guard on his way to the gallows: "I, John Brown, am now certain that the crimes of this guilty land will never be purged away but with blood." At the gallows, Brown asked why only military personnel—more than two thousand by one account—and not citizen witnesses were allowed to be there. Seeing prosecutor Hunter and Charlestown mayor Thomas C. Green, he said, "Gentlemen, good bye." He also bade farewell to jailer Capt. John Avis and Sheriff James Campbell. "I am ready at any time," Brown said. "Don't keep me waiting." At 11:15 AM, the drop fell, and the body remained suspended for thirty-seven minutes.

"The great event of modern times has been enacted," the *Virginia Free Press* editorialized in its December 8 edition, "and the Captain General of mad cap murderers and blood thirsty fanatical Abolitionists, has paid the forfeit of audacious foolhardiness, and the majority of southern rights has been justly asserted through an ignominious but deserved penalty." Governor Wise, for his part, had a different view of Brown. "He is a man of clear head, of courage, fortitude, and simple ingenuousness," he said after interviewing him in jail. "He is cool, collected, and indomitable."

But what of Copeland, Green, Cook, and Coppoc? The night before their scheduled executions, Cook and Coppoc attempted an escape from their first-floor cell. They had used a knife Shields Green had given them to fashion a hole in the wall behind one bed large enough for them to climb through. Both men managed to make it into the jail yard, but no farther. Their fates were sealed.

The raiders, who had been united in life, were segregated in death. Copeland and Green would be hanged together first, then Coppoc and Cook an hour later. All four had been sentenced together, and the judge gave no explanation for the racial divide in their executions; it just seemed in keeping with the prevailing culture that separated black from white. Except this time, the black prisoners had the dubious honor of going first.

Anna Hill, whose husband, Hamilton, was the Oberlin College treasurer, wrote to Governor Wise on behalf of Copeland's mother, asking that Copeland be allowed to write to her "a few lines, informing her of his feelings." Permission granted, Wise forwarded her letter to the condemned man.

So, from his jail cell, John Copeland wrote. Copiously. He wrote to his parents on November 26, more than a month after his capture. He wrote on December 10 to his brother, to schoolmate and longtime friend Elias Toussaint Jones, and to Addison Halbert, another Oberlin friend. To his brother Henry, he compared "the noble but unfortunate" Brown to George Washington, who, he wrote in a revisionist if incorrect flourish, "entered the field to fight for the freedom of the American people—not for the white men alone, but for both black and white." With obvious pride, he recalled that Crispus Attucks, a man of color, had been the first to fall in the Boston Massacre in 1770, widely regarded as the first fatality of the American Revolution.

"I have been treated exceedingly well—far better than I expected to be," John Anthony wrote Henry. "My jailor is a most kind-hearted man, and has done all he could, consistent with duty, to make me and rest of the prisoners comfortable." He especially praised Captain Avis, "a gentle man who has a heart . . . as brave as any other," and another jailer, John Sheats, saying he "has been very kind to us and has done all he could to serve us."

On December 11, "with only five short days remaining between me and the grave," he addressed his "Friends and Brothers of the Oberlin Antislavery Society": "Struggle on dear brothers now and ever until there shall not be a single slave to tread the fair soil of America and until the clanking of a single chain shall not be heard on the Southern plantation."

Finally, in words both moving and poetic came a last letter to his parents, three brothers, and two sisters on December 16, the date of his execution.

"I have seen declining behind me the western mountains for the last time," he wrote his family.

> Last night for the last time, I beheld the soft bright moon as it rose, casting its mellow light into my felon's cell, dissipating the darkness and filtering it with that soft pleasant light which causes such thrills of joy to all those in like circumstance with myself.
>
> This morning, for the last time, I beheld the glorious sun of yesterday rising in the far-off East, away off in the country when our Lord Jesus Christ first proclaimed salvation to man, and now as he rises higher and high bright light takes the place of soft moonlight, I will take my pen, for the last time, to rite you who are bound to me by those strong ties. (yea, the strongest that God ever instituted) the ties of blood and relationship.
>
> *I am well, both in body and in mind.* . . . But think not that I am complaining, for I feel reconciled to meet my fate. *I pray God that his will be done, not mine.* And now dear ones I must bid you that last. long sad farewell. . . . Your Son and Brother in eternity.

Copeland's eloquence continued on the day of his execution. Leaving his cell, bound for the gallows, he said, "If I am dying for freedom, I could not die for a better cause. I had rather die than be a slave."

Though surely it did not take long for news of the December 16 executions to spread, the Charlestown *Virginia Free Press*, likely due to its production schedule, did not print its own account until six days

after the hangings of Copeland and Green in the late morning and of
Cook and Coppoc in the early afternoon. It preceded its report with
verses written by an Irish archbishop and inspired by "The Law of
Love" from 2 Kings 4:6:

> *Pour forth the oil—pour boldly forth;*
>   *It will not fail; until*
> *Thou failest vessels to provide*
>   *Which it may largely fill,*
> *Make channels for the streams of love,*
>   *Where they may broadly run;*
> *And love has overflowing streams,*
>   *To fill them everyone.*
> *But if at any time we cease*
>   *Such channels to provide,*
> *The very founts of love for us*
>   *Will soon be parched and dried.*
> *For we must share, if we would keep*
>   *That blessing from above;*
> *Ceasing to give, we cease to have;*
>   *Such is the law of love.*

The prisoners were transported the few blocks from the jail to the
gallows in a wooden furniture wagon driven by a Mr. Sadler, the undertaker, accompanied by his assistant. Sheriff Campbell and Captain Avis
escorted Copeland and Green to the gallows.

In contrast to Brown's execution, where tight security precluded
much of a public presence, there were an estimated four to five thousand
onlookers, in addition to eight hundred military personnel, for what
was uniformly treated as a solemn occasion.

When the prisoners reached the platform, a Presbyterian minister
offered "a prayer to the throne of Grace." The passage, from the New
Testament's book of Hebrews, reads, "Let us then approach God's throne
of grace with confidence, so that we may receive mercy and find grace
to help us in our time of need." It was "most affecting and appropri-

ate," according to the *Free Press*. "During the delivery," the paper said, Copeland and Green "seemed much affected and deeply humiliated. Copeland stood with head erect and eyes closed, clasping his hands across his breast and seemed listening intently, his lips moving as if following [the minister] in prayer."

"Green," the paper reported, "stood with hands closed in front, and rocked to and fro, frequently casting his eyes towards Heaven and then dropping his head on his breast, glancing, now and then to the right and left; he appeared deeply affected."

Copeland sought to address the crowd, but the hangman lowered hoods and affixed ropes around their necks before he was able to speak. "As they were ascending the steps, Copeland stumbled and was near falling," the *Free Press* reported. Despite Copeland's near fall, the Vincennes, Indiana, *Western Sun* reported, "The prisoners mounted the scaffold with a firm step."

At "the drop," their feet were also bound. At 11:40, the drop fell, "and the souls of the poor, misguided creatures were ushered into the presence of Him whose judgment is final."

Green went quickly, but Copeland lingered in painful transition between life and death for several minutes. His struggle, the reporter noted, "was really most painful to look upon, and as we watched him writhing in agony we could be feel how terrible, indeed, such death must be."

There they were left to hang for thirty minutes, until three doctors ascended the scaffold and declared them dead. The jailor and four guards then took the bodies, placed them in coffins, and buried them in an adjacent field. Cook and Coppoc would meet similar ends an hour later. "The hanging of four persons in one day, is indeed, a most awful incident in the history of any place," the *Free Press* opined. "May our town never again be doomed to so terrible a visitation."

―――――――

On a warm July day, about a mile from the hanging ground, in the Charles Town suburb of Ranson, the surviving founders of the Jefferson

County Black History Preservation Society, formed in 2000, meet for their regular coffee and donuts in the basement rec room of treasurer George C. Rutherford. Also present are James L. Taylor, president, and James A. Tolbert Sr. They are all in their eighties, the keepers of the flame.

The men are all descendants of slaves, and they are "just about the last generation to say we met and talked to [former] slaves," then as old as they are now, Rutherford says.

For generations, Copeland and Green were erased from local history, even from the history taught in the segregated black schools of Jefferson County. "We didn't know about Copeland and Green or anything like that when we were growing up," Taylor says.

There was one notable exception: on September 25, 1929, black veterans of the First World War formed the Green-Copeland American Legion Post 63 in Charles Town. Tolbert's father, Edward, a World War I veteran, was a charter member. The post continued to meet until after the Second World War, eventually joining with another black post and losing its distinct name and separate identity. It was the only legion post in the country named after the men.

"I'll bet anything," Rutherford speculates, "when they submitted the name to the state American Legion, [the state legion officials] probably had no idea who Green and Copeland were, because they wouldn't have permitted it." In a sense, Taylor is thankful for his ignorance—about the five men and more about slavery—because otherwise, he says, he would have been consumed for decades with anger.

"If we had known," he says, "we would have been bitter and tried to get revenge," but the older generation shielded them from the horrors of the past. "Instead, they kept us focused on the future. Had they passed down all that hate to us, we wouldn't have made all the progress we made. We concentrated on the future, education, church, being patriotic. That's what they stressed." But now, there was new knowledge of an old legacy, and not bitterness but pride.

Eleven years after forming their association, the men of the Jefferson County Black Historical Preservation Society formally paid tribute to the two forgotten men. "When we found they were not given a proper burial as were the others," says Taylor, "we decided to have a proper memorial service for them."

So they met at the former site of the "Coloured Cemetery" on South Seminary Street on August 19, 2001. It was after church on a Sunday afternoon, and several of the local black ministers were among the twenty-five or so mostly African Americans present.

The ministers gave the invocation and the benediction. Also on hand were members of American Legion Post 102, the group that had absorbed the Green-Copeland members, and Masonic Star Lodge 1, where the veterans continued to meet in Charles Town. Members of the Jefferson County NAACP, including Tolbert, its president, were also there.

The program lasted about twenty minutes, Tolbert recalls. There had been so much press coverage of Green and Copeland's trial and executions. For this memorial tribute, there was none.

8

Remains of the Day

J ohn Brown's body lies a-moldering in the grave, his soul goes marching on . . . but where lie the others?

It is a cool, cloudy afternoon in June when I reach North Elba, near Lake Placid high in the Adirondacks. In a grass circle where John Brown Road ends in a cul-de-sac is a towering statue of John Brown and a young African American boy. Looming over the site is a ski jump from the 1980 Winter Olympics. Nearby is the enormous glacial boulder next to which Brown and seven of his compatriots rest eternally, some fifty feet from the modest farmhouse he and his family called home. After moving to North Elba from Springfield, Massachusetts, in 1848, he had acquired the 244-acre farm in 1851 from Gerrit Smith, one of the Secret Six abolitionists who funded his ill-fated assault on Harpers Ferry.

Brown's initial reason to move to North Elba in Essex County was to help Smith establish a free black settlement, known as Timbuctoo, which never thrived and eventually withered, its last resident dying in 1942. For decades, into the 1950s, the John Brown Memorial Association, composed largely of African Americans from Philadelphia, annually visited the burial site; when the hotels were restricted in the 1930s, they stayed in private homes. It is now a New York State Historic Site, still a mecca for Brown partisans and visited by others more curious than passionate about the Harpers Ferry martyr and his abolitionist band.

Brendan Mills is the site manager, and he is employed by the New York State Office of Parks. As a kid growing up in East Islip, Long Island, he did a book report on John Brown. "I've been doing that book report ever since," he tells me. The house is open to visitors May 1 to October 31. "By next week, when schools let out, it will be busy from then to Columbus Day," Mills says. But, surprisingly perhaps, he adds, "There are very few African American visitors."

John Brown's journey to his final resting place would not be quite the cortege that accompanied Abraham Lincoln's body in repose to his grave in Springfield, Illinois, a little more than six years later, with sorrowful crowds lining the route, but authorities in Virginia would be amply solicitous to Brown's widow, far more so than to the families of the black raiders. But then the world—even the abolitionist world—cared more for the white martyr than it did for his black raiders.

———

In their final visit at the Jefferson County jail before his execution, John Brown told his wife, "Mary, I would like you to get the bodies of our two boys, who were killed at Harpers Ferry, also the bodies of the two Thompsons, and after I am dead place us all together on a woodpile and set fire to the wood. Burn the flesh, then collect our bones and put them in a large box; then have the box carried to our farm in Essex County, and there bury us." Of the others who died at Harper's Ferry or who were to follow him to the gallows, he said nothing.

But John Brown's body was in demand. The New Orleans School of Medicine offered to pay Virginia $500 for his remains "for dissection." The request came in a letter to Governor Wise dated November 19, 1859. The correspondent, a W. C. Hicks, MD, further pledged that "as soon as his skeleton is properly dried and arranged, I will rattle it through the New England States until I frighten every Scoundrel Abolitionist out of the country. . . . My object is not to show his skeleton for money, but I do expect, should I succeed in obtaining it, to be well paid by the Northern Abolitionist *not* to show it to them."

Wise may have sympathized with these sentiments, but he had another request. Mary Brown had also written to him asking for her husband's remains, and Wise had agreed. Lewis P. Starry, a Charlestown undertaker, made a coffin of solid walnut. Brown's body, according to a newspaper account, was "conveyed to Harpers Ferry in a special train at 6½ PM to be delivered to his widow." And it was, as Governor Wise said, "with dignity and decency."

A few hours after the execution, Pennsylvanians James Miller McKim, a Presbyterian minister and abolitionist, and Hector Tyndale, later a Union general, received Brown's remains at Harpers Ferry on behalf of the widow. The next day, a Saturday, they took a train to Baltimore and then to Philadelphia, arriving around noon. They planned to stay until Monday, but police dispersed an excited, if not admiring, mostly white crowd, as the mayor insisted the body continue without delay. Seven hours later, they reached New York City. They boarded a Hudson River train Monday morning for a seven-hour trip to Troy, where more admirers met the entourage. Then, on to Rutland and Vergennes, Vermont, a boat trip across Lake Champlain back into New York, where, in Elizabethtown, the Essex County seat, his coffin lay in state at the courthouse, guarded overnight by six men. The next morning, the cortege embarked on the arduous twenty-six-mile trek on rutted mountain roads, made nearly impassable by mud and melting snow, through the Adirondacks to the Brown farm at North Elba. They reached this remote spot in the wilds of northern New York late Wednesday night. John Brown's final trip had taken five full days.

Before his burial near the eight-foot-tall boulder on December 8, the funeral began at the house at 1 PM. McKim, who had not known Brown, relied on the testimonies of others in extolling him. He noted the widow had sought—and been denied—visits with the other prisoners in the Charlestown jail. Of Copeland and Green, he had heard nothing while he was in Harpers Ferry. "They belonged to the oppressed and hated class, and if anything could be said to their disadvantage, it would be ere [before] this."

The bodies of John Copeland, Shields Green, Lewis Leary, and Dangerfield Newby did not rest in peace.

Of the raiders who died at Harpers Ferry, the remains of Watson Brown and Jeremiah Anderson went to the medical college. That left eight more corpses. Lewis Leary would presumably join the remains of Newby and other deceased raiders wrapped in the shawls they wore to the Ferry—or not.

The eight dead raiders were left in a pile on the town streets until the next day. No Harpers Ferry cemetery would take them. Instead, two local men, James Mansfield and his brother-in-law James Giddy, were hired for ten dollars to find a suitable, out-of-the-way site and bury them there. They loaded the corpses into a wagon, arms and legs dangling over the side, and drove to a spot a half mile upriver from the town on the east bank of the Shenandoah. There they placed the remains in two wooden storage boxes—four or five in one, three in the other. Newby at least was among them. Their unmarked graves were close enough to the river where spring freshets would regularly wash over them.

And there they remained for forty years. Enter Dr. Thomas Featherstonhaugh, born in France in 1849 and a New Yorker before moving to Washington, DC, to work for the Pension Bureau, which was then in the Interior Department, as a medical examiner. In May 1893, he was promoted to medical referee, ruling on the pension requests of Civil War veterans. His discretionary rulings—not always in favor of the veterans—prompted an Indiana newspaper to allege, with stunning inaccuracy, that he was "an ex-surgeon of the Rebel army."

Featherstonhaugh was a huge admirer of John Brown. For years, he had been collecting images of the raiders and of Harpers Ferry dating back to the 1850s. Featherstonhaugh had also lent his name to a campaign to erect a monument to Brown at Harpers Ferry on land where the arsenal's engine house had once been. That campaign succeeded in 1895 when the railroad erected a nine-foot-tall granite obelisk there memorializing Brown.

Featherstonhaugh had been in close touch with Brown family members, who reminded him of the patriarch's last wish that his

Grave diggers who unearthed remains of Harpers Ferry raiders in 1895, with L. A. Brandebury, an associate of Brown enthusiast Thomas Featherstonhaugh. *Library of Congress, USZ62-11704*

dead sons join him in the North Elba burial ground. Featherston-haugh was determined to fulfill the martyred man's wishes. This, as it turned out, was no simple task. As syndicated columnist Bob Davis wrote in 1932, one day a "mysterious visitor" showed up at the house of Dr. Ezra S. McClellan, the medical officer at Saranac Lake in the Adirondacks, saying he knew where the other raiders were buried. Davis's version, while dramatic, may have been somewhat apocryphal, but not too far off.

Dr. McClellan's daughter Katherine had written an illustrated bound sketchbook on Brown that was for sale at the farm. Featherstonhaugh happened to see one and wrote her of his plan to unearth the raiders' remains and have them ceremoniously reburied at North Elba, complete with military honors. Would she help? Yes, she replied. There ensued a robust correspondence between them as the plan began to unfold.

In July 1895, Featherstonhaugh journeyed to Harpers Ferry in search of the remains. He was joined by L. A. Brandebury, an Interior Department associate and Civil War veteran whose wartime post was at the executive mansion (later to be known as the White House). Local resident James Foreman, who'd been present during the initial burials, and his son Lewis led them to the grave mounds. Featherstonhaugh and Brandebury also found that James Mansfield, the original grave digger, though old, was still alive, and he confirmed the location. The find was breathlessly reported in the *New York World*, with the headline "Rescued from Oblivion." The publicly stated plan then was to reinter the raiders near John Brown's fort along with erecting a monument. But that was perhaps just a cover story.

Featherstonhaugh placed flowers and two stones on the mounds, and there the raiders remained untouched again for four years while the unlikely grave robber formulated further plans. He returned on July 29, 1899, accompanied by E. P. Hall, another Pension Bureau associate, and Orin Grant Libby, a University of Wisconsin history professor spending the summer doing research in Washington. Libby had somehow gotten wind of Featherstonhaugh's plans and wanted in, at least in part to boost his own academic career and fortunes.

On the appointed day, Libby arrived by train from Baltimore with two small storage boxes. Featherstonhaugh and Hall came from Washington, also by train. Using picks and shovels, they dug three feet before reaching the first wooden box. It was made of pine, six feet long, four feet wide, and three feet deep. The box contained the remains of garments and the skeletons of four men. Three more were found in the second box. An additional femur led them to believe they had recovered the remains of not seven but eight of the raiders.

The boxes, Featherstonhaugh wrote, "were, of course, much decayed, but from being constantly wet, by proximity to the river, were remarkably preserved. Most of the smaller bones had crumbled away, but the long bones of eight men were recovered."

"The cover of the box . . . was partially decayed and was sunken in, but was still in a very fair state of preservation. We finally uncovered the whole top of the box and I raised the cover, to which the whole backbone of a man was adherent." The bodies had been closely packed, he reasoned. Some of the blanket shawls, or their remnants, were there, judging from the masses of woolen tissue around each of the remains.

"One of the skulls that I picked out from the ooze was all in pieces as if it had been shattered, and this may have been the skull of Newby, who, it will be remembered, was shot through the head and neck by a great spike."

The diggers replaced the lid and refilled the grave. Word got around and there were doubters. To dispel them, Featherstonhaugh obtained an affidavit from Mansfield dated April 21, 1899, testifying to the veracity of the unearthed "store-boxes."

Libby repacked the remains in traveling luggage, to not invite suspicion. While in New York City en route, he tried, without success, to sell the story to newspapers. The press would cover it anyway. The luggage was delivered to Katherine McClellan, where it remained in her attic on Old Military Road near the Brown farm until just before the ceremonies while arrangements were made. This also entailed obtaining permissions from the families of the deceased.

The reburial took place on August 30, 1899. President William McKinley, vacationing nearby at Lake Champlain, was invited but declined to come. Similarly, Vice President Theodore Roosevelt and Secretary of State Elihu Root were invited but, without explanation, did not attend. However, a contingent from the Twenty-Sixth US Infantry, stationed in Plattsburgh, did and accompanied the funeral procession from Lake Placid to the Brown farm, and a small detachment "fired a volley" before the flag-draped casket was lowered into one deep grave. As could be expected, reaction to this was mixed along regional lines, with Southern newspapers decrying this military salute and Northern organs celebrating the posthumous reunion.

A committee of black Philadelphians had voted on December 2, 1859, the date of Brown's execution and two weeks before the African American raiders would be hanged, to petition Wise—first for executive clemency for Copeland and Green, whose guilt they acknowledged, and then, failing that, for their bodies for a decent burial. Their letter elicited no response from the governor.

Rather, it evoked criticism from other "colored citizens" of Philadelphia who objected to what they regarded as its obsequious tone and description of the men as "poor" and "miserably misguided." It was no less than "a blot upon their dear and cherished memories" and exhibited "a total want of dignity, frankness, and independence, and violate[d] the sentiment and feelings of every true man, by bowing and virtually kissing the heel that would crush its authors."

Copeland and Green still had four more days to live when Dr. Edward Mason, medical director of the Medical College of Virginia in Winchester, wrote to Governor Wise on December 12, 1859. "I dislike to trouble you about small matters," he began, "but I would like, Sir, to obtain the bodies of the two blacks to be executed on Friday next. My object is to place their skeletons in the museum of the [college]." Two days later, Wise responded favorably, absent any demand "by their proper relatives" for the remains.

But there was a "proper demand" from Copeland's family back in Oberlin—and Wise's response would be equivocal. The Copelands could retrieve the body, but not even a free person of color could do the deed. On December 12, by Western Union, Wise wrote, "Yes to your order to some White Citizen. You Cannot Come to this State."

Despite the antiblack decree, this was enough for the *Oberlin Evangelist* to give the news a positive spin: "Item: Gov. Wise has ordered the body of John Copeland, on application of his father, to be delivered to his friends. It will accordingly be brought to Oberlin for burial."

Copeland's remains were already at the medical school in Winchester for dissection when his parents prevailed upon white abolitionist James Madison Monroe, an Oberlin professor, to undertake the mission.

As Monroe recalled later, the Copelands came knocking on his door on South Professor Street the day after their son's execution. It was, he said, "one of the most pathetic experiences of my life." John and Delilah Copeland were "people, in part, of African blood, of respectable standing in the community, and of amiable and Christian deportment." They were in "deep distress," especially the mother, who "exhibited such intense suffering . . . that it was a question whether she would not sink to the floor, in utter exhaustion." It was not so much her son's execution that brought her to this state but rather a report that his body would go to the medical college at Winchester for dissection.

This had kept her up all night, and only a mission to recover her son's body could mitigate her suffering. Monroe was pessimistic; Brown's remains had been respectfully treated, but he "did not belong to the despised race," he reasoned. Still, he agreed to go. Armed with a letter of introduction to the sentencing judge and another letter from Copeland's father authorizing him to act as his agent, Monroe scraped together enough money to make the journey and left Oberlin on December 19 for a two-day train trip, slowed by heavy snows, to Harpers Ferry and Winchester. Concerned his actual address might arouse suspicion, given Oberlin's reputation as a hotbed of abolitionism, he registered in the hotel as "James Monroe, Russia," the Lorain County township where Oberlin is located. Monroe went directly to the home of Judge Richard Parker, who had sentenced the conspirators, and there was invited for tea and dinner; the judge seemed inclined to help.

After dinner, Monroe and Parker went to see the president of the medical college. A faculty meeting was convened. "It was unanimously agreed that the body of Copeland should be delivered to me to be returned to the home of his parents." The college undertaker promised to have the "sorrowful fright . . . decently prepared for delivery at the express office." Monroe went to bed happy. "I thought I saw my way clear to take back the body of the young soldier of liberty to his sorrowing family to be buried in the soil of Oberlin."

Alas, it was not to be. A committee of medical students objected. "Sah, this nigger that you are trying to get don't belong to the Faculty," Monroe quoted one saying.

> He isn't theirs to give away. He belongs to us students, sah. Me and my chums nearly had to fight to get him. The Richmond medical students came to Charlestown determined to have him. I stood over the grave with a revolver in my hand while my chums dug him up. Now, sah, after risking our lives in this way, for the Faculty to attempt to take him from us, is mo' 'an we can b'ar. You must see, sah, and the Faculty must see, that if you persist in trying to carry out the arrangement you have made, it will open the do' for all, sorts of trouble.

A formerly sympathetic professor told Monroe that the faculty would adhere to "their contract with you" but that it had now become impractical. During the night, students had broken into the college's dissecting rooms, removed Copeland's body, and hidden it in an undisclosed location out in the countryside. He added that "if, under these circumstances, we were to persist . . . the whole country about us would soon be in a state of excitement." Instead, he told Monroe to abandon the idea. "The result was a great disappointment to me," Monroe wrote, "but it seemed to be inevitable."

With a few hours to kill before a carriage would take him to the train in Martinsburg, Monroe went with a young faculty member back to the medical college, where they visited the dissecting rooms. "The body of Copeland was not there, but I was startled to find the body of another Oberlin neighbor whom I had often met upon our streets, a colored man named Shields Greene [*sic*]. . . . It was a sad sight. . . . A fine, athletic figure, he was lying on his back—the unclosed, wistful eyes staring wildly upward, as if seeking, in a better world, for some solution of the dark

James Madison Monroe, who tried and failed to bring home the body of John Anthony Copeland. *Oberlin College Archives*

problems of horror and oppression so hard to be explained in this." Rebuffed on Copeland, he made no effort to obtain Green's remains.

On December 24, Monroe returned to Oberlin without either Copeland or Green. He related his unsuccessful efforts to Christmas Day worshippers at Oberlin's First Church. He dreaded meeting Copeland's parents but was relieved to learn they found comfort in his efforts on behalf of their son. "They were grateful to God and grateful to their neighbors," he recalled. "Their satisfaction was increased by the accounts which came in of the manly bearing of their boy in the time of the terrible ordeal."

Monroe's Christmas Day accounting took place during the afternoon memorial service for John Anthony Copeland. In addition to the speeches, a collection was taken up to erect a monument to Copeland and Leary in Oberlin; Green would also be added as an adopted son. "Green so far as is known had never been at Oberlin," noted the Oberlin Evangelist, contradicting Monroe's recollection. "Copeland was a member of the Institution [college] here a short time; Leary had resided here about three years, as a Mechanic, and left here his wife and child." Three thousand persons reportedly attended the memorial service "to mingle their tears with those who wept."

A December 29 fundraising letter from an eleven-member Oberlin committee that included Monroe added Shields Green to its appeal, though he "was but little known to us excepting as he has been made known to the nation and the world by his manly conduct, his patient and heroic endurance in prison, and his pious, courageous and consistent deportment as he stood on the fatal gallows." The letter noted Monroe's sight of Green's corpse "naked, frozen and bloody." Those at the funeral gave nearly $175 for the monument. "The more money we raise the more noble the monument we rear to the memory—not of a man only—but of a race," the appeal concluded.

In January, a fundraising flier circulated in Oberlin. In Boston, on February 24, black abolitionist and publisher William C. Nell reported that a committee at the Baptist Tremont Temple, having met on January 24, had raised fifty dollars: ten dollars for the monument and forty dollars for Leary's widow.

The eight-foot marble cenotaph was duly erected in 1860 at Westwood Cemetery, in the original two-acre burial ground south of Plum Creek established shortly after the founding of the Oberlin Colony in 1833. Its inscription reads, "These Colored Citizens of Oberlin, the Heroic Associates of the immortal John Brown, gave their lives for the slave. *Et nunc servitudo etiam mortua est, laus Deo.* [And thus, slavery is finally dead, thanks to God.]" Then these names and dates:

S. Green, died at Charleston, Va.,
December 16, 1859, age 23 years.
J. A. Copeland, died at Charleston, Va.,
December 16, 1859, age 25 years.
L. S. Leary, died at Harper's Ferry, Va.,
October 20, 1859, age 24 years.

Of their survivors, Lewis Leary's widow, Mary, married John Mercer Langston and moved to Kansas, where Lois, her daughter with Lewis, received an education partly paid for by James Redpath, the journalist, abolitionist, and John Brown biographer. Their daughter Caroline Mercer Langston married a James Hughes, and they had a son, James Mercer Langston Hughes, the Harlem Renaissance poet better known as Langston Hughes.

John Anthony's brother William L. Copeland enlisted in the Second Regiment, Ohio Cavalry, a white unit, during the Civil War. He studied law and was a Reconstruction-era Arkansas state legislator, later becoming a police officer. On December 30, 1885, he became the first Little Rock police officer killed in the line of duty, leaving his white wife, Anna, and an eight-year-old son, Willie. From his photograph, William Copeland could have easily passed for white, and he was listed as such in the 1880 Census, as was his son. His name is inscribed on a memorial to fallen police officers in Washington, DC. Another brother, Henry E. Copeland, served in the Independent Colored Kansas Battery and was a sergeant in Douglas' Battery of the First Kansas Colored Infantry during the Civil War. He and his wife, Lizzie, would both be identified as white in the 1870 Census, then mulatto in 1880.

As an eager recruiting agent in 1863 for the US Colored Troops, Frederick Douglass did not hesitate to invoke the names of John Anthony Copeland and Shields Green. "Liberty won only by white men would lose half its lustre," he declared. He urged those hesitating to "remember Shields Green and John Copeland, who followed noble John Brown, and fell as glorious martyrs for the cause of the slave."

Also in 1863, John Anthony's parents, John C. and Delilah Copeland, moved from their home on Morgan Street to an eleven-acre farm on Hamilton Street, just outside town and not far from Westwood Cemetery. On August 15, 1881, "a pleasant company" of about forty assembled at their home. The occasion, their fiftieth wedding anniversary, was deemed significant enough to warrant local newspaper coverage. At the celebration, a "bountiful supper was served" and gifts included "$50 in gold coin, two gold-lined silver cups, numerous floral offerings, and other articles." Deacon W. W. Wright offered a prayer. James Madison Monroe made what were described as "congratulatory remarks."

John C. Copeland died December 29, 1893, at the age of eighty-five, having outlived his wife and four of their eight children. The *Oberlin News* hailed him as "one of the most prominent representatives of Oberlin's pioneer colored citizens" who for "a number of years . . . lived a quiet life." "His existence was scarcely known to many citizens. . . . For half a century he lived a quiet, peaceable citizen," his obituary said. But John Anthony's execution had made him also "historic."

———————

I visit Westwood Cemetery on a quiet summer day. The burial ground, expanded to its current forty-seven acres in the mid-1860s, contains some ten thousand graves. It adjoins a public golf course, and as I solemnly study the gravestones, golf carts are temporarily parked nearby as duffers move from hole to hole. Breaking the silence is the sound of riding mowers driven by attentive groundskeepers. What is most striking is that the cemetery is integrated; there is no black-white division, no separate "colored" section, the norm in Southern and border states, even today. Scattered throughout are headstones indicating the remains of those who fought as enlisted men in US Colored Troops regiments.

The Copeland family plot is in section U. I find the headstone for George Copeland, who died in 1851 at the age of seventeen. His marker identifies him as the son of "J. C. & D. E. Copeland." James Monroe, who had tried and failed to bring home John Anthony's remains and then spoke at his memorial service, and at John C. Copeland's, is also buried at Westwood, as is Allen Jones, who with his own family had

Oberlin's Westwood Cemetery, where Copeland family members are buried, adjoins a public golf course. *Eugene L. Meyer*

accompanied the Copelands on their trek from North Carolina to Ohio so many years before.

From the cemetery, I drive to Martin Luther King Jr. Park to see the cenotaph, moved there in 1972 to be in a more conspicuous location, adjoining downtown, and another more recently erected memorial commemorating the twenty Oberliners who went to jail "for the crime of rescuing John Price from slavery." Underneath a group photo of the rescuers, the inscription continues, "With their comrades in the Abolition cause they kindled hopes of freedom for us all." It is around the corner from Main Street shops but is easily overlooked, and no one else is there. Across Vine Street from the park is a modest, privately owned house built in 1856 by Wilson Bruce Evans, Delilah Copeland's brother. Oberlin practically oozes history, but it's easy to miss.

No one is home at the former Copeland farmhouse on Hamilton Street. But I reach its current owner, Nancy Hendrickson, by phone.

She is worried about a natural gas pipeline whose right of way is through the land immediately behind the original farm, which has expanded to close to forty acres, including a small orchard and fields where they grow hay and corn and raise cows. The farm remained in the Copeland family until the 1920s, when John Anthony's youngest sister and last surviving sibling, Mary Jane Copeland, a teacher, died at seventy-one on August 23, 1922, after falling from a ladder while picking pears. Delilah's granddaughter Lottie Copeland, Mary Jane's heir, sold the house in 1925, and the property was subdivided. Today, it remains largely undeveloped.

Hendrickson and her husband, Ronald, a veterinarian, bought six and a half acres of it—including the farmhouse—in 1986, and they have been welcoming Copeland descendants, with forty-one relatives, for family reunions since 2002 and most recently in 2008, planned around the 150th anniversary of the Oberlin-Wellington rescue. For details, Nancy directs me to Brenda Pitts, the reunion organizer and a great-great-grandniece of John Anthony's who lives in Columbus, Indiana. The Copeland reunions in Oberlin have entailed a full two-day itinerary. "Nancy usually invites us out to visit the farm, provides refreshments, and gives a tour of the house," she tells me. The cemetery is also on the agenda.

Brenda Pitts is steeped in the history of the Copeland family, and, she says, it is purposely passed on to each new generation. A 2015 book, *The "Colored Hero" of Harper's Ferry*, focusing on John Anthony Copeland, has become something of a family bible. "My grandson is only eleven months old, but he has it," she says. "When he came home from the hospital, we started reading and talking to him about John Copeland. I have a photo of him being read to when he was six months old. I know they do it with some of the other [family] lines as well."

Though John Anthony Copeland never received a proper burial, his spirit lives on.

9

The Aftermath

The sole survivor of John Brown's band to bear witness to the raid at Harpers Ferry did not fare well in its aftermath. His father rejected him, some historians dismissed him, and he died young of "consumption" at age forty, a pathetic, impoverished figure in a city that barely knew him—until his death.

His book, *A Voice from Harper's Ferry*, was no bestseller. No one would hail him as the hero of Harpers Ferry. He had not been martyred, not even injured. He may even have suffered survivor's guilt, as he gave speeches, first to raise money to publish his book, and then to sell copies of the slim volume.

I first became acquainted with Osborne Perry Anderson in the fall of 2000, through Dennis Howard, a collateral descendant who, for some time, had been celebrating his ancestor's life, based on oral history handed down from his grandmother. Tasked to do a family history in eighth grade, he had discovered Anderson. He'd been obsessed with him ever since.

We met at National Harmony Memorial Park, a cemetery in suburban Maryland where Anderson is believed to be buried, near FedEx Field, home to Washington's National Football League team. It is also the final resting place of Mary Ann Shadd Cary, Anderson's former employer and mentor, and of a who's who of other prominent nineteenth-century black Washingtonians.

Dennis Howard, a descendant of Osborne Perry Anderson, kneels at a cemetery plaque dedicated to his ancestor. *Eugene L. Meyer*

A bronze plaque memorializing him was being dedicated on Saturday, November 11, Veterans Day, near a fence far from the entrance, where unidentified remains are buried. Cemetery officials could not vouch for the precise location of his actual grave, since records no longer existed, but there was other evidence of his interment. This day of remembrance was organized by Patricia and Paul E. Sluby Sr. Paul had extensively researched black cemeteries in the area. There were politicians' speeches, ministerial prayers, the singing of the national anthem, a high school color guard, and a rifle salute by Civil War reenactors representing Company B of the Fifty-Fourth Massachusetts Voluntary Infantry Regiment of the US Colored Troops, the vaunted fighting force portrayed in the epic 1989 film *Glory*.

For me, this was the beginning. For Osborne Perry Anderson, this was the end.

Sensing the futility of John Brown's deteriorating situation at the barricaded engine house, Anderson, along with Albert Hazlett, had escaped. The fugitives headed into Maryland and north along Elk Ridge toward Pennsylvania. But Hazlett was hungry, tired, and complaining of sore feet, and the two split. Traveling under the assumed name of William Harrison, Hazlett was carrying a Sharps rifle, pistol, and cartridge belt when he was captured in his home town of Carlisle, Pennsylvania. He was then extradited, tried, convicted, and hanged in March 1860. Anderson made it first to Chambersburg around 2 AM on Thursday, and then the next night to York, Pennsylvania. There he was hidden by William Goodridge, a prominent black businessman and Underground Railroad stationmaster who also owned an actual railroad, known as the Reliance Line.

Goodridge put him on a train bound for Philadelphia. During his flight, Anderson later wrote, he changed clothes three times to avoid detection.

Anderson wasn't safe even above the Mason-Dixon Line. He later told Brown's daughter Annie that when he returned to the family home in Chester County, Pennsylvania, "His own father turned him out from the door, threatening to have him arrested if he ever came again; and that most of the colored people he met turned the cold shoulder to him as if he was an outcast."

Anderson made his way back to the welcoming abolitionist county of Ashtabula, in northeastern Ohio, to the home of abolitionist T. Smith Edwards. He then traveled to nearby Cleveland, where he met up with Charles Plummer Tidd, the white member of Brown's rear guard who also escaped but later died in the Civil War. From there, Anderson crossed the border and returned to Chatham, most likely by boat across Lake Erie.

Arriving in the city that had welcomed and absorbed so many African American refugees, he was not a well man. Isaac Holden, a black emigre from Louisiana and Chatham's first black alderman, later recalled that Anderson had "escaped to the mountains, through which he wandered for weeks" and "came back . . . a gaunt, living skeleton."

On April 9, 1860, at the Coloured Regular Baptist Church in Toronto, Anderson pleaded for funds to publish his account in order to rebuff the "false and willful statement . . . that the slaves of that section . . . refused to join in the insurrection—that they were pressed into service, and as soon as the opportunity offered itself deserted their liberators." Further, in his unprepared remarks, referring to his fellow black raiders, he said he wanted to rescue from oblivion "the heroism of the colored men who so nobly seconded the effort of the immortal John Brown."

When he had finished his oration, the *Weekly Anglo-African* reported, "the edifice shook under the repeated approbation of an overwhelming audience."

In late June, while still a fugitive from Virginia, Anderson made a surprise appearance before the Fugitive Aid Society in Cleveland. Sworn to secrecy, the audience was delighted by his presence. "All rushed forward to the stand to take him by the hand, and to rejoice that he had the good fortune to escape Virginia's bloody halter," a correspondent identified only as "Charlie" reported. "Old ladies cried a la mode, and stout-hearted men were not a little affected by the scene." Anderson, it was further noted, would "publish soon" his own account of the raid, promised to be about 150 pages in length, double its eventual size. It was sure "to find ready sale and its author ample compensation," which the correspondent said was needed, for Anderson was "in great want of pecuniary aid," since, "having been afraid to make himself known . . . has had no work to do. . . . What little money he has been able to get has been spent in preparing his book, and as he has been almost wholly unknown, he has been unprovided for. So he is destitute." Eighteen dollars was raised on the spot and requests made for more, which were to be mailed to Anderson in Chatham, Canada, "and donations will be thankfully received by him."

Soon afterward, Anderson was in North Elba, New York, at Brown's 270-acre farm to attend a memorial service that several of Brown's closest supporters, principally Brown biographer James Redpath, had arranged. There were readings of the Declaration of Independence and the Sermon on the Mount. It was the Fourth of July 1860, the first time, Anderson told the estimated crowd of one thousand people, he had ever felt inclined to celebrate this national holiday styled as Independence Day. Until the raid on Harpers Ferry, which he viewed as the opening round of the coming civil war, he said, he'd felt the holiday had been a lie. He predicted that Brown's sacrifice would be rewarded.

The gathering was set to adjourn when Brown supporter Richard J. Hinton stepped forward to call out the names of Leary, Newby, Copeland, and Green and to recognize the presence of Anderson, "of Chatham, Canada West, but late of Harper's Ferry," for whose capture the "pirate-State of Virginia" had offered an award of $1,500. Should there be any Democrats present, he added, "we have good revolvers and strong arms, wherewith to defend our friends."

Anderson ascended the speaking stand, "a tall, handsome mulatto, with thoughtful face, sadly-earnest eyes, and an expression of intellectual power," the *Liberator* noted in its account of the gathering. "By the light of that [Brown's] grave's sacrifice, he knew the Declaration of Independence held more than 'glittering generalities.' He had gone to Virginia, not as a mulatto, but as a man. Thank God for the struggle."

Financially, the man who had urged other blacks not to beg was reduced to relying on the monetary support of others. "If you can send me 20.00 Dolars pleas do so soon," he wrote on October 13, 1860, to Hinton.

In February 1861, Anderson was still on the run, wanted for his role in John Brown's raid. But that did not stop him from making a discreet appearance in Boston to promote his seventy-two-page book, printed "for the author" in that city. The book was written with an unacknowledged assist from Mary Ann Shadd Cary, who, working from his notes, had helped craft it. The 1861 Chatham Census lists O. P. Anderson, black, Church of England, "book agent." Since his book had just been published, the job description fit.

"Mr. Anderson is a young colored man, and the only man alive who was at the Ferry during the entire time, and is thus enabled to record the facts as they actually occurred," noted *Douglass' Monthly*. "The narrative is published for his benefit, and no doubt will find ready purchasers." The *Monthly* then reported on the recent meeting held in Boston by "some of the most influential colored members" of the city, who raised $100 "for his benefit." At yet another gathering, at the Twelfth Baptist Church on January 1 and made known to only a few "for prudential reasons," Anderson read passages from his book, and an impromptu committee raised forty dollars for him "as an acceptable New Year's present." And in Rochester, Anderson "disposed of quite a number of his books," which sold for 20 cents each and could be bought at Hall's news depot.

After issuing the Emancipation Proclamation in 1863, President Abraham Lincoln authorized the formation of black regiments in the Union Army. He also made Martin R. Delany, the physician and abolitionist who had participated in Brown's Chatham conference, the army's first black commissioned officer. Delany's immediate task was to solicit black recruits, and in this effort, both Mary Ann Shadd Cary, by now a widow with two children, and Anderson assisted. Recruiters also received bonuses, another incentive for both. Records indicate they were actively recruiting in Indiana and Arkansas, and Shadd Cary in Connecticut as well.

Later in the war, Hinton wrote in 1894, Anderson himself joined the army, though there is no record of his military service. The Buxton National Historic Site and Museum, in North Buxton, Ontario, contains a plaque of black residents who enlisted and fought for the Union forces. Anderson is among the 107 names but listed under "regiment unknown." It has been written that Anderson mustered out in 1865 in the District of Columbia, but again documentary evidence has yet to be found, although there is speculation he may have enlisted under an assumed name.

What is documented, however, is that in 1866 Anderson lived in Michigan and represented Battle Creek at a black convention. Soon thereafter, he moved to Philadelphia and then to Washington, DC, residing in both cities with Alfred M. Green, ten years younger than Anderson and an early proponent of raising "colored regiments" to fight for the Union. Meanwhile, Shadd Cary also made her last move, in 1869, to the nation's capital, where she owned a house at 1421 W Street NW, became a public school principal, and, after first enrolling in Howard University's law school in September 1869, eventually received her degree in 1883—the second woman to do so. In 1885, she delivered a speech on "Race, Pride, and Cooperation" at the Mayersville, Mississippi, courthouse. An active suffragist, she tried registering to vote in the District of Columbia in 1871; a seven-member board that included two prominent black elected officials turned her down. She died of cancer in 1893 at the age of sixty-nine and was buried initially, as was Anderson, in the Columbian Harmony Cemetery on Rhode Island Avenue in northeast Washington.

"Anderson, Osb'n P.," occupation "messenger," is the listing in the 1873 Washington directory, published before his death. His address was the same as Green's. Together, Anderson and Green would twice visit Harpers Ferry and the Charlestown jail where John Brown had been held. He also visited in 1871 with Hinton, part of Brown's rear guard who was not in the raid, and noted where the battle had occurred. With several friends a few days before he died, Anderson would make a final, nostalgic visit to Harpers Ferry.

He was suffering from late-stage consumption, known today as tuberculosis, the symptoms of which include difficulty breathing, chest pain, fatigue, weight loss, and coughing up blood. Whatever medical care he was getting, if any, is not recorded. But his condition became increasingly known. The first hint that Anderson was "dangerously ill" appeared in Douglass's *New National Era* newspaper in June 1872. In October, Anderson visited Philadelphia, where those attending a Bethel Church tribute donated $69.02. One of his friends asked him to accept the money "not . . . as a gift; it is only a partial payment for services rendered. As you are the last of [John Brown's] apostles, we owe you unfading honors, and sustenance as long as you may live." Will H. Smith regretted he could not attend but sent a donation, asking Anderson to "please therefore accept my humble contribution, and may God bless the people of Philadelphia in their noble effort to chase the lonely days of a most deserving man."

As Anderson's health continued to decline, according to an account in the *Washington Chronicle*, his supporters met at the District's Fifteenth Street Presbyterian Church on the evening of Wednesday, November 13, 1872, "for the purpose of raising pecuniary aid . . . to enable him to procure nourishment in his distress." Anderson "is in feeble health," the *National Republican* reported; an advance announcement promised that several prominent citizens were expected to attend "and do all within their power to aid the man in his need." He had "lately returned from Boston." Indeed, they raised seventy-five dollars for the "sick and suffering man."

They passed resolutions by which "the citizens and sojourners of this city, this night assembled, rejoice in an opportunity to do honor to the memory of John Brown and the only survivor of that grand struggle for human freedom . . . but regret to know that Mr. Anderson's health is in such a shattered condition, the result of his exposure and trials for us. Resolved. That we extend to Mr. Anderson our profoundest obligations for the great service rendered us on that memorable 16th day of October 1859—a day that will yet stand in American history as the dawn of our political freedom."

The *Belmont Chronicle* of Saint Clairsville, Ohio, reported, "His disease is consumption, and his days are nearly numbered. . . . It would be a thing for Americans to blush over if the last of the brave men who followed Old John Brown down into the very jaws of death should be permitted to die as a pauper in a garret."

Not everyone was sympathetic. From the unreconstructed *Spirit of Jefferson* in Charlestown, West Virginia, still mourning the Lost Cause and regarding the Harpers Ferry raiders as treasonous, came a full fusillade of condemnation. The newspaper took note of recent fundraising for Anderson at the Fifteenth Street Presbyterian Church, netting, it said with sarcasm, "the enormous sum of $75 . . . for a sick and suffering man to whom the Radical [Republican] party owes more than to any man now living."

Here, Osborne is referred to not as a hero but as "the midnight assassin who eluded the penalty of his crime . . . by abandoning his leader and escaping to Canada!" Anderson was merely John Brown's "companion in crime" who "took part in that memorable 'raid' upon a peaceful Virginia community, and committed murder."

A month later, on the morning of December 10, 1872, Anderson succumbed, according to an obituary in the *Washington Star*, at Green's home at Fourteenth and C Streets NW, where the US Commerce Department is now located. He was forty-two. "The deceased was a man of good character, and was quite effective as a political speaker," the paper said.

Anderson "was truly a noble and devoted lover of freedom for all mankind," opined the *New National Era*, a newspaper Frederick Douglass published in the District of Columbia from 1870 to 1874. Funeral services were Friday, December 13, at the Fifteenth Street Presbyterian Church, then between I and K Streets NW, with three ministers and ten African American pallbearers, who included Lewis H. Douglass, a son of Frederick Douglass; John M. Langston, inspector general of the Freedmen's Bureau and later a congressman from Virginia; and George T. Downing, a Newport, Rhode Island, hotel and restaurant owner who for ten years was in charge of the café dining room of the House of Representatives. Also present was Anderson's "aged father," who had turned him away shortly after the raid, but attended the funeral, where "he was the recipient of the sympathy of all," according to one newspaper account.

A week after Anderson's death, the *New National Era* published a eulogy by Daniel A. Straker, another pallbearer, under the headline "Osborne P. Anderson, a Hero." "The greatest hero . . . in the struggle for liberty has gone to his rest," he wrote. "His was no money sacrifice . . . but it was personal sacrifice." Anderson's death, Straker wrote, was "deeply lamented by all lovers of freedom. . . . Let us cherish his memory to our latest generation."

For lack of funds, Anderson's remains would wait months before being interred in Harmony Cemetery. They were to be removed later to West Chester, Pennsylvania, according to the *Daily Morning Chronicle*, but that never happened. Instead, they went to Harmony, "north of the Capitol." Nearly a century later, they were exhumed, along with an estimated thirty-nine thousand others in 1960, and reburied in the newly established Harmony National Memorial Cemetery in the Washington suburb of Landover, Maryland.

Though Anderson had no known offspring, Dennis Howard long believed, based on oral history, that he was a direct descendant three generations removed. There was little doubt, however, that they were kin. Though Anderson was born in southeastern Pennsylvania, his father was born in Virginia in 1804. Thomas Anderson, possibly an uncle, was born in the Scott district of Fauquier County in 1798. The 1850 Census locating Thomas there describes him as a mulatto and a free person of color. His direct descendants would migrate one jurisdiction north, to Loudoun County, Virginia, today an affluent suburb of Washington, DC.

Dennis, a retired army officer turned DC social worker, resided in a rambler in the also affluent Fairfax County, Virginia, the most populous county in the Washington metropolitan area. He had grown up in northern Virginia and attended segregated schools, but integration was just beginning when he entered junior high school. He began researching family history when his eighth grade English and government teacher assigned students to research their family crest back to England and report back in six weeks. Howard was the only black student in the class at the newly integrated Stratford Junior High School, and at first, he was livid.

But three of his four grandparents were still alive, and they filled him with family history and lore. One grandmother passed along stories she'd heard from her elders, that they had been slaves in Virginia who had plowed their masters' fields barefoot, stepping carefully in the warm footprints left by the oxen in front of them. The stories included Osborne Anderson, the son of a mixed-race father and white abolitionist mother with red hair. The connection was always vague and remains undocumented but rests on some strong circumstantial evidence.

The teacher and class loved his report, which included a lesson on "race mixing," and Howard was launched on a lifelong quest to document his family history. His research has taken him to forty-eight states. "I'm still doing the assignment," he says.

As he researched Osborne Anderson, Howard didn't find any information about Anderson's brothers. Then, in 2016, he learned of military records for the Fifty-Fourth Massachusetts, which led the Union assault on Fort Wagner, near Charleston, South Carolina, on July 18, 1863—immortalized in the film *Glory*. The white commanding colonel Robert Gould Shaw and 272 of his black troops died in the battle. Two enlisted sons of Frederick Douglass, Charles and Lewis, the future Anderson pallbearer, participated and survived.

Altogether, there were forty-six soldiers from Chester County, Pennsylvania, in the Fifty-Fourth Massachusetts, of whom fifteen were killed or wounded at Fort Wagner. Among the wounded was a thirty-three-year-old laborer, James Anderson, in Company G. Also on the roster was shoemaker John Anderson, twenty-two. Both would be discharged on August 20, 1865. They were Osborne's younger brothers. Dennis Howard could hardly contain his excitement at getting this belated news. "That makes me very proud," he said.

For the family and descendants of Dangerfield Newby, there were both challenges and opportunities during chaotic times of civil war, Reconstruction, Jim Crow, and beyond.

Sometime during the first half of 1860, the widow Jennings sold Harriet Newby and some of her children south to a Louisiana planter. The evidence of Harriet's absence is found in the 1860 Census for Prince William County, which has Virginia Jennings owning only two slave boys, both of whom she had hired out to others.

In Louisiana, Harriet met William Robinson, sixteen years younger—precisely when and under what circumstances are unclear. He was born in 1840 in Berkeley County, now West Virginia, home to many free blacks. Census records from 1850 show a William Robinson, age nine, residing in Berkeley's Ninth District, in a large household headed by John T. Henderson, a fifty-eight-year-old innkeeper. Only William and Jane Robinson, born "about" 1841, are racially identified (as black). Presumably, the others in the household were white. But how did Robinson get to Louisiana?

William Robinson may have enlisted in the US Colored Troops formed after President Lincoln issued the Emancipation Proclamation. New Orleans and Baton Rouge were occupied by federal troops from 1862 through the rest of the war, during which three hundred thousand Louisiana slaves were liberated. So it is possible that Harriet and her children were among those liberated and that she and William met in a camp for "contrabands," escaped slaves or those affiliated with Union forces, in the Baton Rouge area.

There is another possibility: in May 1861, the First Louisiana Native Guard formed in New Orleans mostly from free persons of color to fight for the Confederacy. It disbanded in April 1862 after the state legislature decreed that only "free white males capable of bearing arms" could belong. In September, some members joined the Union Army, under the same name; it later became the Seventy-Third Regiment Infantry of the United States Colored Troops, drawing recruits from beyond the immediate vicinity. The regiment participated in the long and ultimately successful 1863 siege of Port Hudson, a cotton and sugar exporting center twenty miles north of Baton Rouge.

Civil War pension records contain yet another tantalizing if strange clue to their relationship. They show a Harriet Robinson as "widow" and "dependent" linked to William H. Robinson, whose service was with the First Regiment of the US Colored Infantry. Two claims were filed from Virginia for "soldier" William H. Robinson, alias Henry Robinson, alias Henderson Robinson, the first for Robinson as "invalid" in 1888, the second for his widow, in 1893. But Harriet had died in 1884. The processing officer deemed these claims to be fraudulent.

At some point from 1863 to 1865, Harriet Newby met and married William Robinson and had three children with him in Louisiana. At the war's end, they traveled north. Harriet went to Ashtabula in search of a lost son from her marriage to Newby, possibly Dangerfield Newby Jr., not finding him but receiving a warm welcome. "She came north after the Emancipation, was a light mulatto and intelligent," recalled resident Alfred Hawkes in a 1909 interview. "She never knew what became of her son. She came first to the Edwards' [house] and was a seamstress, a very bright-looking woman."

Her return as "Harriet Robinson" to Virginia, initially to King George County, on the Northern Neck between the Potomac and Rappahannock rivers, was on March 22, 1866. The arrival coincided with the marriage of her and Dangerfield's daughter Agnes to a Thomas Proctor a week later, on March 29. In the 1880 Census, the Proctors were living in Alexandria. Next to each of their three children is the letter *M* for mulatto. Among them was a son, Dangerfield G. Proctor, undoubtedly named for his grandfather killed at Harpers Ferry. He would find work as a waiter and eventually move to York, Pennsylvania, where he died in 1959, aged eighty-nine, a full century after his grandfather Dangerfield died at Harpers Ferry.

In addition to Harriet's children with Newby, she had three daughters with William Robinson. The 1870 Census shows them living in Falls Church, Fairfax County: William was a farmhand; Harriet was keeping house. Gabriel, fifteen, a Newby son born in Virginia, is listed as an employee in a cooper (barrel) shop. Also with them was Anna, ten, also born in Virginia and most likely the Newby child Harriet was pregnant with at the time of Dangerfield's death. Next were Elizabeth, seven; Irena, six; and Louisa, four; all three born in Louisiana—her children with William Robinson. Elizabeth's date of birth, 1863, suggests the timing of the union between William and Harriet.

On August 17, 1872, Freedmen's Bureau records took note of Gabriel Newby, a son of Dangerfield and Harriet's, then working on the railroad. William Robinson was listed as his stepfather, Harriet his mother. His siblings were Laura, Alice, Agnes, and "three or four" others. The record indicates he was born in Waterloo, Fauquier County, Virginia. Gabriel eventually moved west, turning up in an 1887 city directory for Kansas City, Missouri, and also St. Louis in the 1880 Census and a 1902 city directory. He married but had no children.

In Fairfax County, William Robinson became a significant land owner. He acquired some property from the Mason family, the large formerly slaveholding clan that had included George Mason, who wrote the Virginia Declaration of Rights in 1776 but refused to sign the US Constitution in 1787 because it lacked a bill of rights and failed to immediately abolish the slave trade. Robinson initially purchased ten acres of Mason land between Mount Vernon and Alexandria, today a stretch of high-priced real estate along the George Washington Parkway. By 1880, Robinson and one of his daughters with Harriet owned nearly forty acres.

By the June 15, 1880, Census only three remained in the Robinson household, then in Mount Vernon, Fairfax County: William, forty, still a farmhand; Harriet, fifty-six, and their daughter Louisa, fifteen. Four years later, Harriet died at the age of sixty. In 1888, Robinson remarried. His new wife was Sarah Johnson, a widow whose family had been enslaved on the George Washington plantation at Mount Vernon and continued to work and live there after emancipation. He would live to age sixty-eight and die in 1908, she in 1920.

Meanwhile, the Newby family saga continued to play out on both sides of the Ohio River—in Bridgeport, Ohio; Wheeling, West Virginia; and beyond—as the Civil War broke out. Dangerfield had left an estate, and Harriet and their children would get none of it.

The money Dangerfield had saved to purchase his wife and children had remained in the Bank of Ohio in Belmont County. The account held three deposits totaling about $742—the equivalent of more than $20,000 in 2016. Since he'd left no will, the court appointed an administrator, and legal notice was published in the *Belmont Chronicle* on January 22, 1863. It listed some of Dangerfield's siblings and his parents as plaintiffs, while Harriet and her children with Dangerfield were the defendants. Should the defendants not respond by February 14,

1863—less than a month after the posting, and while Harriet was still in Louisiana—the notice said, the petition of the plaintiffs would "be taken as true and judgment rendered accordingly." Thus, Dangerfield's entire estate would go to Henry and Elsey Newby's grown children and none to Harriet and her children—all of them given the surname Jennings, that of her former owner, as if Harriet and Dangerfield's union had never happened.

While the court was working to close the books on Dangerfield's estate, the rest of the Newbys and their relatives, some of whom had taken on the surname Bywater through marriage, settled into a traditional life in Belmont County and neighboring Wheeling, right across the Ohio River. The 1860 Census for Bridgeport, Ohio, counted twenty-one in Henry Newby's household, including ten Newby children: Henry, Ailsey (Elsey), and nine named Bywater. Altogether, in Bridgeport that year there lived twenty-five Newbys and twenty-six Bywaters. They worked as laborers, domestics, servants, miners, waiters, barbers, and as a nurse.

Henry passed away on December 31, 1861, at the age of seventy-eight. Strikingly, in his will, he formally acknowledged Elsey as the mother of his children and left almost all of his property to her. Their union, not legally recognized by the Commonwealth of Virginia, had endured for forty-three years. Elsey would continue to live in Bridgeport until her death at seventy-eight in 1884.

Dangerfield's three other brothers enlisted to fight for the Union as soon as it was allowed. Though the men were initially paid ten dollars monthly, three dollars less than white soldiers, Congress equalized the amounts in 1864. Still, the Newby recruits in the US Colored Troops were often paid late, if at all, according to claims for pensions their widows filed later.

John and William would be detailed to Company C, Fifth Regiment of the Ohio Colored Volunteers. John mustered in on September 10, 1863, at Camp Delaware, Ohio, as a corporal. The war would take them to the outskirts of Petersburg, Virginia, the supply center for the Confederate Army. The city's eastern flank was then defended by only 2,200 Confederate troops. Their commander was Brig. Gen. Henry A.

Wise, the former governor of Virginia who intervened personally to ensure that John Brown and his captured accomplices—including John Copeland and Shields Green—were tried and executed in Charlestown less than five years before.

On June 15, 1864, William's regiment distinguished itself during the battle, engaging in a two-hour assault, pushing back rebel troops, and capturing Confederate artillery. Despite the successes of the US Colored Troops, Union general William F. Smith decided not to push forward to capture the city, and the war went on for nearly another year. In his memoirs published in 1893, Smith defended his decision, writing, "My white troops were exhausted by marching day and night and by fighting most of the day in the excessive heat. My colored troops who had fought bravely were intoxicated by their success and could hardly be kept in order."

Despite Smith's demurral, fighting continued. Twenty-two-year-old William, who was over six foot two and described as a "mulatto" in official papers, was wounded at Petersburg on June 28, 1864, and died the next day "of a gunshot wound rec'd while on duty in front of Petersburg," the commanding officer of Company C later wrote. He had not been paid since February 29. On October 22, 1864, nearly four months after her son's death, Elsey, then sixty-four, filed a "Mother's Declaration" for an army pension. In her application, she stated she was the widow of Henry Newby, whom she had married on December 1, 1818. "And she further states that she believes there is 'no' public record of her said marriage," she affirmed, by signing the form with an *X* ("her mark"). After her husband's death in 1861, she had depended on her sons for support. "For at least five years previous," William had often contributed "the greater part of his earnings and wages to her," paying for food, clothing and "all the . . . other things necessary to house keeping." But after enlisting, he didn't send her money because, he wrote her, he hadn't been paid. Meanwhile, neighbors affirmed, she had no property nor income, "only what she receives from her labor."

Also enlisted in the Forty-Fifth, Company F, but surviving the war was Pvt. Lafayette Bywater of Belmont County, Ohio. Born in Culpeper in 1847, he was the son of Dangerfield's sister Elmira Newby Bywater. He was eighteen when he enlisted in Wheeling on February 18, 1865. After the war, on October 16, 1867, he married Sophia Henderson. They had six children. In the 1880 Census, the entire family is classified as *M* for mulatto. His wife's occupation is given as housekeeper. His oldest child, Mary E., then eleven, was a "Scholar." A coal miner as well as a Civil War veteran, Lafayette would live to be only thirty-seven and pass away on January 2, 1884. Whether his occupation was a factor in his demise is not known.

John would be honorably discharged from the service on September 20, 1865, marry Virginia Hughes on December 16, 1868, and live out his life in Bridgeport, Ohio. He died on December 10, 1884, leaving Virginia with three children to house, feed, and clothe. In support of her application for a widow's pension on July 11, 1890, two neighbors testified that the Newby house was mortgaged and far behind on payments. "[Virginia] has no means of support except her own labor and the little the two oldest boys can do for her, the oldest child a girl is delicate and not able to do much to assisting . . . but [is] often an expense to her," they said. Two of the three children were younger than sixteen.

Dangerfield's brothers, James and Gabriel, who worked together as barbers in Bridgeport, also joined the Union cause. James had married his wife, Elizabeth, on June 20, 1864, and the following February 16, at the age of twenty-seven, he signed up in Wheeling for one year "or during the war." Described as six feet two inches tall, with black eyes, hair, and complexion, he was assigned to Company C of the Forty-Fifth Regiment of the US Colored Infantry and promoted to the rank of corporal on May 13, and then to sergeant on July 1, 1865. James was promised a cash bounty of $100 to enlist, but records show he received only a third. He was last paid his soldier's salary on June 30, 1865. His unit would be sent in May 1865 to the Mexican border in Texas. On November 4, 1865, he was mustered out in Brownsville, at which time he owed the government $49.19 for "cloth'g in kind or money adv'd."

He died August 13, 1883. His widow filed for a pension in 1891, with her sister testifying to her remaining unmarried and in need.

During the war, Gabriel was a servant to Col. Christian L. Poorman, in the white Ninety-Eighth Ohio Infantry. The two may well have been acquainted beforehand: Poorman, the Belmont County auditor, lived in nearby St. Clairsville. As a servant rather than an enlisted man, Gabriel would have joined Poorman well before the US Colored Troops were formed in 1863. If so, he would have seen action with Poorman at the bloody Battle of Perryville, Kentucky, on October 8, 1862. Union forces lost 894 dead, 2,911 wounded, and 471 missing or captured; Confederate losses were 532 dead, 2,641 wounded, and 228 missing or captured.

Gabriel died May 4, 1900, at age seventy-seven, after a two-month illness. His obituary described him as "highly respected" and "one of the most prominent colored men in this town," where he had "made many friends." Gabriel's funeral was "very largely attended," according to a newspaper account. He'd had three marriages and lived in Bridgeport for more than forty years. "He was one of the best known colored men in this vicinity," another local newspaper reported.

The lost son Harriet had hoped to find in Ohio after the war may have been Dangerfield F. Newby Jr., born in 1856. He appears in 1870 and 1880 Census records in Durham, North Carolina. His occupation was listed as "minister." His 1913 certificate of marriage (not his first) lists his parents as Harriet and Dangerfield Newby. His daughter, Viola Annie, would die in 1932 at the age of fifty-three of pellagra, in Durham. Dangerfield and Harriet's last surviving child, Dangerfield Jr., would die at age eighty-one in 1936, of apoplexy, his wife Mary reported. His widow would later work as a hostess at the Algonquin Tennis Club in Durham.

Evaline, also known as Emily, another daughter of Harriet and Dangerfield's, had been owned by Henry Newby, her grandfather, who freed her in 1857. She remained in Virginia but not in the Culpeper-Fauquier area. Instead, she moved with her three children some sixty miles west to Shenandoah County, between the Blue Ridge and Allegheny mountain ranges in the heart of the Shenandoah Valley and also home to a large Quaker population. In manumission papers he filed with the Culpeper Court Clerk on September 22, 1858, Henry Newby "doth emancipate and set free forever" Evaline Newby, twenty-six, and her children: John Newby, twelve; Leander Jackson Newby, four; and Luther Newby, fourteen months—all of them "being slaves the property of said Henry Newby."

It is uncertain exactly how many children Dangerfield and Harriet had together, but several sources put their offspring at seven. Among them was a daughter, Elmira, who had her first child in 1859 with Edward M. Groves, an eighteen-year-old white youth from a neighboring farm. Elmira had been the property of the Dodd family and lived on their land. Once freed, she would remain in Fauquier County. In 1860, Elmira married Eli Tackett, a light-skinned man with whom she had more children. Tackett, a former slave of John Fox, had led the ultimately successful lawsuit on behalf of Fox's other former slaves to acquire the property their last owner willed to them. After Tackett's death, Elmira married George Jefferson Brown.

Mira (Elmira) Brown was a light-skinned black woman living on the white side of Remington, a small town several miles south of Warrenton and still in Fauquier County. Her daughter Agnes, Agnes's husband Felix, and other family members lived in the colored section "up on the ridge." Mira served as the sexton, or caretaker, for the white Remington Baptist Church. Sometimes described as "Indian" in appearance, she died in 1929 and is interred in Hollywood Cemetery, a black burial ground on the west side of town. Mira Brown's Newby maiden name appeared under the space for "mother" on the death certificates of her children Agnes Pinn, Carrie Brown, and Washington A. ("Wash") Tackett.

Ashton M. Robinson III, a descendant of Dangerfield and Harriet Newby living out west, was in the early stages of a long and emotionally difficult journey into his family's past when he and his wife, Ellen, first drove by the house that Carrie Brown's son Elmore had bought for her in 1900 and where she lived out her life. It was now the late 1990s, and it was for him still just a tentative but not a tenuous connection he was not quite ready to confront at this time and in this place. They did not stop.

The second time, a few years later, Ashton came by himself and knocked on the door of the three-bedroom, two-story house on Piney Lane, just east of US 15, the James Madison Highway. A woman answered the door. She was friendly, "a real nice lady," Ashton recalls, but she did not invite him inside. Her name was Virginia Pinn, and she was Agnes Brown Pinn's daughter-in-law.

"We just stood there in the doorway, and we talked about all of the old people, and she told me about how she was connected and what she remembered," Ashton says. Their conversation was more nostalgic than historic. Small talk. Neither mentioned Dangerfield. In truth, the Dangerfield Newby connection might not have set well with the white—and perhaps even some of the black—residents in town. Fauquier County, was, after all, still in the heart of "Ole Virginny," with all of the cultural baggage and contradictions that entailed—the lawful and social conventions of segregation contrasting with often cordial relations between the races. Given the racially mixed backgrounds of so many residents, the informalities continued, if at times uneasily, even during the days of legally enforced separation, and after.

But Ashton had not grown up in this world, and he was only coming to it in middle age. So there he was, standing in the doorway, trying to imagine all who had come through it over the generations and what their lives had been like: "Here I am talking to a descendant, and I'm feeling them all, there in the doorway." From the house, he went to Mira's grave and stood there, alone, grappling with his emotions, trying to comprehend the meaning of it all.

A week later, a distant cousin he'd never met called. Her name was Sherrie Carter. A local resident, she also descends from Harriet and Elmira and had separately been digging into the family's history. They exchanged information, and two years after, they went to the house together. Virginia Pinn had died in 2003. Now the house was empty, between rentals, and they got to go inside, led by Virginia's daughter. The family tree stretching from Dangerfield and Harriet seemed to have sprouted new branches that were blooming. Better late than never.

10

Hapless Haywood Shepherd

I n 1931, the Baltimore *Afro-American* newspaper boldly proposed the erection of a monument to the five African Americans who comprised slightly more than a quarter of the raiding party with John Brown at Harpers Ferry. The idea was not well received locally, and it did not happen then. Nor has it happened in the years since. Anderson, Copeland, Green, Leary, and Newby would thus remain unrecognized in a monument or plaque devoted solely to them. Not so, Haywood Shepherd.

It is among history's ironies that the first fatality of the raid mounted to free black slaves was a free black man with no connection to Brown and who was, by all accounts, shot in the back by one or two white members of Brown's little army. More ironic, perhaps, Shepherd would become an unlikely martyr to the Lost Cause, posthumously misrepresented by unreconstructed Southerners who sought to use his death to rewrite history. In life a free man, Haywood Shepherd in death came to symbolize the "loyal slave" who did not rebel but instead lived happily and faithfully as the property of another human being.

In fact, members of the Shepherd family had been free persons of color for generations in and near Martinsburg, in what is today Berkeley County, West Virginia. There, many family members are buried in a family cemetery on Douglass Road. Where exactly Haywood was born has not been determined. Winchester—twenty-four miles southeast of Martinsburg—claimed him, according to a 1901 local newspaper story.

In the article, he is described as having been tall and dark complexioned, with African features. According to one descendant, the family has rumored French-Dutch ancestry dating back more than three hundred years in America.

Clearly, Haywood Shepherd was born free and not a slave who was later manumitted. There is no record of his manumission in either Jefferson or adjoining Frederick County, Virginia, and the evidence strongly suggests he was never a slave. But by the 1850s, he was unquestionably a free man with a growing family and ownership of property in Winchester, the seat of Frederick County and home to a large free black community. Exactly when he married Sarah Elizabeth Briscoe, from another well-established free black family in Winchester, is another unknown, but after his death she never remarried. A death certificate for their only son, John H. Shepherd, in 1920, indicated both his parents were born in Winchester.

On April 20, 1853, the City of Winchester recorded the birth of the Shepherds' fourth daughter, Fanny, giving Haywood's occupation as "labourer." The following year on October 27, 1854, Haywood purchased a house and lot near the depot of the Winchester and Potomac Rail Road Company for $500. Four years later on September 21, 1858, Shepherd added to his holdings, paying $120 for an additional lot.

Patrick Higgins, the other night watchman the night Shepherd was shot, would remember him as "a very noice nagur [*sic*], and was, too, very well off, being worth upwards of $15,000," more than $400,000 in 2017 dollars. Clearly, Haywood Shepherd was a free black man of means.

Most accounts describe Shepherd as an employee of the Baltimore and Ohio Railroad, but he has also been linked to the Winchester and Potomac Railroad, which ran a daily passenger train to and from Winchester and Harpers Ferry. Shepherd may have commuted from Winchester or lived at the Ferry while his family remained in Winchester. Either way, his job was variously described as baggage handler and porter at the Harpers Ferry train station. There his supervisor was Fontaine Beckham, the train stationmaster and mayor.

By all accounts, Beckham, aged sixty-three in 1859, and Shepherd, then thirty-four, were close, and Beckham was described as "the Best friend of the Negro," although he owned slaves. Supposedly, he had once owned Shepherd and had freed him fourteen years before the fateful raid, though records do not support this. Shepherd had been a railroad employee for twelve years before his death.

Indeed, there is no record of Shepherd having ever been anyone's slave. Had he been, he could have been subject to Virginia's draconian "black laws" affecting former slaves. An 1851 state constitutional amendment decreed, "Hereafter emancipated slaves shall forfeit their freedom" if they remained in the commonwealth for more than twelve months. Virginia law also allowed freed persons who wanted to stay to return to servitude, a provision known as "voluntary enslavement." Several sources assert that Shepherd was "attached" to Beckham so he could continue to live and work in the state. Since all indications are that Shepherd was born free, and therefore exempted from the law, there would be no reason for him to invoke this bizarre clause.

Following Shepherd's death, an agitated Beckham walked the town streets, putting himself in harm's way, and at 4 PM on Monday was fatally shot by one of Brown's raiders. In yet another ironic twist, under the mayor's will, Beckham's four (or seven, depending on the source) slaves were freed.

The Charlestown *Virginia Free Press* would eulogize Beckham as "this most highly and respected and worthy citizen," a B&O employee since 1835 who had variously also been a merchant, postmaster, justice of the peace, sheriff, and finally mayor. "We all miss him and mourn him as though he had been of our own household." The town council quickly followed with a resolution testifying to "the high toned worth of his citizenship and the modest but manliest sincerity of his friendship" and extending sympathies to his family. Council members would wear a badge of mourning for thirty days.

In Shepherd's case, he was just doing his job on the night of October 16 and into the early morning hours of October 17, when he ventured out onto the Potomac River bridge around 1:30 AM to see what the

Sketch of Haywood Shepherd, 1859, seated on a baggage truck. *West Virginia State Archives*

fuss was all about, was ordered to halt, and instead reversed course and was shot in the back, dying some twelve hours later.

The *Virginia Free Press* raged, "He was shot down like a dog. A humble negro as he was, his life was worth more than all of the desperadoes of the party, and his memory will be revered, when theirs will only be thought of with execution."

Joseph Barry, a Harpers Ferry resident and witness to the raid who published his recollections in 1903, speculated that Shepherd's death had dampened the prospects of any slave uprising and was "in fact the only thing that prevented a general insurrection of the negroes, for some of the farmers of the neighborhood said that they noticed an unusual excitement among the slaves on the Sunday before the raid. If it is true that the negroes knew anything of the intended attack, it is probable that they were deterred from taking part in it by seeing one of their own race the first person sacrificed."

"This was the first victim of the foray," wrote Alexander Boteler in an 1883 essay in *Century Magazine*, "and there is a suggestive significance in the fact that it was an inoffensive free negro, and that his assignation was as cowardly as it was cruel, and uncalled for." Boteler was no dispassionate observer. Representing Jefferson County in the US Congress from 1858 to 1861, he became an ardent secessionist, a member of the Confederate Virginia House of Delegates, and an officer in the Confederate Army attached to the legendary Gen. Thomas "Stonewall" Jackson.

Also with a decidedly Southern spin, the Winchester *Republican* reported on the "insane plot to incite a servile insurrection," noting that the regular Winchester–to–Harpers Ferry passenger train of the Winchester and Potomac Railroad, which left only the Monday morning of October 17, as the raid was proceeding, returned to Winchester at noon without reaching its destination but with "startling news of the raid." This included the death of "HAYWARD SHEPPARD, the faithful colored watchman at the railway office, who died in discharge of his duty, refusing to join the rebels." Shepherd "went to Harper's Ferry from this place, and his family still lived here. His remains were brought up Tuesday, and were interred with the honors of war by the military companies of town, accompanied by the mayor, the commonwealth's attorney and others, and followed by a concourse of his colored friends."

In Winchester, Shepherd was mourned, it was said, by the entire town. The state militia fired a salute at his burial in what was described as the "Old Colored Cemetery." Townspeople were said to be raising money for his widow and their children, though there is no evidence of a gift received. Still, the family was bereaved but not bereft. Shepherd left an estate: $623 in the bank (nearly $17,500 in 2017 dollars), plus property. Sarah was named administrator for the children, and records indicate payments made as late as 1868.

In the 1860 Census, Sarah Shepherd, thirty-six, still lived in Winchester with children Martha, sixteen; Mary, twelve; Lucy, nine; Fanny, seven; and John H., four. Under race, all were identified as *M* for mulatto. She is described as a "housekeeper" with real estate valued at $500 and personal property at $50. The Census, taken on July 20, also indicates she was born in Virginia and was unable to read or write. Soon afterward she moved with her children from Winchester to the District of Columbia, where her aunt Betsy Briscoe lived, thereby avoiding the horrors of war that repeatedly swept over Winchester in the much fought over northern reaches of the Shenandoah Valley.

In 1883 and 1885, Haywood's widow and heirs sold the Winchester properties, according to county land records. Sarah and daughter Lucy seemed to fare well in Washington. On June 5, 1889, at the Fourth Baptist Church on R Street NW, between 12th and 13th NW, Lucy attended a fundraising event for "needy schools in the rural districts." The admission was ten cents. The following year, the *Washington Evening Star* reported the sale of a lot in square 236—now in the heart of the gentrified U Street Corridor—from Sarah E. Shepherd to A. Lipscomb for an undisclosed sum. At the time of her death in 1920, Lucy, a seamstress with assets, lived in a comfortable two-story row house built in 1890 with a bay window, at 1453 Corcoran Street NW, then as now in a desirable neighborhood.

Clearly, Haywood and Sarah's progeny achieved solid black middle-class status in the nation's capital. At the age of seventeen, daughter Fanny Shepherd had an account in the Freedmen's Savings and Trust Company, into which she deposited seventeen dollars on September

20, 1870. Freedmen's Bureau documents describe her as "yellow" in complexion and living at 56 Lincoln Street in Georgetown. By 1878, a city directory shows her living at 1134 Connecticut Avenue NW, an upscale move, and her occupation as "dressmaker." Her brother, John H. Shepherd, a barber, is listed at the same address. He was also a member of the Capital City Guards, precursor to the DC National Guard, which performed at the city's Germania Schuetzen Park on June 14, 1882.

While Haywood Shepherd's widow and family got on with their lives, his grave was shamefully forgotten, according to a front-page story in the August 29, 1901, Winchester *Evening Star*. "Shepherd, the unconscious martyr, sleeps silently. Four long and terrible years of war swept over his head and close by his grave marched the tens of thousands of armed men," the newspaper wrote. Then ignoring reality, to be sure, in the era of Jim Crow segregation the paper reported, "Nearly forty years have passed and his people are now enjoying the privileges of the free born, but his grave remains solitary and impoverished and neglected."

Sarah Shepherd died, according to a "Deaths in the District" item in the November 19, 1902, *Washington Evening Star*, at the age of eighty-eight years and one month. The *Star* further noted she had passed on Monday, November 17, at 11:40 PM at the "residence of her daughter, Lucy E. Shepherd, 1106 Connecticut Avenue." She was, the notice said, the "beloved wife of the late Hayward Shepherd," without identifying him further. Her death certificate said she died from "senility" and "exhaustion." She had lived in the District for forty-two years, meaning she had moved there in 1860, shortly after Haywood's death.

Following the funeral at the residence, she would be buried on a hill in Woodlawn Cemetery, nearly twenty-three acres, located east of the Anacostia River in the then rural outer reaches of the District of Columbia, along with such African American notables as Blanche K. Bruce, a US senator from Mississippi during Reconstruction; Mary Robinson Meriwether, the second black female graduate of Oberlin College and a teacher in the District's first black high school; and John Mercer Langston, US congressman from Virginia and inspector general of the Freedmen's Bureau. Lucy and several other Shepherds would also be interred there.

"Winchester papers please copy," Sarah Shepherd's obituary notice said. The *Winchester Evening Star* did just that, headlining a November 21 page-one story "Wife of Famous Negro Is Dead." "In the death of Mrs. Shepherd there passed away a character of more than ordinary note . . . and up to within a few weeks of her death [she] was in possession of all of her powers, while her five senses were strong up to within a few hours of her death." A daughter, Mary Shepherd, still lived in Winchester on South Braddock Street, the paper said. She was a dressmaker, and present when her mother died.

The *Evening Star* then went on to extol Sarah's late husband, "keeper of the station gate" at Harpers Ferry. "He was born in Winchester and lived here until a short time before his tragic death," the paper wrote.

> It will be remembered that Haywood Shepherd was the first man killed by John Brown and his men. His refusal to give up the keys resulted in his being shot. Shepherd was a prominent figure at Harper's Ferry and Winchester. At his burial he was accorded public honors by the State of Virginia, his funeral being attended by a detachment of the Virginia State militia. He was a tall black man, six feet five inches in height, with decidedly pronounced African features. He was much respected for his loyalty to duty, which characteristic led to his untimely death.

His widow was "a woman of sterling worth, great industry and courage. Her success in holding her family together after the tragic death of her husband marks her as one of more than ordinary ability. She was small in stature, modest in manner, and ever kindly and generous in disposition. In her death one of the old land marks of days that are now known to few but as history is removed."

But not for long, as it turned out.

By the turn of the twentieth century, the notion of the happy slave had become part of the national narrative. The South had lost the war but was winning the postwar. Not only did states enact Jim Crow laws throughout the South, but the mythology of a war over states' rights, righteous slaveholders, and happy slaves had firmly taken hold, a rose-colored view famously celebrated in the D. W. Griffith film *The Birth of a Nation* in 1915. During this period, towns large and small south of the Mason-Dixon Line erected statues of Confederate soldiers, and the United Daughters of the Confederacy became the unofficial keepers of the flame that continued to burn brightly more than fifty years after the South had surrendered its arms.

The West Virginia panhandle, most directly affected by John Brown and his raiders, was a UDC stronghold. The local Jefferson County chapter even paid for a subscription to its magazine to be placed in the library of the segregated Jefferson County High School in Charles Town. John Brown and his raiders were vilified; his five black raiders never mentioned.

Though Shepherd was not a slave, he was a black man in antebellum Virginia who did not heed the call of the raiding abolitionists—and that was good enough. The Berkeley Springs *News* even suggested that the old John Brown fort, then newly purchased by Storer College president and reverend Nathan Cook Brackett and soon to be moved to the hilltop campus above Harpers Ferry, display a "proper and historically correct motto" over the door that would say, "The first victim of this fanatical insurrection was an inoffensive colored man."

The UDC rediscovered him—or at least a twisted idea of him—in the first decade of the twentieth century. But its initial proposal, at a 1905 chapter conference in Memphis, Tennessee, was for a "monument to the faithful old slaves who remained loyal and true to their owners in the dark days." As conceived of by Mary M. Solari of the J. Harvey Mathews Chapter, this "Monument to the Blacks" would not only tell the traditions, romance, poetry, and picturesqueness of the South but would speak the pathetic scenes enacted in many grand old Southern homesteads. No one who was rocked to sleep by the sweet lullaby of the faithful black "mammy," listened to her weird ghost stories, nursed at her breast, or played about her cabin door would be willing to have these tender memories die out. There is the side of sentiment, the side of gratitude, that those who have felt the touch can never give up, nor can they forget the debt due the faithful "ten per cent of slaves that remained with their masters after freedom."

If "this is not the time for erecting monuments to the old slaves," one will never be erected, for the men and women who hold them in tender remembrance will ere long be called to a greater reward, and they alone can fully understand the motive of such a work and necessity to leave a mark by which their children's children may perpetuate the heroic deeds of the slaves who were devoted and true to their ancestors in times of deadliest peril. Erect the monument; it will result in much good, as it will tell future generations that the white men of the South were the negro's best friends then and that the men of the South are the negro's best friends to-day.

By the early 1920s, the idea had evolved into a monument to Haywood Shepherd. The UDC by then had joined with the Sons of Confederate Veterans to promote it, and together they sought permission to erect it on B&O Railroad property at Harpers Ferry. Julian S. Carr, North Carolina commander of the United Confederate Veterans, wrote B&O president Daniel Willard on May 12, 1922, with the request on behalf of the UDC and SCV, "to commemorate the memory of the faithful slave, Haywood Shepherd, a negro who was the first victim of the John Brown raid on Harpers Ferry." So, once again, a free man of color had been portrayed as a "faithful slave."

Enter Henry T. McDonald, the white president of Storer College, founded in 1867 for black students. McDonald was also secretary on the Harpers Ferry town board, and he succeeded in convincing his council colleagues to reject the idea. "I have to report to you that it was the unanimous vote that we gratefully acknowledge the desire of the Daughters of Confederacy and the Sons of Confederate Veterans to perpetuate the memory of faithful slaves," he wrote Willard on June 2, "but that we earnestly request you to advise the organizations that we look with disfavor upon the placing in our midst such a monument as proposed, . . . as being likely to occasion unpleasant racial feeling in a community where we are so entirely free from it. We see no good purpose that can be served . . . and believe that harm would result to our community."

Responding for the railroad, George H. Campbell wrote on June 23, "It would appear to me the action taken by the Council was the only action it could take, in view of all the circumstances. The argument is unanswerable that while everything is getting along harmoniously it would be a very grave mistake to inject anything into the situation that might disturb the existing pleasant relations."

That, however, did not end the matter. Memorial proponents found a private property owner, pharmacist W. E. Dittmeyer, who agreed to have the granite stone and tablet on the sidewalk adjacent to his build-ing in the lower town. It would be on Potomac Street, not on railroad property but close and within sight of the train trestle and a John Brown obelisk erected in 1895.

The inscription on the memorial noted that Shepherd, "an industri-ous and respected colored freeman . . . became the first victim of this attempted insurrection," and it continued, "This boulder is erected by the United Daughters of Confederacy and the Sons of Confederate Veterans as a memorial to Hayward Shepherd exemplifying the character and faithfulness of thousands of Negroes who, under many tempta-tions throughout subsequent years of war, so conducted themselves that no stain was left upon a record which is the peculiar heritage of the American people, and an everlasting tribute to the best of both races."

About three hundred whites and one hundred blacks attended the dedication on October 10, 1931. Seated in the front row on the left was Shepherd descendant James W. Walker, a Storer College graduate and farmer from Bunker Hill, a hamlet south of Martinsburg. Also present was Madison Briscoe, a distant Shepherd cousin who kept the family ties to himself. "My husband wouldn't tell them he was related," Marie Briscoe, his widow, recalled in 1995 shortly after her husband had died at the age of ninety. "He said, 'Anyone who would run out in front of a firearm is crazy. I didn't want them to know he was my cousin.'"

The NAACP implored the Storer College president not to participate. "This attempt to destroy the truth and to perpetuate a story that colored people did not participate of their own free will in the struggle for their emancipation, and the effort to vilify the name of John Brown, will be heartily condemned by all individuals, North and South, and of both races."

Rejecting their pleas, McDonald had carefully crafted a high-minded introductory speech. "We come here with forward-looking vision; with confidence in a newer and better day; with pride in a generation which has emerged from the wreckage of a dead past, to build simply and sanely for a more enduring future. . . . Always when men and women meet with high and unselfish motives, there are the dawnings of a better and happier day. Always when men and women unite in a passion for finer and better understanding, the imaginary barriers fall."

In pre-event remarks to the Baltimore *Afro-American* newspaper, McDonald said, "This unique gathering, in what is said and what is done, will voice the spirit of fellowship and enduring good will. It is a fine expression of a new era of interracial understanding."

But if McDonald truly believed the dedication of the memorial he had once rejected as divisive would now not be, he was dead wrong. "Confederates to Dedicate 'Uncle Tom' Monument," declared the *Afro-American* on the day of the event. No matter that George F. Bragg Jr., a black Episcopal minister from Baltimore, was to give the benediction, for which he, too, would be roundly criticized. "Local Pastor to Pray for Rebels," said the headline on the story's jump page. Bragg defended his benediction "to the unveiling of a monument to a faithful Negro slave," one he said was being "erected to one illiterate, and without mental enlightenment, but who had a loyalty of heart. . . . We of this generation certainly cannot hold that slave guilty of wrong-doing when his motive was that of a loyal subject."

All of the scheduled speakers were white.

After McDonald's platitudinous opening, the program took on a decidedly *Gone with the Wind* flavor. There was a major address by Matthew Page Andrews, a native of Shepherdstown then residing in Baltimore, historian, and member of the Sons of Confederate Veterans who had invited Reverend Bragg to give the benediction. Andrews had been instrumental in crafting and revising the words on the memorial tablet. His speech paid a passing tribute to Shepherd as "a popular and capable colored freeman . . . the innocent subject of this memorial." But in the main, he attacked Brown as an "alleged liberator . . . self-selected, self-proclaimed, self-esteemed" responsible for Shepherd's murder and worse. Echoing traditional Southern tropes, he referred to the slave as "ignorant" and "when left to its own devices . . . was known to stagnate or drop back."

If McDonald had any postevent misgivings, he did not share them with Andrews, to whom he wrote on October 15, "I consider this monument one of the most significant erected in the last decade in this land of ours. There was such a fine and understanding spirit manifested. The new and best South was in action. I was glad to be identified therewith. . . . The present day Negro needs to be shielded from the self appointed leaders of his own race. And by the same mark he needs— although he may not know it—white friends—if ever he needed them."

The main speaker was UDC president Elizabeth Bashinsky of Troy, Alabama. Her remarks, addressed to "members and chairman of the Faithful Slave Memorial Committee," were bathed in nostalgia for the Lost Cause. "The Anglo Saxon of the South had reverence for human life and a sympathy for the downtrodden. During that period, the Negro in the South was well clothed, well housed." She then proceeded to wax nostalgic about "that old black mammy who shared our lives, nursed our children, was our confidant. . . . Mammy is now old and decrepit, but she lives in a little rose-covered cottage in my yard, and there she will live until her spirit goes marching on. . . . We of the South are true to the Union; we are true to the stars and stripes, and yet, in a higher and truer sense, to the stars and the bars."

At this point in her oration, the *Afro-American* report noted, "Handkerchiefs were in evidence, and the weeping of the rebel girls was audible."

Another highlight was spirituals Storer students sang under the direction of Pearl Tatten, the college music director, who was not scheduled to speak but could not contain her outrage. "I am the daughter of a Connecticut volunteer, who wore the blue, who fought for the freedom of my people, for which John Brown struck the first blow," she told the assembled crowd before leading the choir in "'Tis Me, Oh Lord, Standing in the Need of Prayer." "Today we are looking forward to the future, forgetting those things of the past. We are pushing forward to a larger freedom, not in the spirit of the black mammy but in the spirit of new freedom and rising youth." It was, the *Afro-American* account said, "like a bolt from the blue, and it struck home."

As the celebration was ending, she was handed a note from a UDC member. "I wonder at your temerity," it said. "Your untimely remarks were out of place, in poor spirit, and most discourteous. Such ignorance is colossal." Pearl Tatten later said that she just "could not stand there and hear those things without being deeply hurt. It was all spontaneous. I just had to speak out and say what was crying to be said. I had no idea the celebration was to take this form. We were informed that this was to be a celebration of interracial good-will."

Interviewed afterward, McDonald said he had spoken the truth and he disagreed with "some of those things" said by others and did "not want to be understood as approving all that was said." Indeed, he added, he viewed Brown "as the greatest American reformer."

The *Afro-American* called Tatten the "Barbara Fritchie in Black at Harpers Ferry," a reference to the elderly white woman who famously confronted Confederate troops marching through her town of Frederick, Maryland, telling them, "Shoot if you must this old gray head, but spare your country's flag." Dr. O. Wilson Winters, a dentist in Norristown, Pennsylvania, in an October 16 letter praised Tatten's "courage and exemplary action" at the monument unveiling. He offered her a year's free membership in the John Brown Memorial Association. Notably, he sent the letter on behalf of the Shields Green Chapter of the association, an indication that not all of the African Americans with John Brown at Harpers Ferry were forgotten. A month later, one William Pickens had some suggestions for the UDC. Writing in the Baltimore *Afro-American* on November 7, he asserted, "Next to Brown himself, Green was undoubtedly the greatest hero in the fighting at Harpers Ferry. If the Daughters of slaveholders want to make a lasting impression on all posterity, let them build a monument there" to him.

"Most of the better thinking people of Harpers Ferry look upon the whole thing with disgust," said S. H. Hill, identified by the Afro-American as "a woman of great prominence" in the town. Also present, and seated in the front row, was Jimmie Moton, the African American porter who now held the job once held by Shepherd. "I haven't got anything to say," he said after the celebration. "It was for a man who was faithful to his duty."

Thus, the Haywood Shepherd memorial, if not universally revered, remained on the sidewalk adjoining the old drug store. Then, recognizing the historic importance of the entire lower town, the National Park Service began acquiring and restoring properties to their mid-nineteenth century appearance. In the 1970s, the Park Service moved to acquire the building and sidewalk with the Shepherd memorial. During the remodeling, the nine-hundred-pound stone and tablet were moved into storage, supposedly a temporary situation. But rumors started flying that the memorial was being "held hostage" by those who didn't like its message.

In the early 1980s, Confederate groups began lobbying for its return to public view, eventually enlisting North Carolina's US senator Republican Jesse Helms in their cause. So the Park Service promised to "remove the Heyward Shepherd Monument from storage and display it." But after it was returned to its former site, park superintendent Don Campbell sheathed it in plywood, citing anonymous threats to deface the memorial. And there it sat for several years. The controversy flared into the open again in the mid-1990s, with the Sons of Confederate Veterans demanding its unsheathing and the Jefferson County and West Virginia NAACP in opposition.

It was as if nothing had changed in sixty years—or a hundred years.

Campbell defended the memorial, like it or not, as part of history. But James A. Tolbert, president of the West Virginia NAACP, demurred. "The only history is Heyward Shepherd was killed. Caught in the cross-fire. That's the history," he said.

Then, quietly, without public announcement, the Park Service removed the plywood on the morning of June 9, 1995. For the sake of what they regarded as balance and context, those in charge added a nearby smaller interpretive sign that provided additional information. The SCV objected to that too. "We feel any monument speaks for itself and doesn't require interpretation by the National Park Service," said George Elliott Cummings, the group's Maryland commander. The West Virginia NAACP wrote the US Department of the Interior demanding the memorial be removed from public view. "Personally," said Tolbert, "I'd rather see the thing taken to the Potomac River at its deepest point and dropped."

Yet there it remains today with the added interpretive sign, near the corner of Potomac and Shenandoah Streets for anyone passing by to pause and ponder the dueling narratives. And inside the Harpers Ferry train station, where commuters wait on benches for DC-bound trains, there is a framed photograph of the stolid-looking mayor with bushy, long sideburns, killed at Harpers Ferry. It is in the Mayor Fontaine Beckham Memorial Room, dedicated on October 10, 2009, to his memory on the occasion of the John Brown raid sesquicentennial.

"We've heard nothing on it," says George Elliott Cummings, the former division commander of the Sons of Confederate Veterans, when I interview him again in the spring of 2016. "The monument's on display there, with the interpretation next to it. We're fine with that. I did think that [was inappropriate], I probably still do, but it's twenty years ago, so it's time to move on."

Cummings was now seventy-six and living in Towson, a northern suburb of Baltimore. He is still proud to count nineteen ancestors who fought for the Confederacy. He is concerned about the movements of the moment to remove Confederate statues and monuments from courthouse lawns and town squares throughout the South and border states, like his own state of Maryland. A native Baltimorean, he is retired from the Social Security Administration, where he worked on budgeting and purchasing. Just another fed, it turns out, but with an interesting family history.

"Who's to say a hundred years from now they won't tear down the wall to Vietnam vets?" he muses. "If groups oppose us and want to take our monuments down, and want to raise money to put up a monument to anyone they deem worthy, I'm fine with that. Just leave ours alone."

Despite his long involvement in the Haywood Shepherd monument controversy, he admits to little knowledge about the man the tablet purports to honor: "My understanding is he was killed by Brown's party. Whoever. I don't know that documentation. It was a long time ago. I haven't got time to research something like that." Nor to plum the details of Shepherd's life—and death. "I didn't know that Shepherd had a wife, family, a will, property, an estate, or that Winchester citizens raised money for his family and a white militia fired guns as salute at his funeral," he says.

Gilbert Shepherd, a direct descendant of Haywood several generations removed, grew up in Manhattan, the Bronx, and Camden, New Jersey. But his deepest family roots were in the West Virginia panhandle, in Martinsburg, home to generations of freeborn blacks where he also lived for a few years as an adult caring for an elderly aunt. Gil had not known of Haywood until he was in his early twenties, in the 1970s, and even then he didn't know much.

"He was with John Brown when they raided Harpers Ferry" is what he'd learned, he told me from his home in Winston-Salem, North Carolina. "I don't know the whole story. If you have an ancestor who was involved in trying to help free the slaves or whatever—that's what I was told, anyway—you feel good about that."

He learned more in 2009 when he went with his children and four grandchildren to Harpers Ferry "to see what it was all about. That's when I saw the plaque about Haywood."

What does it mean to him today, I ask. His answer surprises me. "You never know what God has planned for you, you know?" he says. "It might have been his purpose to be used by the Confederates. To me it was heavy on my heart, because pitting brothers against brothers, family against family, because you had people from North and South, fighting each other—for what? Love is an antidote, but lots of times we can't show that. We show discord more than anything."

———————

Where lies Haywood Shepherd? The "Old Colored Cemetery" in Winchester seems to exist only in old newspaper accounts of its sorry state at the turn of the twentieth century.

But there is more to tell. On a sultry summer morning, Jan Fontaine meets me at historic Woodlawn Cemetery, in southeast Washington, DC. She is the keeper of the cemetery records, secretary of the Woodlawn Cemetery Association, and she knows where the bodies are buried.

From the front gate on Benning Road SE, she drives us in a blue SUV up the hill, pointing out the resting places of long forgotten notables. We come to a stop near a shade tree where she has placed two lawn chairs, in lot 85, section B, at grave 245. There a small monument, perhaps three feet tall, marks the spot.

Not only is Sarah, his widow, interred there. But so are their daughters Lucy and Fanny and Sarah's aunt Betsy Briscoe. In all, nine Shepherd family members are there, according to cemetery records, though not all are acknowledged on the family monument. But engraved on it above Sarah's name is another name. It is of the man also presumably buried there, or perhaps reburied there after his wife's death. It says, simply, "Haywood Shepherd."

11

To Preserve This Sacred Shrine

Logan Anderson of Purcellville, Virginia, due south of Harpers Ferry, did not attend classes or graduate from Storer College, the school established in 1867 at Harpers Ferry for people formerly enslaved. But on graduation days, he would dress up in his finest clothes, rent a horse and buggy, and drive eighteen miles along dusty country roads to attend the graduation ceremonies on Camp Hill.

Born in 1876 in Fauquier County, Anderson revered the school and the town because, according to family tradition, he was related to Osborne Perry Anderson, one of five black raiders in John Brown's revolutionary army in 1859 and the sole survivor. For Logan Anderson, better known as "the dynamite man" for his work with explosives on road construction, it was a matter of great pride that his distant relative had participated in this ill-fated—some would say quixotic—raid that led, ultimately, if cataclysmically, to civil war and emancipation.

The black raiders' ties to Harpers Ferry and to Storer would be long-lasting. The college had come into being here only because of the federal arsenal that made the town John Brown's preferred target; its first buildings had formerly housed arsenal officials. Further, the town's strategic location made it a natural destination not only for Brown and his raiders but also, at the war's end, for former slaves in need of pretty much everything, including an education.

Osborne Anderson himself had returned to Harpers Ferry in 1871, the year before he died, with Richard J. Hinton, the London-born journalist who would publish a two-volume work in 1894 entitled *John Brown and His Men*. Whether Anderson visited Storer College then is unknown. But it is fair to conjecture that he, too, might have taken pride in the new school for freedmen that then had only recently been established, a pedagogical monument of sorts to his efforts twelve years before to break the bonds of slavery.

As if to underscore the failed raid, the ultimate success of the mission, and its link to the school, John Brown's fort, the arsenal's fire engine house where he and his embattled band had barricaded themselves against storming militia, would be moved to the Storer campus in 1910. There it would sit for nearly a century, until the National Park Service restored it to its more historically accurate place in the lower town.

But the connection between the school and the black raiders was publicly recognized early on. On May 30, 1881, Frederick Douglass, then a Storer trustee and recorder of deeds for the District of Columbia, addressed the small graduating class on the school's fourteenth anniversary. Seated on the platform behind him was Andrew Hunter, the man who had prosecuted Brown and his captured accomplices—including John Copeland and Shields Green. After Douglass's address, Hunter shook hands with him, congratulating him on his speech, and surmised that if Robert E. Lee were still alive, he would do the same.

The *Bucks County Gazette* in Pennsylvania reported that "quite a number of Confederates and old Virginians gathered to hear him."

Douglass, who had spurned Brown's appeal to join him in the raid but had instead given him Shields Green, the fugitive slave he'd brought with him from Rochester, launched into long and lavish praise of the band's leader as "our noblest American hero."

But he reserved special praise for Green, "who had attested his love of liberty by escaping from slavery and making his way through many dangers to Rochester, where he had lived with my family, and where he met the man with whom he went to the scaffold." Douglass recalled their fateful meeting with Brown in Chambersburg, Pennsylvania, and Green's decision to "'go wid de old man;' and go with him he did, into the fight, and to the gallows, and bore himself as grandly as any of the number." And when Brown was surrounded and Green could have escaped, Green gave the same answer: "'I b'l'eve I'll go down wid de old man.' When in prison at Charlestown, and he was not allowed to see his old friend [John Brown], his fidelity to him was in no wise weakened, and no complaint against Brown could be extorted from him."

Then, Douglass added, "If a monument should be erected to the memory of John Brown, as there ought to be, the form and name of Shields Green should have a conspicuous place upon it." That would not happen, and even efforts to erect such a memorial to Brown at Storer failed to win over the school administration, which in 1932, the year after it had participated in a memorial ceremony to Haywood Shepherd, refused the request made by the NAACP. John Brown would finally get his plaque at Storer in 2006, but it makes no mention by name of Green, Anderson, Newby, Copeland, or Leary.

The school where Douglass spoke of Brown and Green had its origins in the aftermath of war, when thousands of newly freed former slaves, following the victorious Union Army, found their way to the northern end of the Shenandoah Valley, and thus to the region that included Harpers Ferry. The town itself, battered by war, was in ruins, and the needs were great. But a surprising political development would help to set the stage for the new school.

It was the May 28, 1863, vote in thirty-nine counties to secede from Virginia and form the new state of West Virginia. The number of men then away and fighting for the Confederacy greatly affected the tally in the eastern panhandle. The stationing of Union troops outside the county's two polling places might also have intimidated some voters. Thus, fifty-two of fifty-three votes in Harpers Ferry supported West Virginia. In Shepherdstown, there was a single vote for Virginia and 196 for West Virginia. The small turnout—compared to the 1,857 votes cast in Jefferson County in the 1860 presidential election—reflects how these votes did not reveal the popular sentiment.

After the war, the recently established state required local officials to establish public schools for black students. Still, it took a strong push from the federal government's Freedmen's Bureau, which opened an office in Harpers Ferry in 1865, to make this happen in Jefferson County. In the county seat of Charlestown, there was delay. In Harpers Ferry and the neighboring town of Bolivar, there was outright defiance. Joseph Barry, who would serve on the Harpers Ferry town council in 1877 and later write his firsthand eyewitness account of the raid, was then the county's superintendent of free schools. It was his job, he wrote military authorities in 1867, to fairly distribute tax money based on the school census; to deny black residents a school would be to deny them their equitable share of the tax revenues. An appropriate authority, he declared, should "insist on right being done . . . in the teeth of deep prejudices against the colored population." It was enough to lose their slaves, Charlestown residents complained, but too much to also pay to educate them.

Nonetheless, and in the face of a threat from the Ku Klux Klan, plans for Storer College proceeded, initially under the auspices of the Freedmen's Bureau, to whom the War Department had conveyed several buildings that had formerly housed arsenal officials. There were also donations from Northern abolitionists to support the effort.

Members of the Free Will Baptist Church had arrived from New England right after the war to preach and teach. Again, with help from the Freedmen's Bureau, they opened schools in Jefferson and Berkeley Counties. Rev. Nathan Cook Brackett of Phillips, Maine, led the efforts. He would later become the first president of Storer, serve in that capacity until 1897, and stay on as treasurer until his death in 1910.

But the Baptists developed more ambitious plans to launch the state's first school of higher education for people of color, and thus was Storer College born. John Storer, a Stanford, Maine, philanthropist who had made a fortune in shipbuilding, had developed a close relationship with Freewill Baptists in his home state. He offered to launch the school that would be named for him with a $10,000 donation, to be matched by a like amount from the formerly enslaved and others. The donation stipulated that the school be open to all, regardless of gender or race.

For nearly twenty-five years, Storer would be the only West Virginia college open to African Americans.

The state's charter for this new college met with local resistance. There were still strong antiblack feelings in a county that had contributed 1,600 men and 16 percent of its white males to the Confederate Army and retained its strongly Southern antebellum attitudes. This was consistent with its demographics: in 1860, neighboring Jefferson and Berkeley Counties had 30 percent of the state's slaves, numbering 5,610, in what would become West Virginia. Indeed, 27 percent of the county's population consisted of slaves; in 1870, the now free black population was 26 percent.

But Jefferson, like it or not, was now part of a new state where different views prevailed, despite unreconstructed dissenting voices. The Storer charter easily passed the state senate by a 13–6 vote. "Every vote in favor of the Bill being radical!" railed the *Weston Democrat*. Then after the House of Delegates concurred, the *Wheeling Daily Intelligencer* noted that all but three Democrats in the House of Delegates voted for the bill. "Are the Democrats going in for 'nigger equality,' 'nigger schools,' &c., &c.?" the newspaper asked. "Do the Democratic members want their daughter to 'marry a nigger?' If not, what means this vote to allow colored youth to go to college alongside of white children, just as they do at abolition Oberlin?" Jefferson County's white citizens did not quietly accept the legislative outcome, petitioning the legislature to repeal the charter. Their request was referred to "the Judiciary" committee, where it apparently remained.

Classes began on October 2, 1867, shortly before approval of the school's charter. Storer's initial enrollment consisted of nineteen students. The following year, by act of Congress, the federal government turned over buildings and land to the new college. By 1871, the *Spirit of Jefferson* newspaper reported, the school had more than 150 pupils "of all ages and sexes, and . . . all shades and colors." The total cost per student for room, board, tuition, laundry, fuel, and books was $110.

Initially offering little more than a high school curriculum, Storer would become the state's first and only teachers' college for black students. The high school department, which awarded an associate degree after two years, continued until 1938, when the school began offering a curriculum leading to full degrees. The first full college class of seven graduated in 1942.

Despite the school's academic achievements, Storer students and faculty would endure insults and worse from the townspeople. Residents regarded Storer as a "colored school with nigger teachers." One black teacher said, "It is unusual for me to go to the post office without being hooted at and twice I have been stoned on the streets at noonday."

The Ku Klux Klan also made its presence known, allegedly threatening Storer students. After a football game in November 1922, students on their way to a local store were accosted and at least one assaulted by local whites. A fight broke out, and three students were suspended. Other students staged a half-day walkout, and two left for home. Storer president Henry T. McDonald denied any Klan involvement. Twenty-two years later when Storer inaugurated its first black president, Richard I. McKinney, a cross was burned in his front yard.

Despite such tensions, Harpers Ferry's black population thrived. In 1890, African Americans numbered 4,116, composing 26.5 percent of the residents. Two-thirds were homeowners. Most lived in the upper town near Storer. In 1888, Thomas S. Lovett, a black 1876 Storer graduate, built Hilltop House, a hotel on a high bluff overlooking the confluence of the Potomac and Shenandoah Rivers and Maryland Heights. It would survive fires in 1912 and 1919 and host such prominent figures as Alexander Graham Bell, Mark Twain, and Presidents Woodrow Wilson and Bill Clinton.

Among Harper Ferry's summer regulars was Oberlin graduate and suffragette Mary Church Terrell, founder and president of the National Association of Colored Women. As a young mother, she and her two daughters would spend a month there. Her husband, Robert H. Terrell, who in 1910 became the District of Columbia's first African American judge, would come too, usually staying for a week. She recalled, "We had quarters at Storer College, a splendid school for colored youth, whose lawn was an ideal play ground for children."

Also among the black guests were Anna Evans Murray and her two sons. In August 1883, they stayed in Lincoln Hall, a three-story building set aside for black summer boarders. The connection to John Brown's African American raiders was ever present: Anna was a niece of Lewis Sheridan Leary and also related by marriage to John Copeland. By the 1890s, the Murrays were regularly vacationing at the Ferry, with Anna and the children staying in a cottage and joined by her husband on weekends.

In the 1880s and 1890s, Storer sought to capitalize on its scenic location, as well as the town's rail access and historic status, by marketing its facilities for summer use to the black elites of Washington and Baltimore. It also welcomed whites, though housed them separately. "Camp Hill, which had previously been like a graveyard in the summer, has become the center of life in the town, having all available rooms filled to overflowing with an excellent class of summer boarders," noted Kate J. Anthony, the school historian. "This gives business to the town, and employment to a considerable number of students, while the guests are sure of having intelligent, honest, and faithful attendants."

The *Washington Bee*, a black newspaper, reported that "the visitor to Harpers Ferry is doubly paid, for he not only feels the thrilling impulses which come from a contemplation of the movement of the first martyr of a true and not spurious American freedom, but the natural beauty of the place appeals strongly to the most relaxed and exalted part of the being." The martyr referenced, of course, was John Brown (Anna Murray was on the board of the John Brown Memorial Association); no mention was made of fellow "martyrs" Leary and Copeland.

Storer's entrepreneurial experiment took a rightward turn, however, in 1896 when President Brackett suggested to the trustees that black boarders might no longer be welcomed during the summer months, for financial reasons, implying their presence would dampen white interest in the seasonal offering. Facilities continued to be made available to white boarders, though their presence also failed to be profitable.

Storer College returned briefly to the national spotlight in August 1906 with the convening of the second annual meeting of the Niagara Conference, following the first meeting the prior year at Niagara Falls, Ontario, to act as a militant counter force against Jim Crow laws. Founder W. E. B. DuBois, a Massachusetts-born, Harvard-educated black intellectual, had offered a philosophical counterpoint to the go-slow views of Booker T. Washington, who held that blacks should learn trades and eschew militancy.

"We shall assemble at Storer College," a flier for the conference announced. "The grounds are beautiful, the lawns inviting, and there is ample room for all. . . . Carriages are cheap; tennis and croquet on the grounds; fishing and boating; mountain excursions, music; etc."

Trains brought guests from Washington, and carriages took them the rest of the way, up the hill from the station to Storer for the four-day meeting. The demands the Niagara Movement espoused at Harpers Ferry were "clear and unequivocal," according to an address to the country read to the entire group on the final day. These included "full, manhood suffrage . . . now, henceforth, and forever," an end to discrimination in public accommodations, equal treatment under the law, including enforcement of the fourteenth and fifteenth amendments, and that "no State [be] allowed to base its franchise simply on color."

The meeting drew some one hundred attendees and wide press coverage in papers ranging from the *New York Times* to the *Montana Plaindealer*, putting Storer in the national spotlight. "Negroes Demand Equality" was the succinct headline in the *Daily News* of Frederick, Maryland. Storer president McDonald, addressing the assemblage, termed it fitting that the meeting should be held where the first blow for universal liberty in America was struck, "in the spirit of John Brown."

Friday, August 17, was John Brown Day for the Niagara Movement at Storer. It began at 6 AM with a silent walk to the John Brown fort, which was then on a nearby farm. Marching barefoot in single file around the building, they sang "John Brown's Body" and "The Battle Hymn of the Republic."

That afternoon, conference attendees heard from a speaker who was not listed on the official program. She was Henrietta Leary Evans, the older sister of Lewis Sheridan Leary, one of John Brown's black raiders. Described as having high cheek bones with an Indian cast and nearly straight hair, the seventy-nine-year-old was frail and spoke from her chair about her brother Lewis and her nephew John Copeland, captured, convicted, and hanged for his role. Jesse Max Barber, editor-in-chief of the monthly *Voice of the Negro*, and one of the Niagara Movement's founders, would later recall:

> Mrs. Evans was asked to say a word. In a voice made slender by age she told of the bravery, the love for freedom and the self-sacrifice of her kinsmen in dying as they died for the race. Of her brother she said his enemies paid him the tribute of saying that he was a very brave man. The whole audience hung with bated breath upon every word uttered by Mrs. Evans and what she said made a great impression.

The Niagara Conference made its own impression, though not universally favorable. DuBois, as general secretary, wrote to McDonald in March 1907 to inquire if the Storer campus would again be available. Despite his kind welcoming words in 1906, McDonald was less than enthusiastic. He asked DuBois "to sympathize with me when I say I do not feel justified in saying that we can entertain that annual meeting until the trustees have had an opportunity to express themselves." He claimed that while he did "not think that the Niagara Movement in any way has injured this institution, there are some who will not agree with me, and, in view of the unexpected lessening of our annual appropriation, there might seem to be a foundation for their argument." DuBois received no further correspondence from McDonald, and the organization met in Boston instead. In 1911, DuBois was one of five incorporators of the National Association for the Advancement of Colored People, the successor to the Niagara Movement.

Henrietta Leary Evans, Lewis Sheridan Leary's older sister, in a 1906 portrait by Addison N. Scurlock. *Anacostia Community Museum, Smithsonian Institution*

DuBois would journey again to Storer in May 1932 in connection with a Washington, DC, meeting of the NAACP. It came just a year after the dedication of the Haywood Shepherd memorial and the college's participation, which appalled the NAACP and the black population in general.

Given the school's acquiescence and McDonald's salutary speech at the memorial dedication, it did not seem overly presumptuous for the civil rights organization to propose a memorial tablet to Brown to be placed on his fort during a pilgrimage to Storer from its Washington conference. McDonald at first agreed to the written request, and he even offered to speak and to arrange for a dinner on campus after the event.

But he objected to the wording DuBois had written:

> *Here John Brown*
> *Aimed at human slavery*
> *A blow*
> *That woke a guilty nation.*
> *With him fought seven slaves and sons of slaves.*
> *Over his crucified corpse*
> *Marched 200,000 black soldiers*
> *And 4,000,000 freedmen*
> *Singing*
> *"John Brown's body lies a mouldering in the grave*
> *But his soul goes marching on!"*
> *In gratitude this Tablet is Erected*
> *The National Association for the Advancement of Colored People*
> *May 21, 1932.*

John Brown's "crucified corpse" may have been two words too far. And, to be on the safe side, McDonald brought the wording to the attention of the white-majority board of trustees, which also found reasons to object. The NAACP could come, but its members would be in for an unpleasant surprise once they got there. There would be no plaque dedication.

Floyd J. Calvin, a columnist for the *Pittsburgh Courier*, a black newspaper, counted himself among "those who refused to eat dinner" at Storer "because I felt the insult" from the school's refusal to accept the tablet. The only thing to do "in the face of the growing prejudice and discrimination on every turn . . . is fight back." Personally, he wrote, he would have preferred a "more simple inscription, but carrying the same sentiments Dr. Du Bois expressed." However you look at it, Calvin continued, the college was at fault:

If the college didn't want the tablet, I can't see why it would allow the delegation to drive 72 miles in a bus to stage a demonstration and then take it back. . . . How President McDonald could stand before that audience and speak of the birds and the trees and the flowers, and refer to waters of the passing streams in a touching address of welcome, knowing what was coming, and then to suddenly disappear like a hunted animal is beyond me. His role was . . . insincere . . . and . . . cannot be forgiven.

DuBois made his final appearance on campus in 1950 when he was asked to speak at the college's commencement on June 5. The fiery civil rights leader had not mellowed a bit and had been labeled a Red in the postwar anticommunist environment. In 1961, at the age of ninety-three, he would formally join the Communist Party. He died two years later in Accra, Ghana. For his midcentury appearance, he was offered and accepted a "modest honorarium" of seventy-five dollars. But a tribute to the school's retiring president, Richard I. McKinney, the first black man to hold that position, overshadowed the still-controversial figure's appearance. A story in the *Afro-American* mentioned DuBois as the commencement speaker, but his remarks went unreported.

In 2006, with the campus now owned by the National Park Service, the NAACP was at last permitted to place its once controversial bronze plaque, with the words DuBois had written, on the Storer campus. It was part of a centennial commemoration of the Niagara Movement's hopeful meeting there in 1906 and seemed a fitting way to both mark the historical occasion and recall the event there that had roiled the nation on the cusp of civil war.

George Rutherford, a founding member of the Jefferson County Black Historical Society, was briefly a Storer student in the fall of 1953, a few months after graduating from a segregated high school in Charles Town. The Korean War had just ended that July, and black soldiers were returning home to Jefferson County. "The vets were going under the GI Bill. They would take us under their wings, took me to Storer, got me enrolled," he said in the cozy recreation room of the rambler he'd built himself in Ranson, adjoining the county seat. But he left Storer that November to join the service. He could not then foresee that the school would soon close.

In the postwar world, Storer seemed to be flourishing, if not flush. In 1948, it boasted 220 students from seventeen states, the District of Columbia, and Africa. In 1953, the small college on Camp Hill celebrated its eighty-sixth anniversary. The main speaker was William H. Ansel Jr., West Virginia state treasurer. The choice seemed fitting, since a state subsidy had sustained the school throughout much of its history. It was never a fully self-supporting college. Under the state's segregated system, West Virginia contributed annually in amounts ranging in later years from $20,000 to $30,000.

The following year, in *Brown v. Board of Education*, the US Supreme Court desegregated the South's public schools, and that sounded the death knell for many black institutions that had sprung up specifically because of racially exclusionary policies elsewhere. In this epic struggle, Storer College was collateral damage. West Virginia ended its support, then $20,000, leaving the school on the hill on shaky ground.

An alumni fundraising "Save Storer" campaign came nowhere near its $250,000 goal. But with several new white students and four new staff members, the school managed to reopen in the fall. Rather than a renaissance, it was more like a death rattle. The following spring, the trustees announced that Storer would have to close. Students, alumni, and friends of the school picketed the meeting, to no avail. Eleven faculty members were let go. Diplomas were awarded to six students and the remaining eighty-two were urged to find other colleges.

Storer alumni and friends mounted another effort to reopen the school by September 1958, trying desperately to raise $100,000. A fundraising brochure carried this urgent message: "Storer College—a Sacred Shrine—Preserve It." Still, it was not enough. The only thing left to do was to fight over the remains. Ultimately, after litigation pitting alumni

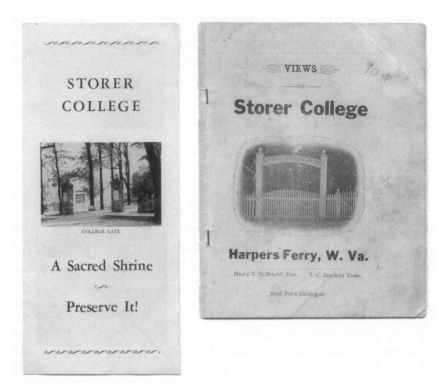

LEFT: A 1957 fundraising brochure for Storer College. RIGHT: The Storer College "Views" pamphlet from 1910. *Author's collection*

and trustees, the school's endowment and archives went to historically black Virginia Union University in Richmond. Any funds remaining in Storer's account would be split between Virginia Union and Alderson-Broadus, a white Baptist institution in Philippi, West Virginia.

A 1962 federal government agreement facilitated the resolution by acquiring Storer's land and nine buildings for some $200,000 to expand Harpers Ferry National Park. Under the agreement, the widow of Henry McDonald, Storer's last white president, was allowed to live out her years in a house on campus.

In 1964, the former Storer buildings would become the Stephen T. Mather Training Center of the National Park Service, named for the industrialist and conservationist who served as first director of the park service from 1916 to 1929.

For Storer College's sesquicentennial in 2017, the Park Service went all out, scheduling monthly events, culminating in an October weekend and alumni reunion to coincide with the 150th anniversary of the state granting a charter to the school. Events were academic, celebratory, nostalgic. The dwindling number of Storer alumni and some of their offspring were there, to wistfully recall the school's final years.

John Brown was remembered. How could he not be? The NAACP's marker finally approved and installed on Camp Hill in 2006 commemorates his role and raid that preceded the school by a mere eighteen years. Not mentioned on the plaque or frequently spoken anywhere are Storer's links to the five African Americans with Brown. But they are there, nonetheless, preserved not only in Frederick Douglass's 1881 tribute to Shields Green and in the presence of Lewis Leary's sister in 1906 but also in the rolls of alumni.

Among the seventy-page list of Storer graduates found online, one name especially stands out: Ida Newby, class of 1884. Born in 1858, in Wheeling, West Virginia, she was also known as Ida "Bell" Newby before she married and spent her last years in Philadelphia as Ida Yarborough. Ida Bell was the daughter of James Newby, a Civil War veteran who served with the US Colored Troops. He was a younger brother of Dangerfield Newby—Ida's great uncle who met his untimely death fighting for freedom on the streets of Harpers Ferry on October 17, 1859.

12

Commemorations

They played at war, staging what was billed as a "sham" battle on Bolivar Heights above Harpers Ferry between Union and Confederate "soldiers," and held a beard-growing contest. The local women's club planted a garden. The wives and children were all decked out in period dress. John Brown was mentioned but not memorialized. The raid was not reenacted, but the capture of Brown was, to the approving cheers of onlookers. Blacks were noticeably absent from the pageantry and from the photographs depicting the weekend activities.

The year was 1959. The month was October. This was the weekend during which the centennial of the John Brown raid was marked not by solemn reflection but by festivities that would sidestep controversies at the heart of the watershed moment in the American story that many historians say led to bloody civil war, resulting in 750,000 deaths, and also to emancipation. If John Brown was downplayed in October 1959, the five African Americans who laid down their lives with him weren't played at all.

The one hundredth anniversary of John Brown's 1859 raid on Harpers Ferry came only three generations removed from that catalytic event. Two other important developments were on the near horizon: the United States was preparing for its big Civil War Centennial, and the civil rights movement was stirring across the South and in border states. The country remained divided and on edge. John Brown was hardly less of a controversial figure than when he'd lived, or died.

There would be no official "celebration" marking the centennial of the Brown raid, and in whatever took place to commemorate or observe the anniversary, the five African American raiders would be conspicuously absent. From a twenty-first-century perspective, this seems remarkable. After all, John Brown's raid was to free slaves and five of his raiding party were African American. But given the times, it was not altogether surprising.

Harpers Ferry in mid-twentieth-century America was a far cry from what it had been during its peak period as a bustling government town anchored by the federal arsenal and armory. Not only had it been devastated by civil war, it had endured multiple major floods that inundated the lower town, leaving water-soaked buildings in ruins. Once a storied nexus of rivers and industry, Harpers Ferry was now down and out, a tattered gateway to depressed Appalachia.

As the centennial approached, Harpers Ferry had only recently achieved national monument—but not yet national historical park—status. The National Park Service was wrestling with how and whether to plan and finance a physical renewal of the historic town, and to which period, a large enough task to consume the full-time attention of government officials and local citizens.

"The downtown section remains a sagging and rotted ghost town," the *Baltimore Sun* reported in September 1957. But with the Park Service newly on the scene, bolstered with $59,000 in initial funding, the *Sun* said, "it no longer has the depressing appearance of a place about which nobody cares, nobody at all." The Park Service was "now working to 'stabilize' the lower end of the town." That may have been hardly a full-fledged renewal, but it was something.

Charles W. Snell, who arrived in 1957 as National Park Service historian, painted a less rosy picture. "Well, it looked like a slum," he said in 1992. "I mean it was run down. . . . There was almost grass growing in the streets when we came here." Park Service employees going to Charles Town to shop and open bank accounts were met with disbelief when they announced they were from Harpers Ferry. "They said 'No way,' it's a depressed area, they weren't interested." Locals perked up, however, when they learned the newcomers were from the federal government, which meant jobs. "They had taken 30 truckloads of garbage out, and there had been squatters living in these buildings rent free, and they had to be put out, and so the Park had a long way to go."

But this urban renewal undertaking was nothing compared to the conflict that was soon to be renewed over John Brown. A temporary exhibit heavy on artifacts and including some information about Brown opened in August 1959, attracting more than 1,100 the first weekend. But the much more significant event marking the centennial loomed rather inauspiciously. It would be a discomforting anniversary to many, including Karl Betts, the executive director of the US Civil War Centennial Commission, who noted that "the Raid came at a bad time in 1859 and that conditions today are such that it would be a bad time to celebrate it in 1959. Such a celebration might have the effect of antagonizing the entire South to the great damage of the proposed Civil War Centennial observances." Betts feared any celebration of Brown would cause Southern senators and conservative Northerners to block funds for the nascent national commission.

If the South would rise again, the Civil War Centennial could be the vehicle of its resurrection. Thus, centennial fever was taking hold across the states of the Old Confederacy. Many of the Southern states created their own centennial commissions. In Virginia, twenty-five of thirty-one cities and fifty out of ninety-eight counties had centennial committees by late 1959. To some in the South, it was a centennial of the War Between the States. By whatever name, Betts was buoyed, oddly. "Any possible complications arising from the integration problem will soon disappear," he reassured Virginia's US representative William M. Tuck, a Democrat and staunch segregationist. "At least that is the reaction we get from all our correspondence from all over the country and particularly in the South."

Betts reported that the B&O Railroad was "not in sympathy with the concept of centennial commemoration at Harpers Ferry . . . and hoped privately for a quiet event." The Park Service Regional Office concurred. "We share their apprehension that the John Brown episode may be a disturbing element in engendering a bipartisan feeling," assistant director Jackson E. Price wrote in a memo to his boss on October 20, 1958.

The Civil War Centennial Commission intended to celebrate and recognize the combatants on each side rather than revive old antagonisms or address unresolved issues. Consequently, the commission asked the National Park Service to "soft-pedal" recognition of the John Brown centennial. That approach meshed well with local sentiment in and around Harpers Ferry and also with the Park Service's top official at Harpers Ferry. "My grandpappy was a Confederate and we're not going to talk about John Brown," said superintendent Edwin M. Dale.

In the late 1950s, segregation still reigned in the West Virginia panhandle, in schools and public accommodations. The 1954 Supreme Court's desegregation ruling in *Brown v. Board of Education* had yet to make a dent—although it gave the state an excuse to withdraw funding from Storer College, which, insolvent, had closed for good in 1957. No, there would be no veneration of John Brown during this centennial year, at least not in Jefferson County, not in Harpers Ferry.

And certainly not among the county's overwhelmingly white population of eighteen thousand. They could venerate hapless Haywood Shepherd, misrepresenting this free man of color as emblematic of the "faithful slave" in 1931—just twenty-eight years before—but, in 1959, neither Brown nor the five blacks who accompanied him.

The keepers of the Lost Cause in Jefferson County, where Confederate crosses mark graves in Charles Town's all-white Edge Hill Cemetery, had no interest in celebrating Brown or his aborted attempt to free the slaves. To them, he was still very much a fanatic, a terrorist, a maniacal man who deserved neither credit nor applause and certainly not glory. The five African Americans who came with him to Harpers Ferry were not even footnotes, much less unsung heroes.

The Park Service solution was to help plan an event if a local group organized and ran it. This task fell to the nongovernmental Harpers Ferry Centennial Commission and the Harpers Ferry Area Foundation, formed in 1957 by leading citizens and businesses to promote the area. Its president was June Newcomer, the last registrar of Storer College, a white woman and a granddaughter of the school's founder, Maine Baptist Nathan Cook Brackett. The Park Service's regional historian, Frank Barnes, urged that organizers involve "colored citizens," including as performers in any pageant or drama re-creating the period and event. "The reenactment cannot be completely realistic," opined the Baltimore *Afro-American* on the eve of the four-day commemoration, "without persons to portray the heroic roles of six [*sic*] colored members of John Brown's dedicated little army." The newspaper overstated the reality of the scheduled reenactment. It would not be "a complete re-enactment of the raid, John Brown's capture and his execution," but only of the capture of Brown.

Ultimately, no persons of color were part of the staged drama. Langston Hughes, writing in his "Week by Week" newspaper column, named all five African Americans with Brown, omitting his family connection to Lewis Leary. "I hope that a great many Afro-Americans will attend this commemoration," he urged. But that would not happen either. This would be a white folks' affair. The National Park Service's inventory of 353 photos contains not one image of a person of color.

The Harpers Ferry–Bolivar Lions Club offered a special "Centennial Cachet" envelope: one-, three-, and four-cent Lincoln stamps and a "historical insert" for twenty-five cents. The B&O Railroad ran special excursion trains from Baltimore, Washington, and Silver Spring, Maryland.

Newspaper coverage also generally steered clear of controversy, instead perpetuating anti-Brown stereotypes. Seven months before the event, the *Washington Post* called Brown "terrible in his righteousness." A *New York Times* Sunday travel section feature opted for "abolitionist fanatic" but did note that the Civil War Centennial Commission had declined to help with or fund the event. The *Washington Post* similarly referred to Brown as "a white-bearded fanatic." "Pageantry, drama, ceremony, and sham battles will be featured," previewed the *Post*.

Almost alone, *Newsweek* magazine tacked directly into the sectional storm, with an October 19, 1959, cover story headlined "John Brown's Raid: The Spark Still Smolders." A sidebar mentioned that Harpers Ferry at the time had a population of 675—"and most are segregationist." "They insisted that it be called an 'observance,' not a 'celebration,'" said another sidebar, by thirty-eight-year-old Benjamin C. Bradlee, who would later become the legendary executive editor of the *Washington Post.*

On the Friday of centennial weekend, Boyd B. Stutler, the premiere John Brown collector and a proud West Virginian, delivered the Historians' Luncheon speech, in which he referred to Brown's "pitiful little army of liberation" and termed Brown's actions "terroristic." He all but blamed Brown and his men for the ensuing civil war, "of death, dying, and long destruction." One assertion was beyond dispute: "One hundred years have done little to give Old John Brown a niche in history on which all can agree. . . . His fame or his infamy still depends very largely on the personal point of view—and all too frequently that point of view is sectional and depends upon the side on which grandpa fought during the Civil War." And that was about as neutral as it got.

As the weekend progressed, the coverage became breezier, lighter, and brighter. "Oratory and old lace blossomed like mountain laurel," waxed Washington *Evening Star* staff writer John W. Stepp. "The gentlemen—some in ante-bellum black and some in 1959 gray flannel—took charge of the rolling syllables department. The ladies, for their part, reveled as models of their great-grandmothers' styles—and never mind how Dior would deplore."

J. E. B. Stuart III, grandson of the "celebrated Confederate cavalry leader" who had a role in capturing Brown, praised his ancestor, admittedly "called an irresponsible, swashbuckling seeker of publicity" but a man who "went forth with a plume in his hat, a song on his lips, and a banjo player at his side," Stepp reported. No one had a good word to say about John Brown.

There would be one afternoon and three evening performances in the high school auditorium of *The Prophet*, a three-act play about Brown's raid written by an assistant professor of drama at Sweet Briar, a women's college near Lynchburg, Virginia. Helen Mozelle Cavalier, identified in the *Star* as "Mrs. Cyrus Cavalier," directed the play. Her husband, who owned a gas station in town and a trailer park in Charles Town, would also play a part. The *New York Times* called it "an authentic chronicle." However, due to the lingering hatred of Brown, the play intentionally omitted his dramatic last statement, in a note handed to his jailer the day of his execution: "I, John Brown, am now quite certain that the crimes of this guilty land will never be purged away but with blood. I had, as I now think, vainly flattered myself that without very much bloodshed it might be done."

The play ended instead with this seemingly more neutral declaration from a Virginia militia commander: "So perish all such enemies of Virginia! All such enemies of the Union! All such foes of the human race!" Next came a rousing rendition of "John Brown's Body." "Everyone in the audience can decide what to think for himself," explained Helen Cavalier. "We didn't want the play to end with a sermon by John Brown."

On Saturday, the dignitaries went to the Hilltop House Hotel, now under white ownership and operation, for a lunch of baked ham, candied sweet potatoes, green peas, hot biscuits, and pineapple sherbet, followed by remarks from West Virginia governor Cecil H. Underwood. He dismissed Brown as a misguided reformer. "But the world is still filled with people like him," the governor said disapprovingly, "and massive destruction—not just an isolated raid—could be touched off by just such a fanatic as John Brown."

After lunch, they adjourned to the Storer College campus, where blue-coated marine reenactors stormed a mock version of John Brown's fort that had been erected on the tennis courts. An estimated seven thousand watched the show. Park Service photographs show a sea of white faces. "Throngs, at least half of them children, cheered" as the marines stormed the fake fort and captured Brown. It was "the biggest splash of color" in the entire commemoration and a "colorful showpiece," the *Baltimore Sun* reported. It was a celebration of Brown's capture, not of his attempt to free slaves.

Civil War reenactors at a mock version the John Brown fort on the Storer College campus during the October 1959 centennial commemoration. *Harpers Ferry National Historical Park*

By the sesquicentennial in 2009, a new ethos had taken hold in the nation and within the National Park Service. The country's first black president had only months before assumed the highest office in the land. Seemingly, the civil rights of all Americans could be no longer denied; nor could African American history be ignored or whitewashed.

Jefferson County had changed too. From 18,665 people in 1960, it had grown by 2009 to 52,750. The landscape was now dotted with subdivisions instead of apple orchards. The racial composition remained overwhelmingly white, but the county was now part of the Washington metropolitan statistical area, with rush hour commuters clogging the main roads on weekdays to and from the District of Columbia and nearby employment centers.

As in 1959, there was a commemorative postal cover and a beard-growing contest. Visitors could also purchase sesquicentennial swag: a kitchen magnet for $2.95; a collectible mug said to be microwave and dishwasher safe for $8.50, a sesquicentennial tote bag for $14.95—all featuring the bearded Brown and available at the Harpers Ferry Historical Association bookshop and in the author tent on Shenandoah Street.

But instead of the sanitized 1959 play *The Prophet*, the sesquicentennial featured *Sword of the Spirit*, a sympathetic portrayal of John and Mary Brown in words and music from folk singers Greg Artzner and Terry Leonino, better known as Magpie. "To us, John Brown is a heroic figure," said Artzner, recalling their 2009 performance, and they played him that way, drawing on his jailhouse correspondence with his wife before his execution. The duet also performed a song based on Copeland's final letters. Completing this cultural medley was Stephen Vincent Benet's epic poem "John Brown's Body," recited by Danny Glover, the prominent African American actor, who greeted visitors that followed him "like a swarm of bees," recalled event coordinator Todd Bolton.

A Park Service document provided the context for this next chapter, and this time there would be no flinching: "Anniversaries provide unusual opportunities to draw attention and stimulate interest in historic figures and events. This observance will provide an unprecedented opportunity to reflect on, and revisit the life of John Brown as it relates to the broader context of slavery, the abolitionist movement and the American civil rights movement. The activities will focus on the theme of John Brown as a watershed event in the chain of African-American history."

As proposed and implemented, the 150th anniversary program would also include a dramatic presentation of the life and letters of John Anthony Copeland. Unlike the centennial, the five African American raiders would be present and accounted for—and share almost equal billing with their martyred captain.

To ensure a more inclusive observance, the Park Service took control of the sesquicentennial. The commemoration began with a three-day academic symposium, followed by a full schedule of public programming over the weekend. Rangers tracked down and invited descendants—

white and black—of the raiders, townspeople, and other players involved in the original drama. They came from California, Virginia, and West Virginia, from Indiana, Wisconsin, and Massachusetts, to be there that October weekend, not sunny, as in 1959, but rainy, as it had been in 1859. Planners rejected proposals to "recapture" John Brown yet again, or to stage a mock hanging in Charles Town. "Of course, we did not support those ideas," park ranger David Fox explained. "Fifty years makes a big difference."

Explained Bolton, officially chief of visitor services at Harpers Ferry, "We wanted to try to not just get the history buffs here. We wanted to have something for everyone. We were trying to reach out to new and diverse audiences. Obviously, we were in a different day and age." Bolton involved the Jefferson County NAACP. "We did not extend invitations to the United Daughters of the Confederacy or the Sons of Confederate Veterans."

Guinevere Roper, a Jefferson Countian whose father and aunt attended Storer, had been hired in 1973 as a 180-day seasonal parks employee, along with several other African Americans. Formerly a beautician, she became a full-time ranger in 1985. Roper and a committee she formed reached out to many descendants. Of the five black raiders, only Shields Green, the fugitive slave from South Carolina who left behind a one-year-old son, went unrepresented. His trail could not be traced. "That was very disappointing," Roper said.

Brenda Pitts, a Copeland family historian from Indiana, contacted dozens of descendants to encourage their attendance. Pitts had organized prior Copeland reunions, and the family was well represented at Harpers Ferry. "It was like a celebration," recalled Thomas J. Hopkins, a Copeland descendant. There were even 150th anniversary Copeland family pens featuring an image of John Anthony and his parting words before his execution: "If I am dying for freedom, I could not die for better cause."

"The family is extremely diverse," Pitts explained. "By that I mean, we have branches that are now white, and some of them were there in 2009. But I can also tell you at one point in time the way I tend to think of it is these descendants tended to follow their hearts and express freedom in every sense of word. If they fell in love with someone white they married them."

Donna Copeland Hill, Henry Copeland's great-granddaughter, grew up white. She had come to her connection to "Uncle John" Copeland and, indeed, to her own racially mixed background only in middle age, when a cousin began doing family genealogy and met Pitts. Her father, a grandnephew of John Copeland, had kept her "completely in the dark," she told me. "My parents were so intent on keeping my heritage from me." She had Hawaiian ancestry, she was told, to explain her olive skin color.

But through reunions, including the 2009 sesquicentennial, she has embraced her black along with her white heritage. "I was Caucasian my entire life. Then after Harpers Ferry, I'd say I'm mixed, both black and white. Then it got too confusing, so I identify as Caucasian." But she said she is still "just in awe that someone in my background would be willing to give his life and was so passionate about abolition."

Another black descendant Pitts reached was Kim Fraser, a Leary from Plymouth, Massachusetts, who brought her daughters and met "sixty-six relatives from other branches." "Walking the ground, knowing what had occurred here, it was pretty moving," said Fraser. "It was a powerful experience. We felt very connected to it all. One of the park rangers cried when she said she didn't think there was anyone related to Lewis Leary . . . and I was kind of teary-eyed myself."

Descendants of Osborne Perry Anderson filled twenty rooms at the nearby Cliffside Inn above the Shenandoah River, recalled Dennis Howard, the keeper of the family flame. His five grown children were there, along with aunts and uncles, sixty to eighty altogether. "I was proud as shit," he said, to see all "the young kids learning about their history." Sherrie Carter, a Newby descendant from Warrenton, Virginia, had been there before, but this was special. On Sunday morning, she joined a rainy Walk of the Descendants of raiders, townspeople, militia, and military that followed the path of Brown and his raiders through the town. "It was just the whole thing of being there and walking and wondering if you stepped in that person's footsteps."

There was a reception for all the descendants—including a great-great-great-granddaughter of John Brown. They all got along famously.

Donna Copeland Hill reading the story of "Uncle John" Copeland on the banks of the Shenandoah River, where he was captured on October 17, 1859. *NPS Photo/Marsha Wassel*

On Friday night, October 16, exactly 150 years after Brown and his band set out from the Kennedy farmhouse for Harpers Ferry, an estimated two hundred people, including descendants, did the same. It was cold and drizzly, as it had been that fateful night in 1859. At the end of the two-hour hike, they gathered in front of the old engine house, John Brown's fort, ringed with carnations. Candles were distributed to twenty-four descendants. As actor Fred Morsell, who also reprised Frederick Douglass's 1881 commencement address at Storer College, read the roll of those who died at Harpers Ferry, each candle was lit. Then they solemnly walked behind the engine house, formed a circle, and extinguished the lights.

Copeland descendant Brian Beatty listens intently to National Park Service ranger at the conclusion of the Walk of the Descendants during the 150th commemoration weekend, October 2009. _Brenda Pitts_

"We had lousy weather, totally lousy weather," Bolton would recall. Yet, he and others concluded, the sesquicentennial observance had been a huge success. "We had great attendance. All our venues were full." The weekend concluded with the soggy two-hour walk led by ranger David Fox to all the relevant sites in the lower town "in the footsteps of John Brown."

In February 2017, the National Park Service announced the selection of a new top official at Harpers Ferry. Tyrone Brandyburg, a thirty-two-year veteran of the service, became the park's first African American superintendent. "He has a great reputation as a leader and motivator," said regional director Bob Vogel, "and [a] passion for making history relevant to modern society."

Epilogue

Cannonville, Utah, is three times zones and 2,170 miles from Harpers Ferry, where Dangerfield Newby died trying to liberate his enslaved wife and children. But to Ashton Morris Robinson III, the distance in time and space is not so great. Nearly 170 years after Newby's death, his spirit and his story live on in Robinson, a descendant who has spent decades seeking to liberate himself by searching for and reconnecting to his hidden roots. It has been a surprising, emotional, powerful, and often painful journey.

From Robinson's desert home, Bryce Canyon National Park can be seen in the distance. It is geological history on steroids, the result of millions of years of wind and water carving stunning spires out of the sandstone landscape. It is a place to gain perspective, a constant reminder that what seem like cataclysmic events to humans are but a blink in time. Closer to Robinson's 1,300-square foot, solar-paneled home is Promise Rock, a smaller monument also fraught with symbolism. Local legend has it that the promise the rock is named for was a marriage vow that was broken, compelling the disappointed bride to plunge from its heights to her death.

An unkept promise leading to tragedy is deeply embedded in Robinson's lineage. Dangerfield Newby had promised to free his wife before she and their children could be sold south, but it was a promise he could not keep.

Ashton M. Robinson III at his home in Cannonville, Utah. *Eugene L. Meyer*

Ashton's own story is admittedly less dramatic, but it is also poignant. He and his wife, Ellen, an artist, photographer, and substitute teacher in a nearby town, live remotely in the home they built in 2013 on a red dirt road two miles from the nearest pavement. The closest civilization is Cannonville, population 162. He is retired from the US Department of Agriculture, where his job was to hunt predators—mountain lions, coyotes, bears—that threatened herds of sheep and cattle.

Ashton's story is one of self-discovery, begun at the age of forty-five with help initially from Mormon genealogists and then teased out, reluctantly at first, from family members. In our race- and color-conscious society, who and what was he? Where had he come from? He had grown up in a white world with light-skinned parents who both passed for Caucasian. His true racial identity was his first discovery. His relationship to Dangerfield Newby—his great-grandfather three generations removed—would flow from that initial, startling discovery.

Inevitably, the Harpers Ferry raid is positioned at the top of the narrative arc, and John Brown's eloquence and execution are rightly portrayed as the catalytic events that further polarized the nation and led to the Civil War. But this compressed narrative is misleading. The bigger picture can be found in the lives of the five black raiders and their descendants.

This is the American story, not just of a quixotic band of raiders led by a fanatical abolitionist with revolutionary results but of a much longer narrative, beginning with the original sin of slavery and then its ongoing consequences, how it affected not only historical figures in the distant past but also people today who continue to grapple with what Swedish sociologist Gunnar Myrdal, from a white perspective, euphemistically termed "an American Dilemma." More accurately, it is America's shame. It is also Ashton Robinson's story—and our story—and the legacy of the five African Americans in John Brown's revolutionary army.

"It's the pebble in the lake—and the ripples that follow" is how Doug Perks, a native of Jefferson County, West Virginia, and assistant curator at the county museum, puts it.

Ashton and I had spoken on the phone and corresponded by email. He had very generously shared his years of research, with his own explanations accompanying dozens of public documents he had obtained. They included Census reports, death certificates, and court records. Now it was early spring in Utah's high desert, and we were inside his adobe house seated on a couch with a side-window view of the mountains. I had shared two chapters with him, one about the Newby family saga, the other about the immediate aftermath of the raid, for fact-checking. He helped correct some errors and clear up some discrepancies in the manuscript.

Now, in his desert home, we turn to his personal story. Over an afternoon, a tightly wound thread slowly unspools. Ashton, born in 1950, is a modest man of medium height and build with Caucasian features and copper skin tone. In these parts, he could be mistaken for Native American. In fact, DNA tests show a trace of Native American ancestry in his genes.

His parents, Ashton Robinson Jr. and Edith Dolores Broughton, both fair-skinned, grew up black in Washington, DC, where they attended Dunbar High School, the elite academic institution for African Americans in the then segregated nation's capital.

Dunbar's teachers were the finest; many had doctoral degrees and could have taught at any of the country's elite white colleges were it not for their race. Its students were among those characterized by W. E. B. DuBois as "the talented tenth," and often the whitest of the black. In those days, it was not uncommon for light-skinned blacks, among them Dunbar students, to pass for white in downtown Washington's racially segregated restaurants and theaters.

Founded in 1870 as the M Street School, Dunbar was the nation's first public high school for blacks. It boasted a long line of achievers that included US senator from Massachusetts Edward Brooke; William H. Hastie, the first black federal judge; Benjamin O. Davis, the first black general; Dr. Charles Drew, who discovered blood plasma; Robert C. Weaver, the first secretary of the US Department of Housing and Urban Development (1966–1968); and Charles Hamilton Houston, the Howard Law School dean who was the architect of the legal challenges that brought down Jim Crow and was also a mentor to the future Supreme Court justice Thurgood Marshall. The school faded from prominence after integration, which some of its graduates blamed for lost traditions coupled with lower academic standards.

Armstrong High School, where Ashton's darker-skinned relatives by marriage went, was primarily the trade school for blacks in Washington, DC. But among its alumni were also many notables that included composer and orchestra director Duke Ellington; crooner Billy Eckstine; DC superior court judge John D. Fauntleroy; the city's first black police chief, Burtell Jefferson; and Lillian Evanti, an internationally known opera star descended, three generations removed, from raider Lewis Leary.

Ashton's parents—and their siblings—all went to Dunbar. Born in 1923, Ashton's father, Ashton Jr., graduated in 1940. In his yearbook picture, "Capt. Ashton Robinson, Jr." is positively dashing in his snappy high school cadet uniform; he commanded Company B. In segregated Washington, the cadet corps bestowed status, whether black or white. Every year, in separate events, white and black cadets competed at Griffith Stadium for top honors in drilling. He was also a member of the Honor Society, Rex (the senior boys' choir), and Rifles and Officers. His career goal: "To be a surgeon." Ashton Jr. went to Howard University for a semester, then to Bowdoin College in Maine, an experience he fondly recalled to his son. At the end of his first year, he joined the Merchant Marines, which did not impose segregation as the armed forces did, and never finished college.

Edith, known by her middle name, Dolores, graduated in 1943. Her yearbook picture shows her with long, straight tresses and a high front pompadour. "CHARMING" is the one-word description applied to her. Her ambition: "To be a pediatrician." Her activities: Correspondence, Dunbar News Reel (the school newspaper), Fleur-de-lis ("Flower of the Lily," a girls club). To her immediate left on page twenty of the yearbook is her sister, Agnes Elizabeth Broughton, a year older but in the same graduating class. And also with long, straight hair. Her ambition: "To be a nurse." The one word describing her: "SINCERE." Her activities: First Aid, House Beautiful, Spanish. There are three other sisters, all Dunbar graduates.

Dolores and Ashton Jr. traveled in the same social circles, and their families knew each other. Ashton was home on leave from the Merchant Marines when he met Dolores. They danced together at a social event, and he told her he would marry her someday. He shipped out again, and when he returned they were married at St. Augustine's Rectory on November 2, 1944, after which he went back to sea. Ashton Jr.'s mother obtained a certificate from Miner Teachers College, the school for aspiring black educators—although she told Ashton she had attended Wilson Teachers College, which was restricted to whites. Whatever her credentials, she was able to put her academic background to good use, a source of pride to Ashton. For many years, she directed the Ridgefield Community Kindergarten in Fairfield County, Connecticut.

Ashton III's older sister was born in 1945 in Washington. In the early postwar era, Ashton Jr. and Dolores, passing for white, moved north, first to a cold-water, fifth-floor walkup on York Avenue in Manhattan, then to Levittown, Long Island, a suburban tract development built for GIs but with racial covenants. Ashton III was born on March 27, 1950, at St. Mary's Hospital in nearby Queens. Ashton Jr. was by then a New York advertising executive who commuted by train to Manhattan. In 1951, the family moved to tony Weston, Connecticut, where Ashton Jr. joined the legions of upper-middle-class men taking the New Haven Railroad into the city.

The town, forty-five miles northeast of New York City, is among the country's richest, with a median household income of $209,630 in 2010, the highest in Fairfield County. Some 20 percent of Weston's working residents commute to the city. In 2010, less than 1 percent of the population was African American. Notable residents have included Robert Redford, Keith Richards, James Thurber, Christopher Plummer, Bette Davis, and Erica Jong. Notably, Eartha Kitt, the sultry-voiced black singer, actress, and activist, moved to Weston in 2002. The Robinsons lived there from 1952 to 1967. In 1960, the town counted 4,039 residents, and virtually all the townspeople were white. Ashton's parents were the sub-rosa exceptions.

"It was a great place to grow up," Ashton says. "It was 100 percent safe. You could walk and ride bicycles everywhere. Just a real small town with one little Weston center with a couple of stores." It was a Republican town, and his father was the first chairman of the Democratic town committee.

Dolores helped at the cooperative nursery school and was a Brownie leader. Ashton was a Cub Scout. "There were no African Americans in town at all," he recalls. It was a purely white-bread existence.

"If I had known I was African American," Ashton reflects, "if I'd been brought up in the culture, if they'd stayed in DC, it would have been different."

There were visits to his paternal grandparents in Maryland but not to his mother's family, who lived nearby and did not hide their race.

His mother would go alone to see them while Ashton, his sister, and their father would stay at his paternal grandparents' house. His father's mother, Constance, had emigrated from Italy. She had met his grandfather when both worked for a family in Philadelphia. In the 1920 and 1930 Censuses, they were identified as black. In the 1940 Census, she is listed as white. As Ashton relates this, he shows me a formal portrait of them, taken in the 'teens. Ashton Sr., who died in 1974, is wearing a suit and standing. He could be African American, but perhaps his racial category might be ambiguous. Constance stands beside him; she has a slightly dark complexion. His dark skin "was not something we talked about," Ashton says. "It was a very formal and 'proper' family. You did not talk about things you shouldn't. You did not ask nosey questions." Ashton Sr. and two of his sisters who remained in the Washington, DC, area weren't passing; but when Ashton and his parents came to visit, they kept the family secret.

"To me the difference was just New England versus Maryland," he says. Upon reflection, he sees now that creating an alternative reality was not unusual for African Americans light enough to pass; often, it was the norm, as they tried to live their lives as best they could in a race-obsessed society they did not create.

Ashton also shows me photos of his mother as a young girl and then after World War II in the early 1950s. In the latter image, she is smiling and has the same long, straight hair as in her Dunbar yearbook picture. She could have been a beauty queen in a whites-only contest. These are among the family pictures treasured in the Robinsons' compact desert home, along with Ellen's outdoor oil landscapes of canyon country.

Ashton has one especially vivid memory from his early childhood. His family made a rare visit to his mother's sister Agnes at the Washington row house at 1532 T Street NW, where Agnes lived with her mother, Lavinia Broughton. It was then in a predominantly black neighborhood that is now largely gentrified and majority white. It was Christmastime. He was no more than a toddler, but he remembers a dark-skinned man named Brumsic bouncing him on his knee. When he asked later about Brumsic, his mother said she didn't remember who he was. Years later, she described him as a friend of the family. "I knew Brumsic was the key," Ashton says.

In fact, he was Ashton's uncle, married in 1950 to Rita, the youngest of the five Broughton sisters. His full name was Brumsic Brandon Jr., as it turned out his father's second cousin, and he later became a prominent cartoonist, introducing *Luther*, the first nationally syndicated cartoon strip featuring a leading black character. Brumsic raised a family on Long Island—his three children are Ashton's first cousins—and died in 2014 at the age of eighty-seven. His wife, Ashton's aunt Rita, had graduated from Howard in 1949 with a major in French and taught junior high in Westbury, Long Island, where they lived. Brumsic's two brothers, Emerson (also known as Al-Hajj Wali Muhammad), a photographer who lives in Atlanta, and Ivan, a journalist who worked for the *Washington Post*, were born in Washington.

Since rediscovering his family, Ashton has reconnected with some of his blood relatives and relations by marriage, including Ivan Brandon, who, as it turns out, was my colleague at the *Post* in the early 1970s. Brumsic's best friend was Leslie Hicks, now ninety, a professor emeritus at Howard and a 1945 Dunbar graduate who has been my next door neighbor since 1996. There had been tension between the Broughton and the Robinson/Brandon clans, Ivan tells me, and it was all about skin color. "Ashton's father bought into that. It was always just weird." Ashton's parents "went away, and suddenly they weren't black anymore. The joke was they were passing as Armenian."

As Ashton would later learn, it was more complicated. Norbert and Lavinia Broughton, his maternal grandparents, had moved from Washington to Buffalo, New York, where they passed for white for several years, and where Ashton's mother and aunt Agnes were born. Eventually, they moved back to Washington to reestablish their family ties and live as African Americans.

But Ashton's parents hid these relatives and their racial makeup from him. If he pressed, his mother would tell him he was part Indian and part Irish. Then when he'd ask what tribe, she would say Cherokee. "I think she tried to give me some kind of ancestry. She was living under my father's rule," and Ashton Jr. was most inflexible on the subject. Ashton had met his maternal grandmother, Lavinia. She was "a little dark but had straight hair. So I believed the story."

"As I got older, I questioned the difference I was beginning to realize was actually there," he says. "Considering the atmosphere in the late '50s and early '60s, and my parents' reaction to my questions, it was obvious that we were certainly not Negroes." He watched black people on television being beaten, chased, and hosed. He felt bad for them, "but I obviously wasn't one, nor did I want to be." But there was an unresolved question: Who was he?

When Ashton was eleven years old, his parents separated, and they divorced three years later in 1964. His father took an apartment in the city, with Ashton a frequent weekend visitor. Ashton attended public elementary and junior high schools in Weston, then public high school for two years in nearby Westport, where he got in trouble for skipping classes.

His father moved to Los Angeles. There Ashton Jr. worked in real estate and married a "full-blooded European woman," as Ashton describes his German-born stepmother. Back in Connecticut, Dolores was having a hard time raising her spirited son. Boarding school in Sheffield, Massachusetts, came next, but Ashton lasted there just half a year. So out he went to live with his dad and attend Montclair Prep, a private school in the San Fernando Valley. There he met his future wife, Ellen, another rebellious teen who had grown up in the Los Angeles area. The two decided to attend college together, and, knowing nothing about Utah or Mormons, they wound up at Cedar City State College (now Southern Utah State University), in a town 5,840 feet above sea level and with a population when they first enrolled of about nine thousand, of which only a tiny percentage was listed as African Americans in the last Census.

While still in college in 1971, they got married. Ashton went to work for the federal government's Animal Damage Control Program. They had a daughter, who is now a physical therapist married to an orthopedic surgeon in Los Angeles. She went to high school in Idaho, among the several western states where the Robinsons would make their home, usually in remote spots. "I've lived outside," Ashton tells me. "You see how we live. We're not part of any culture or any group."

In his midforties, Ashton had brain surgery for what turned out to be a benign tumor, but that and with it the realization of his mortality motivated him to do family research. He and Ellen were living in a camp trailer by Mitchell Creek, in Elko County, Nevada. His half brother Patrick, then attending school in Boston, looked up the family in the 1920 Census and found the letter *B* for black next to their grandparents' names.

"I thought OK, there's a story. I have to dig into it." Ashton called the Elko Nevada East Family History Center, operated by Mormons, and drove there to meet with a librarian, who found the 1920 Census records, which confirmed that his parents, Ashton Jr. and Dolores, were also black. "That hit me hard," he says. "What does that mean?" he asked himself. "I didn't understand mixed race, the one-drop rule, or any of that."

He phoned his mother back in Connecticut. "OK, what's the deal?" he asked. "I don't know, you'll have to talk to Agnes," she replied, referring to her sister still living in Washington, and then she abruptly hung up. Ashton called back to get the phone number, and then he called his aunt Agnes. Did she know of a Brumsic? Relating the story, Ashton pauses, places his head in his hands, and begins to sob. After a time, he continues. "She says, 'Yeah, that's your father's [second] cousin, and he married your mother's sister Rita."

"Then," Ashton continues, "Agnes began to tell me the story. I contacted Brumsic. I'm now good friends with his children." The story expanded from there. For about five years, before he owned a computer, Ashton did his family research tediously in courthouses, record depositories, and libraries, and through mail correspondence and phone calls.

Once he had access to the internet, the trail led him to Sherrie Carter, another Newby descendant, and to Philip J. Schwarz, a Virginia academic who was researching a book, *Migrants Against Slavery: Virginians and the Nation*, eventually published in 2001. Schwarz posted a search on the web for Newby descendants, and both Ashton and Sherrie, who lives in Fauquier County, Virginia, responded. The two would share information—with Schwarz, with each other—and they would travel together with Ellen in a car overflowing with family-related research papers to Harpers Ferry and to the Kennedy farmhouse.

Ashton hadn't known anything about Dangerfield Newby, but the name intrigued him and he learned who Newby was and the part he had played in history. "I got shivers and the hair stood up on the back of my neck," he says. "I felt a pride I had not felt before about ancestral connections."

Ashton's discovery of his true racial identity has not affected his marriage in the slightest, Ellen says, "only that it troubled Ashton and he wanted to get to the bottom of it. When I met his parents and grandparents, I always figured he was part African American. It was vaguely in my mind, and I could tell it wasn't something his family wanted to talk about."

If there was stigma to being black, being descended from Dangerfield Newby in Piedmont Virginia was even worse. Anyone associated with John Brown was more likely vilified than deified south of the Potomac. Elmira, Harriet and Dangerfield's daughter, lived in Remington, in Fauquier. She was a black woman in an overwhelmingly white community, and she didn't make waves. She married Eli Tackett, a former slave, and later a darker-skinned man named Brown. Dangerfield, meanwhile, faded from family history. Elmira's Newby name resurfaced on the death certificates of her children. Otherwise, there was nothing. Ashton and Sherrie would visit Elmira's second great-granddaughter in Remington many years later.

By passing, Ashton's parents, presumably, had hoped to elevate their status in a country where race mattered more than character. They may also have been trying to shield their children from the inevitable social, cultural, and legal segregation that afflicted generations.

"The family history brought out all these strong, deep, and unex-plainable feelings and reactions. I just live with that," Ashton says. "The real issue here is I wasn't told. They pretended they had no black ancestry. It affected me psychologically. It's OK not to tell the public every damn thing. But you should know yourself and know why people are asking. I had cousins [whose parents were] not as extreme. They didn't tell them exactly, but they visited other cousins and figured, OK, I'm part black.

"Also, part of it is that my parents didn't know the full story of their ancestry. It was kept quiet with each generation keeping things from a different generation. It went clear back where everyone knew Mira [Brown] was black, but nobody knew Dangerfield was her father. The next generation down, there was no story of why they looked white. And the next generation—my parents—'No, we're not black.' It went down through levels of secrecy. All practiced keeping secret aspects of their ancestry. I have one cousin, a dark-skinned woman who knew she had African American ancestry, but she didn't have the straight story. Her boyfriend in college, when he found out, he beat her up. There were different ways cousins dealt with being mixed race.

"It's not just as simple as if you knew you were black or white, and what does that mean? I do know I would have been better off if they had told me and helped me, or raised me in DC, like Agnes's kids, lighter than I, but they grew up black in DC."

Ashton's long journey of discovery has revealed more than his own immediate origins. In studying his family's history down through the generations, he has gained a broader perspective on his ancestors "and their problems as they relate to race, mixed race, segregation, prejudice, and passing, as well as the individual or unique problems for each person in each generation," he says. "I come from generations of private people who kept ever-deepening layers of secrets from others, including their offspring."

So, here he is, a direct descendant of Dangerfield Newby—a biracial man who died a horrible death at Harpers Ferry—still struggling nearly two centuries later with the color line in his own life, and with the existential questions: Who am I? What am I?

To some, the past is best forgotten and relegated to the dustbin of history. Yet the legacy of slavery, of American's "peculiar institution" and its "original sin," of race mixing and the one-drop rule, of Danger-field Newby and the four other African Americans with John Brown at Harpers Ferry lives on in remote Cannonville, Utah, in the person of Ashton M. Robinson III.

It is our legacy as well.

Acknowledgments

While I bear sole responsibility for this book, it would not have happened without the help and support of many others.

I am greatly indebted to Ashton Robinson, a descendant of Dangerfield Newby, for generously sharing his family research, and to Ellen Robinson, both of whom welcomed me and my wife into their home and lives. Sherrie Carter, another Newby descendant, shared information about her family history and helped to chart my route to areas of Fauquier County, Virginia, where her ancestors were enslaved. Thanks also to Brenda Pitts, Thomas Hopkins, and Donna Copeland Hill, descendants of John Anthony Copeland; to Dennis Howard, related to Osborne Perry Anderson and who years ago set me on this long path; to Gil Shepherd, in Winston-Salem, North Carolina, and to Jan Fontaine, archivist, historian, and secretary of Historic Woodlawn Cemetery, for taking me to the Shepherd family grave in Southeast Washington, DC.

Thanks to Doug Perks, assistant curator at the Jefferson County Historical Society, for leading me to the grave of Fontaine Beckham and helping to fill in any gaps in my knowledge of local history.

Thanks to Frederica Wilson, for furthering my research of Sylvanus Demarest in Canada West; to Gwen Robinson, a descendant of Mary Ann Shadd Cary; and Susan Solomon, of the Chatham-Kent Black Historical Society in Ontario. Jean Libby, a John Brown scholar in California, has for many years been a long-distance colleague and resource on the five African American raiders with John Brown.

Helpful information and leads came from Harpers Ferry National Historical Park rangers Guinevere Roper, Todd Bolton, David Fox, and Dennis Frye; archivist Michelle Hammer; and Cathy Baldau, executive director of the Harpers Ferry Park Association. James L. Taylor, George C. Rutherford, and the late James A. Tolbert, of the Jefferson County Black History Preservation Society, provided more historical and recent background.

Karen Hughes White of the Afro-American Historical Association of Fauquier County, Virginia, guided me through the organization's vast archives during my research. Kimberly Springle, executive director of the Charles Sumner School Museum & Archives, helpfully provided access and scans from relevant Dunbar High School yearbooks.

To the staff of the Handley Library in Winchester, Virginia, and of the Balch Library in Leesburg, Virginia, thanks for helping me to find resources I might otherwise have missed. Ken Grossi and Louisa Hoffman at the Oberlin College archives were both enormously helpful. Tom Crew from the Library of Virginia in Richmond told me of John Copeland's intercepted letters from jail and led me to the microfiled executive papers of Virginia governor Henry A. Wise during the period of the Harpers Ferry raid and its aftermath.

Martha Hamlyn and Jim Richardson graciously allowed me to be their first writer-in-residence in sleepy Claiborne, on Maryland's Eastern Shore. May they have many more.

Thanks as well to Roger Williams, my savvy and sagacious agent, whose enthusiasm for this book has been inspiring and unflagging, and also, at Lawrence Hill Books, to senior editor Jerome Pohlen and project editor Lindsey Schauer for their helpful comments and careful reading of the manuscript.

Along the way, I have appreciated the friendship, enthusiasm and support of many, including Alice Bonner, Steve Case, George and Elanor Cato, Leslie Hicks, Ivan Brandon, Robert Pierre, Richard Prince, and Jack Wennersten.

Thanks also to Sydney Trent, who bought my pitch many years ago for a *Washington Post Magazine* article about Osborne Perry Anderson and then shepherded it into print; and to Tom Shroder, the magazine's editor at the time who more recently provided invaluable comments as the manuscript progressed. My friend and colleague Miranda Spivack managed to carve time from her own busy work schedule as a journalist and college professor to read portions of the manuscript. David Meyer also read chapters and made helpful suggestions.

I have sought to imbue my sons Eric, David, and Aaron with a sense of history and welcomed them as fellow travelers on my forays into often obscure and forgotten places that illuminated the past and present. Most importantly, my wife, Sandy Pearlman, the love of my life, not only read and commented on chapters but also encouraged and supported my efforts throughout. Day in and day out, she makes my life possible, exciting, and fulfilling. I cannot begin to thank her enough.

Notes

Introduction

"worth a voyage": Thomas Jefferson, *Notes on the State of Virginia* (London: John Stockdale, 1787), 28.

Chapter 1: Beginnings

The success of the American Revolution: "Slave, Free Black and White Population, 1790–1830," University of Maryland, Baltimore County, http://userpages .umbc.edu/~bouton/History407/SlaveStats.htm. See also "Statistics of Slaves," US Census Bureau decennial report, 1860, https://www2.census.gov/prod2 /decennial/documents/00165897ch14.pdf.

The British had played a major role: "British Involvement in the Transatlantic Slave Trade," The Abolition Project, http://abolition.e2bn.org/slavery_45.html.

"Be not then, ye negroes": *Williamsburg Virginia Gazette*, November 17, 1775, quoted in Benjamin Quarles, "Lord Dunmore as Liberator," *William and Mary Quarterly* 15 (October 1958): 494–507, in August Meier and Elliott M. Rudwick, eds., *The Making of Black America* (New York: Atheneum, 1969), 1:130.

From 1800 to 1833, the governor reviewed: James Hugo Johnston, *Race Relations in Virginia and Miscegenation in the South 1778–1860* (PhD diss., University of Chicago, 1937; Amherst: University of Massachusetts Press, 1970), 17.

"While we deprecate the horrors": *The Annual Report of the Auxiliary Society of Frederick County, Va. for Colonizing the Free People of Colour in the United States* (Winchester, VA: Auxiliary Society, 1820), https://archive.org/details /annualreportofau00auxi.

"on the question of general emancipation": Alexander Campbell, *A Tract for the People of Kentucky* (Lexington, KY, 1849), 2, quoted in Johnston, *Race Relations*, 129.

Between 1820 and 1830, 265 slaves: Theodore M. Whitfield, *Slavery Agitation in Virginia, 1829–1832* (Baltimore: Johns Hopkins Press, 1930), 47.

In August 1831, Nat Turner . . . led an insurrection: A decade earlier, Denmark Vesey, who had purchased his freedom, attempted to mount a similar rebellion in South Carolina. Inspired by a successful and bloody slave rebellion in Haiti, Vesey had been betrayed by two slaves who knew of the plan and was hanged in Charleston on July 2, 1822. Vesey directly linked slavery and the Bible, recalling the deliverance of the ancient Israelites from bondage in the land of Egypt.

"I heard a loud noise": Christopher Klein, "10 Things You May Not Know About Nat Turner's Rebellion," History channel website, May 24, 2016, www .history.com/news/history-lists/10-things-you-may-not-know-about-nat-turners -rebellion.

"conspiring to rebel": Southampton County Court Minutes Book, 1830–1835, 121–123.

"The case of Nat Turner": George Washington Williams, *History of the Negro Race in America* (New York: G.P. Putnam's Sons, 1883), 2:90, quoted in Vincent Harding, "Religion and Resistance Among Antebellum Negroes, 1800–1860," in *The Making of Black America*, ed. August Meier and Elliott M. Rudwick (New York: Atheneum, 1969), 1:188.

a public whipping of thirty-nine lashes: W. E. B. DuBois, ed., *The Negro Church* (Atlanta: Atlanta University Press, 1903), 25, http://scua.library.umass.edu /digital/dubois/dubois8.pdf.

"We may shut our eyes": Joseph C. Robert, *The Road from Monticello: A Study of the Virginia Slavery Debate of 1832* (Durham, NC: Duke University Press, 1941; Whitefish, MT: Kessinger Legacy Reprints, 2010), 17–18.

A petition for outright abolition: "Petition from the Society of Friends, Charles City County (December 14, 1831)," Encyclopedia Virginia, www.encyclope diavirginia.org/Petition_from_the_Society_of_Friends_Charles_City_County _December_14_1831. The Encyclopedia Virginia website has all documents regarding the Virginia Slavery Debate of 1831–1832. This and other petitions are also transcribed in Erik S. Root, *Sons of the Fathers: The Virginia Slavery Debates of 1831–1832* (Lanham, MD: Lexington Books, 2010).

At current growth rates: "Petition from the Citizens of Buckingham County (December 16, 1831)," Encyclopedia Virginia, www.encyclopediavirginia.org /Petition_from_the_Citizens_of_Buckingham_County_December_16_1831.

"placed as an apprentice": Erik S. Root, "The Virginia Slavery Debate of 1831–1832," Encyclopedia Virginia, August 25, 2017, www.encyclopediavirginia .org/Virginia_Slavery_Debate_of_1831-1832_The.

"Whilst we were enjoying": "Excerpts from Governor John Floyd's Message to the General Assembly (December 6, 1831)," Encyclopedia Virginia, www .encyclopediavirginia.org/Excerpts_from_Governor_John_Floyd_s_Message _to_the_General_Assembly_December_6_1831.

The House of Delegates proceeded: Robert, *Road from Monticello*, 118.

"removed beyond the limits": Robert, 19.

He envisioned the plan: Whether free persons of color would be allowed to participate was not addressed.

"It in fact operates": Slaves were counted as three-fifths of a person under the Constitution, not two-fifths, as Randolph mistakenly said. "Speech of Thomas J. Randolph in the House of Delegates of Virginia, on the Abolition of Slavery," American Memory, from Slavery to Freedom: The African-American Pamphlet Collection, 1824–1909, Library of Congress, http://memory.loc.gov/cgi-bin /ampage?collId=rbaapc&fileName=23920//rbaapc23920.db&recNum=0&item Link=r%3Fammem%2Frbaapcbib%3A%40field%28NUMBER%2B%40od1 %28rbaapc%2B23920%29%29&linkText=0.

"final and most brilliant": Robert, *Road from Monticello*, v.

In Virginia, the General Assembly declared: June Purcell Guild, *Black Laws of Virginia: A Summary of the Legislative Acts of Virginia Concerning Negroes from Earliest Times to the Present*. (Richmond, VA: Whittet & Shepperson, 1936), reprint comp. Karen Hughes White and Joan Peters (Westminster, MD: Heritage Books, 2011), introduction. Further, free persons of color could own slaves only by inheritance, with the sole exception of the person's enslaved spouse or children.

"Africa gave to Virginia": Barton H. Wise, *The Life of Henry A. Wise of Virginia, 1806–1876* (New York: Macmillan, 1899), 156–160, https://hdl.handle .net/2027/loc.ark:/13960/t9q241571.

"considered the race fit": Wise, 60.

"would fight a regiment": Wise, 161.

In 1860, Virginia had more slaves: Johnston, *Race Relations*, 161.

They were destined to enact a raid: Guy Gugliotta, "New Estimate Raises Civil War Death Toll," *New York Times*, April 2, 2012, www.nytimes.com/2012/04/03 /science/civil-war-toll-up-by-20-percent-in-new-estimate.html.

Chapter 2: One Bright Hope

"SALE OF NEGROES AND LAND": "Sale of Slaves at Brentsville 30 Nov 1844," *Fauquier County (VA) Flag of 98*, Prince William County Newspaper Transcripts, 1784–1860, comp. Ronald Ray Turner, www.pwcvirginia.com/Rons Ramblings.htm.

"ALSO the following Slaves": "Many Slaves (All Named) to Be Sold at Brentsville 12 Jan 1846," *Alexandria (VA) Gazette*, Prince William County Newspaper Transcripts. "Increase of the females" refers to the children born since the deed.

"NEGROES WANTED": "200 Negroes Wanted for New Orleans Market 19 June 1853," *Alexandria (VA) Gazette*, Prince William County Newspaper Transcripts.

"soundness or unsoundness": *Alexandria Gazette*, December 5, 1859, 2. The 1860 Census shows that constable Solomon Brill was twenty-six years old and living with his father, Philip F. Brill—sixty-six, a farmer with real estate valued at $2,800 and personal property at $400—two brothers, and one sister, all born in New York. Also in the household were Samuel Stodard, thirty-seven, a dentist from Connecticut with $1,000 in personal property, and Mary Stafford, an eighteen-year-old "domestic" listed as *M* for mulatto. She was born in Virginia. For her to be listed by name in the Census, she would have had to have been free in 1860.

"that he was an Abolitionist": *Washington National Era*, August 27, 1857.

"The fact that Mr. Underwood": *Baltimore Sun*, August 11, 1857, 2. See also "Brentsville Link to the Underground Railroad," Prince William County, Virginia, website, www.pwcgov.org/government/dept/publicworks/hp/pages /brentsville-link-to-the-underground-railroad.aspx.

Underwood had . . . railed against slavery: Patricia Hickin, "John C. Underwood and the Antislavery Movement in Virginia, 1847–1860," *Virginia Magazine of History and Biography* 73, no. 2 (April 1965): 156–168. Underwood, a transplanted New Yorker, established dairies and cheese factories in adjoining Fauquier and Clarke Counties using free labor. After his Republican Convention speech became known back home, Virginia citizens formed a committee to invite him to "leave the state as speedily as he can find it in his power to do so." *Alexandria Virginia Sentinel*, June 27, 1856.

"It appears that even in Virginia": "Dred—American Slavery," *Quarterly Review* 101 (January and April 1857): 340.

Harriet Newby and her children . . . were "sold south": No record of sale has been located. However, Harriet Newby's owner at the time, Virginia Payne Jennings, lived in Brentsville. It is also conjecture that Harriet and her children were sold at auction at the Brentsville courthouse or in a private sale. The 1860 slave schedules for the estate of Lewis Jennings list only two boys, ages six and ten, strongly suggesting that Harriet and her children had been sold by then. For this and other information on the Newbys, I am indebted to the research of Ashton Robinson. A descendant of Harriet and Dangerfield Newby, Robinson has devoted more than twenty years to researching his roots in Virginia and environs.

providing another source of income for their owners: Eugene M. Scheel, *Culpeper: A Virginia County's History Through 1920* (Culpeper, VA: Culpeper Historical Society, 1982), 158–159.

What happened to the Newby clan: Philip J. Schwarz, *Migrants Against Slavery: Virginians and the Nation* (Charlottesville: University of Virginia Press), 2001.

"This is my Diary of Anne Frank": Schwarz, quoted at a Stratford Hall Seminar on Slavery, www.stratalum.org/2001/01aug2/newby.html.

Prince William's 1860 population: "Population Statistics for Virginia," Virginia Places, www.virginiaplaces.org/population/popgrowth.html.

In 1860, Culpeper's population: James Andrew Davis, *Music Along the Rapidan: Civil War Soldiers, Music, and Community During Winter Quarters, Virginia* (Lincoln: University of Nebraska Press, 2014), 27.

Fauquier County . . . population in 1860: Kurt Schick, "Slavery in Fauquier County," *News and Notes from the Fauquier Historical Society* 5, no. 4 (fall 1983): 4.

"bright mulatto": *Fauquier County (VA) Free Register*, will book 11, 165–166, quoted in Thomas C. Givens, "Manumission of Slaves in Fauquier County, Virginia, 1830–1860" (honors theses, University of Richmond, 1972), paper 298.

Chichester's estate: Robert J. Chichester, "Chichester . . . the History of our Family from 1653–present," March 2, 1992, http://chichesterfamily.com /chichester_family_history.pdf.

"with a hat and blanket": John Fox v. Henry S. Halley, Fauquier County Case No. 1848-015.

Under his last will: "At a Circuit Court of Fauquier County Held on the 6th day of April 1859. The Last Will and Testament of John Fox, Deceased, Was This Day Filed." Fox had traveled to Ohio to investigate how best to free his slaves but settled upon making their emancipation a condition of his will instead.

March Farm was sold in five lots: Schick, "Slavery in Fauquier County," 4.

Elsey Pollard: Her name has been variously spelled as Elsey, Ailsey, Alcy, or Alcey.

referring to the Ohio River: Schwarz, *Migrants Against Slavery*, 157–158.

Washington A. Tackett: Tackett was a laborer who died single in 1938 and is buried in Fauquier County.

"his begging expedition": *Woodsfield (OH) Spirit of Democracy*, November 16, 1859, 3.

"a quiet man upright": Schwarz, *Migrants Against Slavery*, 163; Thomas Featherston-haugh, "John Brown's Men: The Lives of Those Killed at Harper's Ferry," *Publications of the Southern Historical Association* 3, no. 4 (October 1899): 281–306.

"light mulatto": Alfred Hawkes, interview by Katherine Mayo, January 2, 1909, in Oswald Garrison Villard Papers, Columbia University Rare Book and Manuscript Library (hereafter "Villard Papers"). The son may have been Dangerfield Newby Jr., a minister who shows up in later Census records in Raleigh, North Carolina.

"We aren't buying men": Hawkes, interview by Mayo. Hawkes also said that his son taught Newby how to read.

Their probable fate would be: Jennings's widow would move to Missouri with her two children, both of whom died there at the ages of fifteen and eighteen. Philip J. Schwarz, "Harriet and Dangerfield Newby in Slavery and Freedom," PowerPoint presentation, 2009, www.slideshare.net/stratalum/newby-harpers -ferry-schwarz-101709-final.

"Dear Husband": "2009 African American Trailblazers in Virginia History: Dangerfield Newby's Letters from His Wife, Harriet," Library of Virginia Publications and Educational Services, www.lva.virginia.gov/public/trailblazers /res/Harriet_Newby_Letters.pdf.

"The last letter was delivered": Jean Libby, *The John Brown Photo Chronology: Catalog of the Exhibit at Harpers Ferry 2009* (Palo Alto, CA: Allies for Freedom, 2009), 56.

"I want you to buy me": *Governor's Message and Reports of Public Officers of the State, of the Boards of Directors, and of the Visitors, Superintendents, and Other Agents of Public Instruction or Interests of Virginia* (Richmond, 1859) special collections, Library of Virginia, Richmond, 116–117.

Ninety-four percent of the residents are Caucasian: Spokeo, www.spokeo.com /Tackett+Ln+Bealeton+VA+addresses.

Chapter 3: The Oberlin Connection

In stark contrast to most of Ohio: Lorain County Board of Elections, certified results, November 23, 2016, http://media.wix.com/ugd/2568d0 _cfd3044357784ccc8f97cae1776a3e2a.pdf; Jodi Weinberger, "Oberlin Residents, Students Reeling from Election Results," *Chronicle-Telegram* (Lorain County, OH), November 10, 2016, www.chroniclet.com/Local-News/2016/11/10/Ober lin-residents-students-reeling-from-election-results.html. By contrast, Donald Trump carried rural swaths of the county outside Oberlin.

Copeland and Leary were related through marriage: In many accounts, Leary has been incorrectly identified as John Copeland's uncle, noted Brenda Pitts, Copeland descendant, in an email to Guinevere Roper, National Park Service ranger, September 18, 2009.

John Anthony's father, John C. Copeland: John C. Copeland has often been identified as John A. Copeland Sr. and his son as John A. Copeland Jr. This is incorrect, according to family historian Brenda Pitts. John Anthony, as the son was often called, signed his name without the junior suffix.

working . . . on the reconstruction of the statehouse: Copeland's wages were $1.00 a day starting in June 1835 and rose to $1.50 in February 1837. His last recorded pay day on the capitol was July 25, 1840. *Capitol Buildings*, vol. 7, *State Capitol*, Treasurers' and Comptrollers' Papers, State Archives of North Carolina; Carpenters Time Book 1833–1840, State Archives of North Carolina. Salary information provided June 15, 2005, as an attachment to a letter to Nancy Hendrickson (Oberlin, OH) from Leslie M. Kesler, curator of political and socioeconomic history, North Carolina Museum of History.

On August 15, 1831, he married Delilah Evans: Brent H. Holcomb, *Marriages of Orange County, NC, 1779–1868* (Baltimore: Genealogical, 1983). Marriage bonds posted August 13, 1831, two days before the marriage.

Nathanael Greene: Greene, regarded as one of the most effective Revolutionary War generals, took command of the Continental Army at Hillsborough on December 3, 1780.

"pleasure in saying that he has": "John A. Copeland, 20 July 1861," in *William Cooper Nell: Nineteenth-Century African American Abolitionist, Historian, Integrationist, Selected Writings from 1832–1874*, ed. Dorothy Porter Wesley and Constance Porter Uzelac (Baltimore: Black Classic, 2002), 607. Nell's notes were published July 20, 1861, in James Redpath's abolitionist Boston newspaper, *Pine and Palm*.

In Tennessee, they added one more: Reuben (or Ruben) Turner is buried in section Q of Westwood Cemetery, Oberlin, in a plot titled to the GAR (Grand Army of the Republic). A twenty-four-inch-high stone marks the spot where he was buried on September 4, 1865. According to the Westwood Cemetery website, "'Reuben Turner' is listed on Oberlin's Soldiers' Monument as having served in the '3rd USCA' and as having 'died in the service of our country'" (www .oberlinwestwood.org/omeka/items/show/27542).

they headed for New Richmond, Ohio: Some sources say the families headed for New Richmond, Indiana, but that community barely existed in 1843, having been laid out only seven years before. Moreover, it was not known for antislavery sentiment. More likely, they were bound for New Richmond, Ohio, an abolitionist "hotbed" and Underground Railroad center on the Ohio River ("History," New

Richmond, Ohio, website, www.newrichmond.org/history.html). Further, there were no individuals named Tibbitts in or near New Richmond, Indiana, in the 1840 Census, while there was a Tibbitts household of four —including Samuel, who gave his occupation as farmer—near the Ohio town.

"go on and look into the chasm": William E. Bigglestone, *They Stopped in Oberlin: Black Residents and Visitors of the Nineteenth Century* (Oberlin, OH: Oberlin College, 2002), 51.

citizens eschewed any Fourth of July celebration: Nat Brandt, *The Town That Started the Civil War: The True Story of the Community That Stood Up to Slavery—and Changed a Nation Forever* (New York: Dell, 1981), 28.

"Oberlin is peculiar": Robert S. Fletcher, "The Wellington Rescue," *Oberlin Alumni Magazine* 54 (November 1958): 6, quoted in Brandt, 28.

It was truly integrated: It should be noted that integration did not meet total acceptance. The slim majority included John Brown's father, Owen Brown, an early board member. Even after the decision was made, there was some lingering resistance to black and white students mingling in dining halls and classrooms.

"old buzzard's nest": William Loren Katz, *The Black West: A Documentary and Pictorial History of the African American Role in the Westward Expansion of the United States*, 3rd ed. (Seattle: Open Hand, 1987), 102.

"of God in the salvation of men": Robert Samuel Fletcher, *A History of Oberlin College from Its Foundation Through the Civil War* (Oberlin, OH: Oberlin College, 1943), 1:88, https://ia600802.us.archive.org/12/items/historyofoberlin01flet /historyofoberlin01flet_jpg.pdf.

"irrespective of color": Fletcher, 236, quoted in Marlene Merrill, "First Church and Oberlin's Early African American Community," presentation to Oberlin African American Genealogy and History Group, December 6, 2003, Oberlin Public Library, www2.oberlin.edu/external/EOG/FirstChurch/FirstChurch -Merrill.html.

By 1856, the school counted: Steven Lubet, *The "Colored Hero" of Harper's Ferry: John Anthony Copeland and the War Against Slavery* (New York: Cambridge University Press, 2015), 4. In 1841, Oberlin also became the first American college to grant degrees to women.

there John Brown grew to manhood: John Brown married his housekeeper's daughter, Dianthe Lusk of Meadville, Pennsylvania. They had seven children, five of whom survived to adulthood. She died in 1832 in childbirth. In 1833, he married Mary Ann Day, with whom he had thirteen children, seven of whom died as children and two of whom died at Harpers Ferry.

the state legislature tried . . . to repeal the college's charter: Katz, *Black West*, 102.

His father . . . championing the abolitionist cause: In 1852, Copeland's father and John Mercer Langston attended the Ohio State Black Convention, with Langston as president. To assist fugitives, the convention formed county-level committees, and John C. Copeland was one of two men named to head the Lorain County branch. William Cheek and Aimee Lee Cheek, *John Mercer Langston and the Fight for Black Freedom, 1829–65* (Urbana: University of Illinois Press, 1984), 351.

"determined and unyielding": "John A. Copeland," in *William Cooper Nell*, 608.

"sympathetic attention": "John A. Copeland," 608.

"often by the deep scowl": John Mercer Langston, *From the Virginia Plantation to the Nation's Capital, or, the First and Only Negro Representative in Congress from the Old Dominion* (Hartford, CT: American Publishing, 1894), 195, https://archive.org/details/fromvirginiaplan00langiala.

"Bozzaris died": "John A. Copeland," 609.

Sarah Jane Revels: Revels was also related to Hiram Revels, a Reconstruction black senator from Mississippi. The Croatan Indians have been linked, but not definitively, to the Lost Colony of Roanoke, an early English settlement that inexplicably vanished but is believed to have intermarried with the Croatan tribe. The Lumbee Indians of Robeson County, claiming descent, have long sought federal recognition as Native Americans.

African American slaveholder: The 1850 Census identifies Matthew Leary as "mulatto." The Cumberland County, North Carolina, slave Census for that year shows he then owned three slaves: a female, fourteen; and two males, thirty-eight and forty-five.

"A box!": Henrietta Evans interview, March 5, 1908, Villard Papers, quoted in Lubet, *"Colored Hero,"* 73.

Lewis Sheridan Leary: His middle name is sometimes given as Sherrard, the origin of which is unclear.

"Men must suffer for a good cause": "John Brown's Men: Louis Sherrard Leary, 15 December, 1858," in *William Cooper Nell*, 612.

"an intelligent and interesting young colored lady": Langston, *Virginia Plantation*, 194.

Benjamin Wade: Following the Civil War, Wade was a leader among the Radical Republicans forcefully advocating for black civil rights and supporting the impeachment of President Andrew Johnson for what they considered his too conciliatory policies toward the former Confederate states.

"hold the fugitive slave law": William W. Williams, *History of Ashtabula County, Ohio* (Philadelphia: Williams Brothers, 1878), 33, http://solomonspalding.com/SRP/saga2/1878Ast2.htm.

he reportedly rejected offers of money: Lubet, *"Colored Hero,"* 22.

where Price said he "supposed": Nat Brandt, *Town That Started the Civil War*, 92.

"to shoot the damn rascal": Lubet, 95.

"We will have him anyhow": Brandt, *Town That Started the War*, 98.

Lincoln was handcuffed, jailed: Boston *Liberator*, January 13, 1860.

"I have been thinking": "John Brown's Men: Louis Sherrard Leary," 612.

"things are working as they should be": Lewis Leary to "Dear Friend," 18 January 1859, Miscellaneous Manuscripts Collection, Huntington Library, Black Studies Center.

"good looking, bright mulatto": Quarles, *Allies for Freedom*, 34; Bigglestone, *They Stopped in Oberlin*, 52; Langston, *Virginia Plantation*, 193—all quoted in Brandt, *Town That Started the War*, 118.

"a man of incomplete education": Richard D. Webb, ed., *The Life and Letters of Captain John Brown* (London: Smith, Elder, 1861), 352, http://bit.ly/2rPzJJO.

Ralph Plumb . . . would later figure prominently in the case against Copeland: Brandt, *Town That Started the War*, 118–121.

"I felt it my duty to go": Wilbur H. Phillips, *Oberlin Colony: The Story of a Century* (Oberlin, OH: Oberlin Printing, 1933), 34.

He was fined $100: Robert Ewell Greene, *The Leary-Evans, Ohio's Free People of Color* (self-pub., 1989), 29–30.

"Leary did not believe": "John Brown's Men: Louis Sherrard Leary," 611.

"honored himself": Langston, *Virginia Plantation*, 195.

"secured two of the bravest": Langston, 194.

They would in fact receive such assistance: Quarles, *Allies for Freedom*, 148.

"for quite some time": Cleveland *National Democrat*, November 2, 1859.

later said he hadn't asked for specifics: Ralph Plumb testimony before the "Select Committee of the Senate appointed to inquire into the late invasion and seizure of the public property at Harper's Ferry," 36 Cong. 1 session, *Senate Report* 278, 179–186, quoted in Fletcher, *History of Oberlin College*, 414; Langston, *Virginia Plantation*, 190–197.

"Whether on the scaffold high": *Pine and Palm*, July 27, 1861.

Chapter 4: North to Canada

Edward Gorsuch: Gorsuch may have been a distant collateral ancestor of US Supreme Court justice Neil Gorsuch. Although the connection is difficult to trace, a Thomas J. Gorsuch was born in 1814 in Baltimore County, where Edward Gorsuch, the slain slaveholder, was born in 1795.

more than a third of Boston's black population: Lubet, *"Colored Hero,"* 56.

"the head quarters of the Negro": William M. Mitchell, *The Underground Railroad* (London: William Tweedie, 1860), 138, 141. https://ia601404.us.archive.org/35/items/undergroundrail01mitcgoog/undergroundrail01mitcgoog.pdf.

A business census that year: Gwendolyn Robinson and John W. Robinson, *Seek the Truth: A Story of Chatham's Black Community* (Chatham, ON: self-pub., 1989), 129–130. The Census found two blacksmiths, five grocers, five plasterers, seventeen seamstresses, thirteen carpenters, six doctors, four barbers, three painters, two teachers, two watchmakers, two ministers, a gunsmith, a cabinetmaker, a brick mason, a wagon maker, a butcher, a lawyer, a milliner, a teamster, a gardener, and a tavern keeper.

"colored population of Upper Canada": Benjamin Drew, *A North-Side View of Slavery: The Refugee, or the Narrative of Fugitive Slaves in Canada Related By Themselves with an Account of the History and Condition of the Colored Population of Upper Canada* (Boston: John P. Jewett, 1855), v, https://ia800503.us.archive.org/33/items/cihm_49469/cihm_49469.pdf.

"Canada was a good country": Mitchell, *Underground Railroad*, 113.

During these 1857 investigations: C. Peter Ripley, ed., *The Black Abolitionist Papers*, vol. 2, *Canada, 1830–1865* (Chapel Hill: University of North Carolina Press, 1986), 81.

narratives published by Benjamin Drew: Drew, *North-Side View*.

"then a little village": Drew, 247–248.

"As to the negro paradise": Quoted in *Marion (SC) Star*, May 11, 1852, www.teachingushistory.org/documents/marionstar5111852.pdf.

"Becoming weary of Canada freedom": *Clarksville (TN) Chronicle*, August 5, 1859, 1, reprinting a report in the *Cleveland Democrat*.

"Beneath the pale light": Jared Hickman, *Black Prometheus: Race and Radicalism in the Age of Atlantic Slavery* (New York: Oxford University Press, 2016), 435n101.

"thoughtful" tan oval face: "Celebration at North Elba, the 4th of July Among the Adirondacks, the Journey to John Brown's House," Essex County, New York Genealogy and History, Genealogy Trails, http://genealogytrails.com/ny/essex/johnbrown.html.

West Chester . . . counted three hundred free blacks: William C. Kashatus, *Just over the Line: Chester County and the Underground Railroad* (West Chester, PA: Chester County Historical Society, 2002), 57.

a mere 4,509 enslaved persons in 1820: "Statistics of Slaves," US Census Bureau decennial report, 1860, https://www2.census.gov/prod2/decennial/documents/00165897ch14.pdf.

When Mary Ann was ten: "Mary Ann Shadd Cary (1823–1893)," in *Nine Black Women: An Anthology of Nineteenth-Century Writers from the United States, Canada, Bermuda and the Caribbean*, ed. Moira Ferguson (London: Routledge, 1998), 202.

Abraham Doras Shadd, was a conductor there: Mary Ann would also be listed with her father among the 132 Underground Railroad agents in West Chester in 1850. Kashatus, *Just over the Line*, 96.

By 1850, his estate was valued at: Kashatus, 57.

"I have been here more than a week": Kashatus, 62.

"Editors": Ripley, *Black Abolitionist Papers*, 367.

He returned to town on April 30: Richard J. Hinton, *John Brown and His Men, with Some Account of the Roads They Traveled to Reach Harper's Ferry* (New York: Funk & Wagnalls, 1894), 178, https://archive.org/details/john brownhismenw00hint.

John Kagi and Osborne Anderson acted as secretaries: Hinton, 175.

"a Puritan of the most exalted": Osborne Perry Anderson, *A Voice from Harper's Ferry: A Narrative of Events at Harper's Ferry* (Boston: self-pub., 1861), 9.

Delany was wary of his plans: Within three months, Delany would be exploring on behalf of a Chatham committee possible migration of blacks to the Niger Valley in Africa, a path he ultimately rejected.

"Whereas slavery . . . is . . . a most barbarous": Select Committee on the Harper's Ferry Invasion, US Senate, Rep. Com. no. 278 (June 15, 1850), appendix, 44–59.

James Monroe "Gunsmith" Jones: Jones was one of five brothers who attended Oberlin, of whom four graduated, including Gunsmith in 1849.

He would use his gunsmithing skills: Lubet, "Colored Hero," 23.

"He knew well": *New York Times*, August 19, 1883, 5.

"different from the slaves in the French West India Island": *New York Times*, August 19, 1883, 5. The reference is to the slave rebellion that grew into the anticolonial Haitian Revolution (1791–1804) and led to the island nation's independence from France. The successful revolt is said to have inspired Denmark Vesey to plan his aborted slave rebellion in Charleston, South Carolina, in 1822.

Copeland's role in spiriting him there: Two Copeland siblings would later state their belief that John Copeland had taken Price to Canada. See Villard Papers, letter and interview, 1908, quoted in Lubet, "Colored Hero," 101. See also Quarles, *Allies for Freedom*, 88. The presumption that Copeland and Price went to Chatham is based on Copeland's close association with Jones's younger brothers in Oberlin.

Elijah Leonard: Leonard was a native of Rochester, New York.

"A recognition of the injustice": *The Honorable Elijah Leonard: A Memoir* (London, ON: Advertiser Printing, 1894), 47–48, https://ia902303.us.archive.org/35/items/cihm_08560/cihm_08560.pdf.

"As an agent appointed": Ripley, *Black Abolitionist Papers*, 392–393.

"If in releasing this boy": Barrington Walker, *Race on Trial: Black Defendants in Ontario's Criminal Courts, 1858–1958* (Toronto: University of Toronto Press, 2010), 37–38.

Chatham boasted nearly forty-five thousand people in 2011: "Population by Community 2016," Chatham-Kent website, www.chatham-kent.ca/Economic Development/LabourForceStatistics/Demographics/Pages/population%20 by%20community.aspx.

she was awarded the coveted Canadian National Griot: The Griot is awarded by the Canadian National Griot Association of Edmonton, Alberta, to a person of African descent or "individuals who are sensitive to the issues, or share values, goals and objectives of people of African descent." See a flier from Dorothy Williams's website: http://dorothywilliams.ca/pdf/XWF-0004.PDF.

A. D. Shadd Road: A. D. Shadd Road was renamed in 1994 for Abraham Shadd. Highway 401 is also known as the King's Highway, but popularly known as the 401 or MacDonald-Cartier Freeway, for two Canadian Confederation founders, Sir John A. MacDonald and Sir George-Étienne Cartier.

Chapter 5: The Road to Harpers Ferry

The 2016 book John Brown to James Brown: Ed Maliskas, *John Brown to James Brown: The Little Farm Where Liberty Budded, Blossomed, and Boogied* (Hagerstown, MD: Hamilton Run, 2016).

The farmhouse is still visible: See the official website for the farmhouse: http://johnbrown.org/restoration.

"We love our history": South T. Lynn, interview by author, May 10, 2017.

The two-and-a-half-story stone-and-log house: Dr. Robert F. Kennedy purchased the property in 1852. He is repeatedly referred to as "Booth Kennedy" in many accounts. For more information on the history of the house and its ownership, see the Historic American Buildings Survey from the Library of Congress: https://cdn.loc.gov/master/pnp/habshaer/md/md0500/md0587/data /md0587data.pdf. For photographs of the house taken in 1958, see the Maryland Historical Trust website: https://mht.maryland.gov/secure/medusa/PDF /Washington/WA-III-030.pdf.

"horses, mules, oxen": David S. Reynolds, *John Brown, Abolitionist: The Man Who Killed Slavery, Sparked the Civil War, and Seeded Civil Rights* (New York: Alfred A. Knopf, 2005), 278.

Several of the raiders also stayed there: "John Brown House," National Park Service, www.nps.gov/nr/travel/underground/pa2.htm.

an important stop on the Underground Railroad: Magdalena Radovic-Moreno, "Mercersburg's 'Little Africa': Free African American Communities of Franklin County and the Underground Railroad," Franklin County, Pennsylvania, website, http://franklincountypa.gov/index.php?section=archives_blog/little_africa.

Shields Green: According to most accounts, Shields Green, also known as Esau Brown, was born enslaved in 1836 and escaped from a Charleston, South Carolina, plantation, boarding a northbound ship in the harbor, most likely in mid-1857. He eventually resided with Frederick Douglass in Rochester, New York, where he met John Brown in February 1858. He was still in Rochester that July, according to his dated business card announcing his services as a clothes cleaner. The identity of his owner is unknown, but it is possible he was the property of Alexander H. Brown, a Charleston district sheriff and lawyer who also owned a 550-acre plantation on the Ashley River, which flows through the city into the harbor. A. H. Brown, as he is referred to in Census records, was a large slaveholder, with an "inventory" of fifty-eight enslaved men and women in 1850—including a fourteen-year old boy, who may have been Shields (see the Census record available on Family Search: www.family search.org/ark:/61903/1:1:MVZG-1V1). He had fifty-three slaves in 1860. The 1860 slave Census includes a three-year old boy who might have been the son Shields left behind. All of this is conjecture. During the period, the *Charleston Mercury* contains many ads offering rewards for runaway slaves but none easily identified as the elusive Esau Brown/Shields Green, whose name change is also a mystery. Alexander Henry Brown, meanwhile, was a member of the state's secession commission and during the Civil War was assistant provost marshal at Charleston. He died in 1873.

He reportedly worked as a sailor: Sidney Kaplan, "The American Seamen's Protective Union Association of 1863: A Pioneer Organization of Negro Seamen in the Port of New York," *Science and Society* 21 (1957): 155, www .jstor.org/stable/pdf/40400494.pdf?refreqid=excelsior%3A492da0a949967007 2f818b1722c821d8.

"CLOTHES CLEANING": William C. Nell, letter to the editor, *Pine and Palm*, July 6, 1861.

"Shields Green was not one to shrink": Frederick Douglass, *The Life and Times of Frederick Douglass: From 1817 to 1882* (London, 1882), 276–277, http://lf-oll .s3.amazonaws.com/titles/2007/Douglass_1349_Bk.pdf.

"an uncommonly brave man": Nell, letter to the editor.

"a beginning in his work": Douglass, *Life and Times*, 277.

"and told them where and for what": Douglass, 277. The Rev. James Newton Gloucester was an active supporter of the Underground Railroad, financial contributor to John Brown, and friend of Frederick Douglass. He founded the Siloam Presbyterian Church in Brooklyn in 1849 and in later life was also a physician. See "Black Wealth and the 1843 National Colored Convention James Gloucester," Colored Conventions, http://coloredconventions.org /exhibits/show/exhibit-1843/biographies/james-gloucester.

"going into a perfect steel-trap": Douglass, 390.

Douglass . . . declined to go along: Brown cited Douglass's cowardice as one reason for the latter's demurral in an October 31, 1859, letter he wrote from Canada West to the *Rochester Democrat*. John H. Zittle, comp., *A Correct History of the John Brown Invasion, at Harper's Ferry, West VA* (Hagerstown, MD: Matt Publishing, 1906), 235, https://archive.org/details/correcthistoryof00zitt.

"and was surprised by his coolly saying": Douglass, 278.

"Oh, what a poor fool I am": Oswald Garrison Villard, *John Brown: A Biography, 1800–1859* (Garden City, NY: Doubleday, Duran, 1929), 414. Owen Brown dictated his recollections to Ruth Brown Thompson, another Brown daughter.

"to see if any express packages": Franklin Benjamin Sanborn, *Recollections of Seventy Years* (Boston: Gorham Press, 1909), 1:182, https://archive.org/details /recollectionsse01sanbgoog.

"Shields Green was a perfect rattlebrain": Sanborn, 179. Sanborn interviewed Annie Brown.

"found an efficient hand": Hinton, *John Brown and His Men*, 262.

"I walked alone as far as Middletown": Anderson, *Voice from Harper's Ferry*, 23. Middletown Borough, in southern Dauphin County, Pennsylvania, is on the east shore of the Susquehanna River, ten miles southeast of Harrisburg. But it is about seventy miles to the Mason-Dixon Line, not near the line, as Anderson wrote. He may have meant Middleburg, which is just across the Mason-Dixon Line in Washington County, Maryland.

"It nearly broke up the camp": Peter Marshall and David Manuel, *Sounding Forth the Trumpet: 1837–1860* (Grand Rapids, MI: Revell, 1999), 272.

"to cool off": Villard, *John Brown*, 416.

"earnest, fearless, determined company": Anderson, *Voice from Harper's Ferry*, 23.

"accustomed to being confined": Villard, *John Brown*, 419.

"rough, unsightly, and aged": Anderson, *Voice from Harper's Ferry*, 24.

"no less than four": Anderson, 20.

Others related variations: In a letter to his wife Isabell (Bell), in North Elba, Watson
Brown shared Newby's story and wrote of five murders and one suicide in the
area, which he said had only solidified his support for the mission. See also Bonnie
Laughlin-Schultz, *The Tie That Bound Us: The Women of John Brown's Family and
the Legacy of Radical Abolitionism* (Ithaca, NY: Cornell University Press, 2013), 60.

"A fine slave man near our headquarters": Villard, *John Brown*, 423.

And Watson Brown, in a letter to his wife: Villard, 416. Watson Brown wrote his wife
Bell, "There was a slave near where we live whose wife was sold to go South the
other day and he was found hanging in Thomas Kennedy's orchard, dead, the
next morning." In his letter, Watson also shared the story of Dangerfield Newby
and his enslaved family.

"Newby seemed a good-natured": Sanborn, *Recollections*, 179.

"Newby was quiet, sensible": Villard, *John Brown*, 419.

"Poor man": Laughlin-Schultz, *Tie That Bound Us*, 60.

"one bright hope": "2009 African American Trailblazers."

"I never heard John Brown pray": Anderson, *Voice from Harper's Ferry*, 24.

"We applied a preparation": Anderson, 25.

"the negro man with Congo face": Hinton, *John Brown and His Men*, 507.

"The men then sobered down": Villard, *John Brown*, 420.

They departed Oberlin on October 10: Lubet, *"Colored Hero,"* 136.

"a number of the wealthier citizens": James Redpath, *The Public Life of Captain John
Brown: With an Autobiography of His Childhood and Youth* (Boston: Thayer and
Eldridge, 1860), 243.

"induced to leave their masters": Zittle, *Correct History*, 17.

John Brown decided to move the date up a week: Hinton, *John Brown and His Men*, 271.

"applicable to the condition": Anderson, *Voice from Harper's Ferry*, 28.

"It has been a matter of inquiry": Anderson, 15.

Green was accorded the honor: J. Ewing Glasgow, *The Harpers Ferry Insurrection:
Being an Account of the Outbreak in Virginia and of the Trial and Execution of
Captain John Brown, Its Hero* (Edinburgh: Myles Macphail, 1860), 18, http://
historyonline.chadwyck.co.uk/getImage?productsuffix=_studyunits&action=pr
intview&in=gif&out=pdf&src=/bap/bap00026/conv/bap00026.pdf&IE=.pdf.

Copeland was to become a judge: Cecil B. Eby, "The Last Hours of the John Brown
Raid: The Narrative of David H. Strother," *Virginia Magazine* 73 (1965): 169–177.

Owen Brown, Barclay Coppoc, and F. J. Merriam would stay behind: Anderson,
Voice from Harper's Ferry, 28–29.

"Men, get on your arms": Villard, *John Brown*, 427.

"as solemnly as a funeral procession": Anderson, *Voice from Harper's Ferry*, 32.

Chapter 6: The Raid

"Anderson being a colored man": Anderson, *Voice from Harper's Ferry*, 31.

"we met some colored men": Anderson, 34.

"You can have my slaves": Anderson, 34.

"speechless or terrified": Anderson, 35, 41.

The raiders then hustled Washington: Text of indictment of October 26, 1859, in the *New-York Evening Post* 58, no. 258, 1. According to a contemporary account in the *Baltimore American*, excerpted in the *New York Weekly Anglo-African*, October 26, 1858, the raiders took twelve Washington slaves with them from Beallair.

They reached his two-story frame house between 1 and 2 AM: John Allstadt remembered the time as closer to 3 AM when he "heard a rapping on our chamber door" and rose from his bed and Brown's men broke through the front door to confront him. In his version, seven—not six—of his slaves were also taken, and Washington rode in his carriage ahead of the wagon. Zittle, *Correct History*, 48.

"our six negroes": John Thomas Allstadt, interview by Katherine Mayo, in Villard Papers, 641n35.

the fire engine house inside the armory yard: John Thomas Allstadt, the last survivor of the raid, lived until 1923, and the two-story stone house remained in the family during his lifetime. The 1830 house survives, off Route 340, two miles west of Harpers Ferry. It has been on the National Historic Register since 1985. See the National Historic Register of Historic Places inventory nomination form: www .wvculture.org/shpo/nr/pdf/jefferson/85000767.pdf.

"an old colored lady": Anderson, *Voice from Harper's Ferry*, 34.

"I came here from Kansas": Philip S. Foner, *History of Black Americans: From the Compromise of 1850 to the End of the Civil War* (Westport, CT: Greenwood, 1983), 252.

"Thus, the first victim": *Winchester (VA) Evening Star*, August 29, 1901.

"one of the most respectable free negroes": Boteler owned fifteen slaves, according to the 1860 US Federal Census slave schedules. He would later represent Virginia's Tenth District in the Confederate House of Representatives and serve in the Confederate Army. *Century Magazine*, July 1883, 399–411, reprinted in the *Washington Post*, July 1, 1883, 3.

"Had he stood when ordered": Anderson, *Voice from Harper's Ferry*, 35.

"in fact the only thing that prevented": Joseph Barry, *The Strange Story of Harper's Ferry: With Legends of the Surrounding Country* (Martinsburg, WV: Thompson Brothers, 1903), 84, https://archive.org/details/strangestoryof ha00barr.

"Last night a band of ruffians": Mary E. Mauzy to Eugenia Burton, 17 October 1859, Harpers Ferry National Historical Park Archives.

"hurried from cell to cell": John G. Rosengarten, "John Brown's Raid: How I Got Into It, and How I Got Out Of It," *Atlantic Monthly*, June 1865, 711–717.

Shortly before noon: Alexander Boteler, "Recollections of the John Brown Raid by a Virginian Who Witnessed the Fight," *Century Magazine*, July 1883, 399–411.

Newby fatally shot him first: Joseph Barry, a Harpers Ferry resident present during the skirmishes, in his account published forty-four years later, credited Shields Green with the murder of Boerly. Barry, *Strange Story*, 68.

a sniper took Newby down: Who fired the shot or shots that killed Newby is unclear. A man named Bogart, said to be an armory worker, is mentioned in a 1909 account by the Rev. Samuel Vanderlip Leech; Richard B. Washington in others. Leech also wrote that someone else shot Newby in the stomach: "I saw him die, in great agony, with an infuriated crowd around him." *The Raid of John Brown at Harper's Ferry as I Saw It* (Washington, DC: self-pub., 1909), 8, https://archive.org/stream/raidofjohnbrowna02leec#page/n5/mode/2up.

"Newby was a brave fellow": Anderson, *Voice from Harper's Ferry*, 40.

"I saw his body": Anderson, 40.

"The huge mulatto that shot": Redpath, *Public Life of John Brown*, 259.

"rather pleasant face and address": Barry, *Strange Story*, 80.

"Poor doomed Harpers Ferry": Mary E. Mauzy to Eugenia Burton, 8 November 1859, Harpers Ferry National Historical Park.

"African Slavery": "Resolutions Passed by the General Assembly of South Carolina in Response to John Brown's Raid of Harper's Ferry, 1859," Teaching US History in South Carolina, www.teachingushistory.org/ttrove/johnbrown.htm.

"may be considered as the commencement": Barry, *Strange Story*, 95.

"showered it with a shower": *Baltimore Sun*, October 19, 1859, quoted in Gordon L. Iseminger, "The Second Raid on Harpers Ferry," *Pennsylvania History: A Journal of Mid-Atlantic Studies* 71, no. 2 (April 2004): 137.

Thompson . . . was taken to the Wager House: Some other accounts say Thompson was taken to the Gault hotel. See Leech, *Raid of John Brown*, 8.

"a negro of the darkest hue": Barry, *Strange Story*, 83.

"three colored men": Anderson, *Voice from Harper's Ferry*, 49.

"On entering the river": John Anthony Copeland to Addison Halbert, 10 December 1859.

"He was a young man": Barry, 83.

"I was pulled out": Copeland to Halbert, 10 December 1859.

"Stepping between the two": Charles White to his brother-in-law, 10 November 1859, quoted in "John Brown's Raid at Harpers Ferry, an Eyewitness Account by Charles White," ed. Rayburn S. Moore, *Virginia Magazine of History and Biography* 67, no. 4 (October 1959): 390.

"During the affair": White, 390.

"that we could be of no further avail": Anderson, *Voice from Harper's Ferry*, 36.

"The charge of deserting": Anderson, 46.

"a prisoner": Villard, *John Brown*, 445–446.

he and Hazlett walked along the river: In his post-raid account, Anderson wrote that when they left the arsenal, he and Hazlett walked along the Shenandoah. That seems implausible, as the arsenal bordered the Potomac, and the men would have had to cross the Lower Town, heavily occupied by militia and armed citizens, without being seen to reach the other river. It seems more likely that they walked upriver along the Potomac.

"the heavens are illuminated": *Richmond (VA) Enquirer*, quoted in Reynolds, *John Brown, Abolitionist*, 380.

He noted in his diary: Diary of Edmund Ruffin, from the John Brown Raid Miscellaneous Papers (Mss1P4299d) in the collection of the Virginia Historical Society, Richmond. The diary was transcribed by Boyd B. Stutler, West Virginia author and historian. It is also available in the Winchester Historical Society at the Hanley Library, in Winchester, Virginia. The diary was also reprinted in the *Ranson (WV) Jefferson Republican*, September 20, 1951, 12–15, 18, 20, 21, 24. It is also available on microfilm at the Library of Congress (MSS51839).

"Many, who started to join": Redpath, *Public Life of John Brown*, 244.

"People may say what they please": Foner, *History of Black Americans*, 256–257.

"actively informed": Hinton, *John Brown and His Men*, 272–273.

"rallied fifty slaves to his standard": Libby, *Black Voices from Harpers Ferry: Osborne Anderson and the John Brown Raid* (Berkeley: self-pub., 1979), 105.

"The negroes proved ready": Libby, 140.

"For slaveholders": Libby, 125.

Shields Green . . . tried to blend in with the slaves: Tony Horwitz, *Midnight Rising: John Brown and the Raid That Sparked the Civil War* (New York: Henry Holt, 2011), 179.

"repelled the idea that his design": In an address to the Virginia legislature, quoted in Wise, *Life of Henry A. Wise*, 245.

"a fanatic, vain and garrulous": Wise, 247.

"on the ground that his": Whether Allstadt received compensation from the state is not known. One other slaveholder filed a similar claim. Dr. W. McP. Fuller

of Winchester sought compensation for the death of Jim, a light mulatto slave he'd hired out to Lewis Washington who had returned to Beallair after visiting his mother. There he learned of the hostage taking and said, according to his mother's affidavit, "If they have taken Mr. Washington, they must take me too & I am going to see what they are going to do with Mr. Washington." At Harpers Ferry, the insurgents handed him a pike and directed him to the rifle works to stand guard. According to the petition, Jim sought to flee and drowned in the millrace or Shenandoah River. The Virginia Committee of Claims rejected the petition on grounds that Jim "joined the rebels with good will." *Journal of the House of Delegates of the State of Virginia, for the Session 1859–1860* (Richmond: William F. Ritchie), 175. See also "Petition: John H. Allstadt," in Horwitz, *Midnight Rising*, 223.

the Mount Vernon Collection at Beallair: In July 2016, homes were priced from $389,00 to $494,900, except for the three-level "Summerhill" model, with 5,500 square feet, whose price was $650,000, less than the $850,000 it cost to build at the height of the 2000s' real estate boom. Seventy-five homes occupied the old Lewis Washington plantation, of 418 projected.

Louisa Beall Lane: Beall was the surname of Lewis Washington's mother and stepmother.

Chapter 7: Trial and Punishment

The courthouse: In May 1986, the Leetown Chapter #236 United Daughters of the Confederacy succeeded in having a plaque mounted next to the courthouse entrance "in honor and memory of the Confederate soldiers of Jefferson County, who served in the War Between the States." Then, three days after clashes in Charlottesville, Virginia over a Confederate statue in August 2017, six local African American women wrote to the county commissioners, asking that the bronze plaque "sanctifying the Confederacy" be removed. After a contentious hearing, the five white commissioners rejected their request, even though the local UDC chapter did not oppose the removal and suggested another plaque be erected somewhere else honoring soldiers on both sides of the conflict. The controversy underscored the lingering aftereffects of the war fought to end slavery after more than 150 years in the very county where John Brown and his raiders lit the spark that ignited the conflict.

The 1850 Census for Jefferson County: Marcia J. Drucker, ed., *A Bicentennial History: Jefferson County, West Virginia, 1801–2001* (Martinsburg, WV: Jefferson County Bicentennial Committee, 2001), 97.

In the 1860 presidential election: P. Douglas Perks, "'. . . How I Should Love to Know How My Own Dear Husband Is This Night': 1863 in Mr. Jefferson's County," *Magazine of the Jefferson County Historical Society*, 2013, 60n21.

Their cell had one window: Anderson, *Voice from Harper's Ferry*, 49–50.

Shepherd "in and upon the back and side": The indictment uses *Sheppard* instead of the correct spelling of *Shepherd*, according to Census and other records.

"even though he was literate": David Hunter Strother, "Trial of the Conspirators," *Harpers Weekly*, November 12, 1859, quoted in Quarles, *Allies for Freedom*, 134. Though his family had divided loyalties and Strother was unsympathetic to the abolitionist cause, he served as a commissioned officer in the Union Army during the Civil War.

"You will prepare for the execution of Brown": Order of November 24, 1859, Villard Papers, 523, 649n44.

"vulgar letters every day": Henry A. Wise Executive Papers, 1859, Library of Virginia (hereafter "Wise Papers"), 4220:302, 334.

"every mail": Wise Papers, 4219:303–304.

"and his confederates": Wise Papers, 4219:187–201.

"by express": Wise Papers, 4219:340–341. Also in the Wise Papers (4219:336) is a "For Sale" broadside, dated December 19, 1859, advertising "Mementoes of OLD BROWN," including "tears shed by the worshippers of 'OLD BROWN,' warranted genuine. Also a piece of his shirt, price one dollar per square inch . . . A piece of 'OLD BROWN's' had will be in view at the 'Union Meeting' at the Academy of Music to-night."

"They number about sixteen": Wise Papers, 4219:333.

Andrew H. Hunter: After the Civil War, Hunter would file an unsuccessful suit to return Jefferson and Berkeley Counties to Virginia from the breakaway state of West Virginia.

"George Sennott has come": "More Humor of the Local Press," *New-York Daily Tribune*, November 9, 1859, 6.

"doing his damndest": *New-York Daily Tribune*, November 9, 1859, 6. The newspaper used a long dash instead of using the word "damndest," but the term is easily surmised from context.

Green's one-day trial took place on November 3: Hunter was annoyed by Green's "boldly careless bearing." Foner, *History of Black Americans*, 256.

"It was the climax of tyranny": *New York Herald*, November 17, 1859, quoted in Quarles, *Allies for Freedom*, 110.

fifteen dollars in travel money: Accounts vary between $15 and $17.50.

"protested their ignorance": *Baltimore Sun*, November 14, 1859.

"the utmost silence was observed": *Charlestown Virginia Free Press*, November 17, 1859.

"predetermined purpose": *Charlestown Virginia Free Press*, November 17, 1859.

a large Victorian home, at 515 South Samuel Street: The National Register of Historic Places nomination says this was the site of Brown's hanging but makes no mention of the executions there of Copeland, Green, Cook, and Coppoc: www .wvculture.org/shpo/nr/pdf/jefferson/83003238.pdf.

he is buried in the town's Edge Hill Cemetery: "John Thomas Gibson," Find a Grave, www.findagrave.com/cgi-bin/fg.cgi?page=gr&GRid=10302168.

"Copeland was the prisoner who impressed me": *St. Louis Globe-Democrat*, April 8, 1888, quoted in Andrew Hunter, "John Brown's Raid," *Publications of the Southern History Association*, July 1897, 32.

"small silver coin for remembrance": Franklin Benjamin Sanborn, ed., *The Life and Letters of John Brown, Liberator of Kansas, and Martyr of Virginia* (Boston: Roberts Brothers, 1885), 625, https://archive.org/details/lifeandlettersof00san brich. A different source puts the exact amount at a quarter each. Thomas Drew, *The John Brown Invasion, an Authentic History of the Harpers Ferry Tragedy with Full Details of the Capture, Trial, and Execution of the Invaders, and of All the Incidents Connected Therewith* (Boston: James Campbell, 1860), 67, https:// archive.org/details/johnbrowninvasio00drew. The descriptions of the executions of Brown and the others are identical to those contained in Sanborn's book published twenty-five years later.

"The day opened beautifully": Account carried in the *Charlestown Virginia Free Press*, December 8, 1859.

"I, John Brown, am now certain": *New York Times*, December 3, 1859, 4.

"I am ready at any time": Sanborn, *Life and Letters*, 626. Among the Virginia militia at the scaffold was future Lincoln assassin John Wilkes Booth, who had left a stage performance in Richmond to join Company F, which was deployed to Charlestown. Sanborn attributes this to the Virginia correspondent of the *New-York Tribune*, November 28, 1859.

"He is a man of clear head": Wise, *Life of Henry A. Wise*, 246.

"a few lines": Wise Papers, 4218:672, microfilmed July 2003.

"with only five short days remaining": Wise Papers, 4220:83–84.

"Last night for the last time": "The Letters of John A. Copeland: A Hero of the Harpers Ferry Raid," Electronic Oberlin Group, www2.oberlin.edu/external /EOG/Copeland/copeland_letters.htm.

"If I am dying for freedom": *Annual Report of the Anti-Slavery Society* (New York: American Anti-Slavery Society, 1861), 135, quoted in Nat Brandt, *Town That Started the War*, 243.

did not print its own account until six days: *Charlestown Virginia Free Press*, December 22, 1859.

"The prisoners mounted the scaffold": *Vincennes (IN) Weekly Western Sun*, December 24, 1869. Estimates on the crowd varied. The *Weekly Western Sun* said there were 1,600 witnesses to the Copeland and Green executions.

James A. Tolbert Sr.: Tolbert died before the publication of this book, on October 26, 2017. He was eighty-five.

Chapter 8: Remains of the Day

"Mary, I would like you to": Bob Davis, "John Brown's Body," Bob Davis Reveals, *New York Sun*, 1932. The Thompson brothers were related by marriage to the Brown family. Their brother Henry Thompson married Brown's oldest daughter (with his first wife) Ruth (1829–1904), who died in 1832. In 1858, the Thompsons' sister, Isabella, married Watson Brown, John Brown's son who was later killed at Harpers Ferry.

"for dissection": Wise Papers, 4219: page unknown.

"conveyed to Harpers Ferry": *Charlestown Virginia Free Press*, December 8, 1859.

"with dignity and decency": Henry A. Wise, message to the Senate and House of Delegates of the Virginia General Assembly, December 1859, *Doc. No. I. Governor's Message and Reports of the Public Officers of the State, of the Boards of Directors, and of the Visitors, Superintendents, and other Agents of Public Institutions or Interests of Virginia* (Richmond: William F. Ritchie, 1859).

guarded overnight by six men: Foner, *History of Black Americans*, 258.

"They belonged to the oppressed": Webb, *Life and Letters*, 323–341. Webb, identifying himself as the editor, was an Irish publisher and abolitionist.

the remains of Watson Brown and Jeremiah Anderson went to the medical college: John Kagi's body was also handed over to the medical college in Winchester for dissection. When Union soldiers burned the college in June 1862, Jarvis Johnson, the federal doctor in charge, removed the carefully preserved specimen of Watson Brown to his Indiana home. Nearly twenty years later, he "freely and willingly" surrendered the body to John Brown Jr. so that it could be "interred in free soil." This was done at North Elba on October 13, 1882. Featherstonhaugh, "John Brown's Men," 21. The remains of Aaron Stevens and Albert Hazlett, executed by hanging on March 16, 1860, had been buried in what was known as the socialist cemetery in Englewood, New Jersey. See the *Indiana (PA) Gazette*, July 3, 1976, F24, www.newspapers.com/image/14050202. Their remains were also later transferred to North Elba for reburial.

"an ex-surgeon of the Rebel army": *Huntington (IN) Weekly Herald*, June 22, 1894, 2. Born in 1849 to a French father and a mother from Virginia, Featherstonhaugh was an 1870 graduate of the College of Physicians and Surgeons in Albany, New York.

"mysterious visitor": Bob Davis, "John Brown's Body," *Phoenix Arizona Republic*, March 12, 1933, 31. The column also ran in the *New York Sun*, copyrighted 1932.

his plan to unearth the raiders' remains: Alfred Lee Donaldson, *A History of the Adirondacks* (New York: Century, 1921), 2:19–23, http://bit.ly/2tkYcWd. This volume contains the most detailed and local account of the reburial as seen from North Elba.

"Rescued from Oblivion": *New York World*, September 22, 1895.

"were, of course, much decayed": Thomas Featherstonhaugh, "The Final Burial of the Followers of John Brown," *New England Magazine*, April 1901, 133.

"One of the skulls": Featherstonhaugh, "John Brown's Men," 21–24. The 1899 ("John Brown's Men") and 1901 ("Final Burial") articles differ in some details, specifically the number of remains, seven in the first account, eight in the second. Leary's name is not among those listed on the North Elba memorial table of those buried there in 1899. Featherstonhaugh found an extra femur in the remains and, apparently, concluded it belonged to Leary, but that conclusion may not be definitive. Further adding to the mystery of Leary's remains is the fabled shawl that Leary's widow, Mary, told her grandson Langston Hughes belonged to the fallen raider. How she came by the tattered garment is not entirely clear, but Hughes, the famous Harlem Renaissance author and poet, recalled that she covered him with it as a blanket when he was a child. See "Lewis Sheridan Leary's Shawl," *Steam at Harper's Ferry*, August 27, 2014, https://steamathf.wordpress.com/2014/08/27/lewis-sheridan -learys-shawl. According to another second-hand account, "From a friend, Mary Leary Langston received the bullet-ridden, bloodstained shawl worn by her first husband when he was critically wounded . . . that he wore at his death." Carmaletta M. Williams and John Edgar Tidwell, eds., *My Dear Boy: Carrie Hughes's Letters to Langston Hughes, 1926–1938* (Athens: University of Georgia Press, 2013), xxiii, 46. Yet another account can be found in Elizabeth Dowling Taylor, *The Original Black Elite: Daniel Murray and the Story of a Forgotten Era* (New York: Amistad, 2017), 215–216. When donating the shawl to the Ohio Historical Society in 1943, Langston Hughes passed along the family tradition

that "'some good person' had sent the muddy woolen cloth to his grandmother Mary shortly after the 1859 raid. Such a provenance is doubtful, to say the least. . . . It is improbable that a sympathetic soul, who might have retrieved Leary's blanket and sent it to his widow, was on the scene." Taylor speculates that Richard J. Hinton, a comrade and biographer of Brown, gave Mary the blanket shawl during his visit to Kansas in 1900. "It can only be said that it was one of the blanket shawls found with what was left of the bodies, given that just a single set of remains could be individually identified."

Libby repacked the remains: Donaldson, *History of the Adirondacks*, 20.

"fired a volley": *Harrisburg (PA) Telegraph*, September 4, 1899, 4.

Their letter elicited no response: *New York Weekly Anglo-African*, January 14, 1860.

"colored citizens": *Frederick Douglass' Paper*, February 17, 1860.

"I dislike to trouble you": Wise Papers, 4220:133–134.

"Item: Gov. Wise has ordered": *Oberlin (OH) Evangelist*, December 21, 1859, 202–203.

James Madison Monroe: Monroe, a professor of rhetoric and belles lettres from 1849–1862, served as both a state representative and state senator; was US consul at Rio de Janeiro, 1863–1870; and a five-term Congressman, 1871–1881.

"The body of Copeland was not there": James Monroe, *Oberlin Thursday Lectures, Addresses and Essays* (Oberlin, OH: Edward J. Goodrich, 1897), 157–183, https://archive.org/details/oberlinthursday01monr. Monroe's recollection is the only testimony that puts Shields Green in Oberlin prior to the raid. Other sources have questioned whether he had ever visited the town.

"They were grateful to God": In May 1862, Union troops exacted some measure of revenge by torching the Winchester medical college, an act attributed to the army's New England doctors and chaplains. The school was "obliterated" and the ground, belonging to the state, was sold. Monroe, 177.

"Green so far as is known": Lubet says that Monroe "erroneously believed that he had known Green in Oberlin. The mistake was discovered, but it was retained as a gesture of respect for his sacrifice." "A Monument," *Anglo-American Magazine*, January 14, 1860. Additionally, J. M. Fitch wrote to James Redpath about the exclusion of Newby: "At one point, the Oberliners also considered including Dangerfield Newby's name on their monument, but it was ultimately decided to include only those who were once believed to have some connection to Oberlin." July 17, 1860, Richard Hinton Collection, Kansas State Historical Society.

"Copeland was a member": *Oberlin (OH) Evangelist*, February 1, 1860, 23.

"to mingle their tears": *New York Weekly Anglo-African*, January 14, 1860.

gave nearly $175 for the monument: The equivalent of nearly $5,000 in 2017 dollars.

"was but little known to us": *New York Weekly Anglo-African*, January 14, 1860.

forty dollars for Leary's widow: The money was to be forwarded to J. J. Fitch, treasurer of the Oberlin monument committee. "The Colored American Heroes of Harper's Ferry," in *William Cooper Nell*, 579.

The eight-foot marble cenotaph: In 1971, the cenotaph was moved to Martin Luther King Jr. Park on East Vine Street, close to downtown Oberlin and opposite the home of Wilson Bruce Evans, the brother of Delilah Copeland, John Anthony's mother.

L. S. Leary, died . . . October 20, 1859: The date on the cenotaph for Leary's death is incorrect. He was mortally wounded October 17 and died October 18.

enlisted in . . . a white unit: Brenda Pitts confirmed in an email to the author on June 20, 2017, that William served in a white unit, as did his and John Anthony's uncle Wilson Bruce Evans.

killed in the line of duty: *Oberlin (OH) News-Tribune*, July 16, 2002, 7. William Copeland was killed by a jail trustee on work release. See "William L Copeland, 12/30/1885," Little Rock Fraternal Order of Police, Lodge #17, http://www.lrfop .org/?zone=/unionactive/view_article.cfm&HomeID=398676&page=LRPD20 Memorial20Page.

"Liberty won only by white men": Foner, *History of Black Americans*, 357–358.

"a pleasant company": *Oberlin (OH) Weekly News*, August 19, 1881.

"one of the most prominent representatives": *Oberlin (OH) News*, January 11, 1894.

"Brenda Pitts is steeped in the history": Also steeped in Copeland family history was US Army sergeant Jonathon Michael Hunter of Columbus, Indiana, who died from a suicide bomb attack on August 23, 2017, near Kandahar in Afghanistan at the age of twenty-three. "Jonathon was raised with the family history and had attended family reunions in Oberlin," Brenda Pitts wrote in an email on August 5, 2017. "Like his Uncle John, he was sensitive, caring, and generous with a strong desire to make a difference in the lives of others."

Chapter 9: The Aftermath

changed clothes three times: Anderson, *Voice from Harper's Ferry*, 55.

"His own father turned him out": Sanborn, *Recollections*, 1:278; Tom Huntington, "Escape from Harpers Ferry," *American History Magazine*, April 2017, www .historynet.com/escape-from-harpers-ferry.htm.

Anderson made his way: Charley Garlick, interview by Katherine Mayo, January 2, 1909, Villard Papers.

"escaped to the mountains": *Detroit Free Press*, April 24, 1881, 12.

"false and willful statement": New York Weekly Anglo-African, April 28, 1860.

"the edifice shook": New York Weekly Anglo-African, April 28, 1860.

"All rushed forward": New York Weekly Anglo-African, July 7, 1860.

"a tall, handsome mulatto": Boston Liberator, July 27, 1860, 2.

"Mr. Anderson is a young colored man": Douglass' Monthly, February 1861, quoted in "Celebration at North Elba, the 4th of July Among the Adirondacks, the Journey to John Brown's House," Essex County, New York Genealogy and History, Genealogy Trails, http://genealogytrails.com/ny/essex/johnbrown.html.

"for prudential reasons": Boston Liberator, January 11, 1861.

"disposed of quite a number of his books": Douglass' Monthly, February 1861.

enlisted under an assumed name: Anderson may still have worried about the criminal charges he faced from Harpers Ferry, though that seems unlikely, given that the charging state was now at war with the United States. Speculation that he enrolled under an alias revolves around the assumption—without documented proof—that he enrolled at all.

the second woman to do so: J. Clay Smith Jr., *Emancipation: The Making of the Black Lawyer, 1844–1944* (Philadelphia: University of Pennsylvania Press, 1993), 18, 55.

In 1885, she delivered a speech: Smith, 300.

An active suffragist, she tried registering to vote: Jane Rhodes, *Mary Ann Shadd Cary: The Black Press and Protest in the Nineteenth Century* (Bloomington: Indiana University Press, 1998), 195.

"not . . . as a gift": Philadelphia Christian Recorder, October 26, 1872.

"is in feeble health": Washington National Republican, November 12, 1872, 4.

"sick and suffering man": Washington Chronicle, November 13, 1872.

"the citizens and sojourners": Washington Chronicle, November 13, 1872.

"His disease is consumption": Saint Clairsville (OH) Belmont Chronicle, November 28, 1872, 2.

"the midnight assassin": Charlestown Spirit of Jefferson, November 26, 1872, 2, attributing the information and resolutions to the Washington Chronicle, a radical Republican newspaper published in various editions from 1862 to 1875. The *Lynchburg Virginian* referred to the paper as "the President's organ," an apparent reference to newly elected Republican president Ulysses S. Grant.

John M. Langston: Born free in Louisa County, Virginia, John M. Langston was one of the first two African Americans admitted to Oberlin College, where he earned a bachelor's degree in 1849 and a degree in theology in 1852. He was admitted to the Ohio bar in 1854. He recruited for blacks to serve in Union regiments during the Civil War, and in 1868 moved to Washington to become dean of Howard University's law school. He also served briefly as a congressman from Virginia. The great uncle of poet Langston Hughes, Langston is buried in Woodlawn Cemetery in southeast Washington, DC.

"aged father": Exact newspaper is unknown.

Both would be discharged: Kashatus, *Just Over the Line*, 97–98.

Sometime during the first half of 1860: The exact month and date are unknown because no bill of sale has been found.

"free white males": Official Copy of the Militia Law of Louisiana, Adopted by the State Legislature, January 23, 1862, 1, https://archive.org/stream /officialcopyofmi01loui#page/n3/mode/2up.

"She came north after": Alfred Hawkes, interview by Katherine Mayo, January 2, 1909, Villard Papers.

Her return as "Harriet Robinson": Her arrival is documented in records of the Freedmen's Bureau, more properly the Bureau of Refugees, Freedmen and Abandoned Lands, established by the federal government in 1865 to aid former slaves in the Reconstruction South.

By 1880, Robinson and one of his daughters: Scott E. Casper, *Sarah Johnson's Mount Vernon: The Forgotten History of an American Shrine* (New York: Hill and Wang, 2008), 171–172.

"My white troops were exhausted": William Farrar Smith, *From Chattanooga to Petersburg Under Generals Grant and Butler: A Contribution to the History of the War, and a Personal Vindication* (Boston: Houghton, Mifflin, 1893), 24–25, https://archive.org/details/cu31924030905495.

Pvt. Lafayette Bywater: The name is variously spelled Bywater and Bywaters. Official military documents omit the *s*.

Union forces lost: Kenneth W. Noe, *Perryville: This Grand Havoc of Battle* (Lexington: University Press of Kentucky, 2001), 369, 373.

"highly respected": *Wheeling (WV) Daily Intelligencer*, May 5, 1900, 8.

"very largely attended": *Wheeling (WV) Daily Intelligencer*, May 7, 1900, 3.

"He was one of the best known": *Wheeling (WV) Register*, May 5, 1900, 4.

Chapter 10: Hapless Haywood Shepherd

the erection of a monument to the five African Americans: Akiko Ochiai, "Continuing Skirmishes in Harpers Ferry: Entangled Memories of Hayward Shepherd and John Brown," *Japanese Journal of American Studies*, no. 23 (2013): 14.

Haywood Shepherd: Spellings of Shepherd's first name in Census and land records and in secondhand accounts vary. He is variously referred to as Haywood, Heywood, and even Heyward. For the sake of consistency, I use Haywood, the spelling that appears on most official records, except when a different spelling appears in quotes or a headline.

the "loyal slave" who did not rebel: A similar phrase, "Good Darky," was applied to a monument erected in 1927 in Natchitoches, Louisiana, that parallels the Shepherd memorial in spirit if not in its precise wording. After protests in the late twentieth century, city officials moved the statue, also known as "Uncle Jack," from a public corner to the Rural Life Museum of Louisiana State University. Under further protest, the museum sheathed it inside a wooden frame. For more information, including an extensive discussion of the Haywood Shepherd memorial controversy, see Emily Rinaldi, "Threatened by History: Preservation in Preserving the Postbellum Commemorative Landscape" (master's thesis, Columbia University, May 2013), https://webcache.googleusercontent .com/search?q=cache: mfk3TN_UzvkJ: https://academiccommons.columbia.edu/ download/fedora_content/download/ac: 162322/CONTENT/Rinaldi_Emily_ Thesis_Threatened_By_History.pdf+&cd=10&hl=en&ct=clnk&gl=us.

There, many family members are buried: Paul Planchon, "Free Blacks in Berkeley County and the Black Community of Douglass Grove," *Berkeley Journal*, no. 32 (2006): 69–70.

Winchester . . . claimed him: *Winchester (VA) Evening Star*, August 29, 1901.

According to one descendant: Gilbert Shepherd, interview by author, July 25, 2016.

a free man with a growing family . . . in Winchester: Shepherd's and Briscoe's local roots were deep and would remain so: Madison Briscoe, a physician born in 1904 and a descendant of both Haywood and also perhaps distantly of Sarah, would become a trustee of Storer College in its final days and a plaintiff in a failed lawsuit to keep the historically black college open after integration in the 1950s.

"a very noice nagur": Oswald Garrison Villard, "How Patrick Higgins Met John Brown," *Harper's Weekly*, January 26, 1909, 7, quoted in Quarles, *Allies for Freedom*, 93. In 1859, $15,000 was the equivalent of more than $422,000 in 2017.

Shepherd had been a railroad employee: Quarles, 93.

"Hereafter emancipated slaves": Guild, *Black Laws of Virginia*, 209.

"this most highly and respected and worthy citizen": *Charlestown Virginia Free Press*, editorial, November 3, 1859.

"He was shot down like a dog": *Charlestown Virginia Free Press*, October 27, 1859. In trial testimony, John Brown expressed the hope that it wasn't his men who'd shot Shepherd.

"in fact the only thing that prevented": Barry, *Strange Story*, 84.

"insane plot": *Winchester (VA) Republican*, October 21, 1859.

horrors of war that repeatedly swept over Winchester: By some accounts, Winchester changed hands fourteen times during the war. See "Winchester, Virginia: A Town Embattled During America's Civil War," HistoryNet, June 12, 2016, www.historynet.com/winchester-virginia-a-town-embattled-during-americas-civil-war.htm.

"needy schools": *Washington Bee*, June 1, 1889, 1.

reported the sale of a lot: *Washington Evening Star*, on February 18, 1890, 8.

then as now in a desirable neighborhood: The five-bedroom home's estimated value in July 2017 was $1.8 million, according to Realtor.com.

He was also a member of the Capital City Guards: *Washington Bee*, June 10, 1882.

"Shepherd, the unconscious martyr": *Winchester (VA) Evening Star*, August 29, 1901, 1.

she would be buried . . . in Woodlawn Cemetery: Paul E. Sluby Sr., *Bury Me Deep: Burial Places Past and Present in and Nearby Washington, DC* (self-pub., 2009), 39–40; site visit, August 29, 2016; Jan Fontaine, Woodlawn Cemetery Association historian and archivist, interviews by author. The cemetery was established in 1895 and also contains the remains of six thousand whites who had been relocated from the former multiracial Graceland Cemetery.

"proper and historically correct motto": *Berkeley Springs (WV) News*, quoted in the *Baltimore Sun*, December 27, 1909, 11.

"monument to the faithful old slaves": "Monument to Faithful Slaves," *Confederate Veteran* 13, no. 3 (March 1905): 123–124, https://archive.org/stream/confederateveter13conf#page/123/mode/1up/search/123.

"It would appear to me": Henry T. McDonald to Daniel Willard, 2 June 1922; George H. Campbell to Henry T. McDonald, 23 June 1922; Harpers Ferry National Historical Park Archives.

About three hundred whites: Quarles, *Allies for Freedom*, 183.

"My husband wouldn't tell them": Eugene L. Meyer, "NAACP Calls for Memorial to Be Hidden; Harpers Ferry Marker Again Focus of Debate," *Washington Post*, August 19, 1995, B2.

"This attempt to destroy the truth": *Afro-American*, October 17, 1931, 8.

"We come here": A typewritten copy of his speech, with McDonald's deletions and inserts, is in the Harpers Ferry National Historical Park Archives.

"Confederates to Dedicate 'Uncle Tom' Monument": *Afro-American*, October 10, 1931, 1.

"Local Pastor to Pray for Rebels": *Afro-American*, October 10, 1931, 1.

"a popular and capable colored freeman": The typed, twenty-three-page, double-spaced address entitled "Heyward Shepherd: Victim of Violence" is among the documents in the Harpers Ferry National Historical Park Archives.

Elizabeth Bashinsky: As was the custom, she was listed in the program as Mrs. Leopold Bashinsky, using her husband's name.

"members and chairman": Afro-American, October 17, 1931, 7.

"Handkerchiefs were in evidence": *Afro-American*, October 17, 1931, 7.

"I wonder at your temerity": *Afro-American*, October 17, 1931, 1.

"Barbara Fritchie in Black": *Afro-American*, October 17, 1931, 6.

"The only history": Eugene L. Meyer, "NAACP."

a nearby smaller interpretive sign: In 2017, the 1995 wayside marker seems oddly out of date. It appears that the Park Service sought "balance" to contextualize a memorial and an event rather than to state a stark truth: the Shepherd memorial tablet was part of a concerted effort to memorialize not Haywood Shepherd but rather the Lost Cause that mythologized the institution of slavery and the Confederacy that fought to maintain it. But twenty-five years ago, such monuments and memorials that have become belatedly controversial stood largely unchallenged. The Park Service's strangely neutral narrative was further flawed by failing to accurately label the words W. E. B. DuBois wrote memorializing John Brown. They came from an inscription DuBois penned in 1932 for a Brown plaque that was to be displayed on the Storer College campus as a reaction to the Shepherd tablet but that the school rejected. The wayside marker failed to mention any of this. It was not until 2006, when the college campus was under the National Park Service, that the plaque was at last erected at its intended location.

"Personally, I'd rather see": Eugene L. Meyer, "NAACP."

Chapter 11: To Preserve This Sacred Shrine

Camp Hill: The name Camp Hill derives from its use, as early as the mid-1700s, as a place where soldiers camped during the French and Indian War.

"quite a number of Confederates": Bucks County (PA) Gazette, June 2, 1881.

"If a monument should be erected": "Address by Frederick Douglass, May 30, 1881," John Brown pamphlets 5, Boyd B. Stutler Collection, West Virginia State Archives, www.wvculture.org/history/jbexhibit/bbspr05-0032.html.

did not reveal the popular sentiment: Perks, "'How I Should Love to Know,'" 62.

Freedmen's Bureau: The Bureau of Refugees, Freedmen, and Abandoned Lands, its formal name, was charged with establishing schools for freedmen.

Joseph Barry, who would serve: "Harpers Ferry Council Membership 1851–2009 Terms," 2nd ed., April 16, 2008, www.harpersferrywv.us/council/hfcouncils .pdf; John E. Stealey III, "The Freedmen's Bureau in West Virginia," *Magazine of the Jefferson County Historical Society* 2002, 43.

1,600 men and 16 percent of its white males: Stealey, 28.

in 1860, neighboring . . . Counties had: Stealey, 29.

"Every vote in favor": *Weston (WV) Democrat*, October 10, 1870, 2.

"Are the Democrats going in": *Wheeling (WV) Daily Intelligencer*, March 4, 1868, 2.

where it apparently remained: *Wheeling (WV) Daily Intelligencer*, December 12, 1868, 1.

"of all ages and sexes": *Charlestown Spirit of Jefferson*, February 28, 1871, 3.

"colored school with nigger teachers": "Storer College: It Was Here a Century Ago That the NAACP Took Its First Steps," *Journal of Blacks in Higher Education*, no. 51 (spring 2006): 21.

a cross was burned in his front yard: *Afro-American*, November 17, 1922, 1; December 1, 1922, 9, 22.

Harpers Ferry's black population thrived: Andrew W. Kahrl, "The Political Work of Leisure: Class, Recreation, and African American Commemoration at Harpers Ferry, West Virginia, 1881–1931," *Journal of Social History* 42, no. 1 (fall 2008), 64.

Hilltop House: The seventy-six-room Hilltop House hotel closed in 2008 and at this writing is in deteriorating condition, awaiting renovation by a Washington, DC–area developer who purchased the property.

"We had quarters": Patsy Mose Fletcher, *Historically African American Leisure Destinations Around Washington, DC* (Charleston, SC: History Press, 2015), 38.

Also among the black guests: Taylor, *Original Black Elite*, 89.

By the 1890s, the Murrays were regularly vacationing: Taylor, 107.

"Camp Hill, which had previously": Kate J. Anthony, *Storer College, Harper's Ferry, W.Va.: Brief Historical Sketch, with Supplementary Notes, 1867–1891* (Boston: 1891), 18–19, quoted in Kahrl, "Political Work," 64–65.

"the visitor to Harpers Ferry": *Washington Bee*, September 17, 1892, quoted in Kahrl, 59.

Storer's entrepreneurial experiment: Kahrl, 67.

"clear and unequivocal": *New York Times*, August 20, 1906.

"Negroes Demand Equality": *Frederick (MD) Daily News*, August 14, 1906, 2.

the John Brown fort: Storer College acquired the fort in 1909 for $900 from farmer Alexander Murphy and moved it to the campus the following year. There it stayed until 1968, when the National Park Service moved it once again, to a spot in the lower town near its original location. The building was almost lost to Harpers Ferry when it was moved in 1892 to the site of the 1893 Columbian Exposition in Chicago. Funds were raised then to buy it and move it back to Harpers Ferry.

They sang: Quarles, *Allies for Freedom*, 4–10.

"Mrs. Evans was asked": Jennifer Morris, "Sneak Peek from the Stacks: A Voice from Harpers Ferry," *Smithsonian Collections Blog*, November 12, 2012, http://si-siris.blogspot.com/2012/11/sneak-peek-from-stacks-voice-from.html.

"to sympathize with me": Kahrl, "Political Work," 71.

"Here John Brown": Gloria Gozdzik, *A Historic Resource Study for Storer College, Harpers Ferry, West Virginia* (Morgantown, WV: Horizon Research Consultants, 2002), 166.

There would be no plaque dedication: Storer College alumni had been allowed to place a less controversial tablet on the fort in 1918. It read, "That this nation might have a new birth of freedom, that slavery should be removed forever from American soil, John Brown and his men gave their lives."

"If the college didn't want the tablet": *Pittsburgh Courier*, June 4, 1932, 12.

his remarks went unreported: *Afro-American*, June 17, 1950, 9.

the NAACP was at last permitted to place its . . . plaque: NAACP 2006 Annual Report, 10, http://action.naacp.org/page/-/annual%20reports/2006ar.pdf.

Chapter 12: Commemorations

five African American raiders would be conspicuously absent: Lillian Evanti, descended from Leary and through marriage from Copeland, asked National Park Service director Conrad Wirth for "a big celebration" to be held on the Storer campus. "John Brown was thought to be a mad man," she wrote, "but *to day* [*sic*] we know his spirit was dedicated to Freedom and Democracy for all people." To bolster her credentials, she noted, "I had two relatives who joined Brown from Oberlin, Ohio and gave their lives that America might be free." Lillian Evanti to Conrad Wirth, 28 August 1957, quoted in Anne C. Kretsinger-Harries, "Commemoration Controversy: The Harpers Ferry Raid Centennial as a Challenge to Dominant Public Memories of the U.S. Civil War," *Rhetoric and Public Affairs* 17, no. 1 (spring 2014): 82.

"The downtown section remains": *Baltimore Sun*, September 18, 1957, 16.

"Well, it looked like a slum": Charles W. Snell, interview by Dennis Frye, January 22, 1992, Harpers Ferry National Historical Park Archives.

"the Raid came at a bad time": Donald W. Campbell to assistant chief (WASO), Office of Policy memo, "National Park System Advisory Board Meeting," March

8, 1988, quoted in Teresa S. Moyer and Paul A. Shackel, *The Making of Harpers Ferry National Historical Park: A Devil, Two Rivers, and a Dream* (Lanham, MD: AltaMira, 2008).

"Any possible complications": Karl Betts to William M. Tuck, 5 February 1959, folder 5267, Tuck Papers, quoted in Robert J. Cook, *Troubled Commemoration: The American Civil War Centennial, 1961–1965* (Baton Rouge: Louisiana State University Press, 2007), 74.

"not in sympathy": Cal Burroughs to Corbett, notes from telephone call, 16 April 1959, folder H2215 1957–78, admin. coll., BH/HAFE, quoted in Teresa S. Moyer, Kim E. Wallace, and Paul A. Shackel, *"To Preserve the Evidences of a Noble Past": An Administrative History of Harpers Ferry National Historical Park* (Frederick, MD: Catoctin Center for Regional Studies; Frederick Community College; and Center for Heritage Resource Studies, Department of Anthology, University of Maryland, 2004), 146.

"We share their apprehension": Moyer, Wallace, and Shackel, 146.

"My grandpappy was a Confederate": Ryan C. Bixby, "A More Inclusive Civil War: Neglected Themes in West Virginia Civil War Historiography," in *Lesser Civil Wars: Civilians Defining War and the Memory of War*, ed. Marsha R. Robinson (Cambridge: Cambridge Scholars, 2012), 95.

solution was to help plan an event: Jefferson County citizens also hoped to use the event as a catalyst to improve Route 340, the main road between Harpers Ferry and Charles Town, to accommodate the expected tourist traffic. A delegation lobbied the state road commission for improvements to the road near Halltown. *Hagerstown (MD) Daily Mail*, January 25, 1958, 11.

"colored citizens": Frank Barnes to "Dr. Nelligan," memo "John Brown Raid Centennial," 29 August 1958, folder HFNHS 1959, box 29, ent. 414B, RG 79, NARA-MA (Ph), quoted in Moyer, Wallace, and Shackel, *"To Preserve the Evidences,"* 146.

"The reenactment cannot be": *Afro-American*, October 17, 1959, 4.

"I hope that a great many Afro-Americans": *Chicago Defender (National Edition)*, October 17, 1959, 10.

"terrible in his righteousness": *Washington Post and Times Herald*, March 15, 1959, B16.

"abolitionist fanatic": *New York Times*, October 4, 1959, section 2, 1.

"a white-bearded fanatic": *Washington Post and Times Herald*, October 19, 1959, B1.

"Pageantry, drama, ceremony": *Washington Post and Times Herald*, September 8, 1959, A12.

"pitiful little army": Boyd Stutler, speech at John Brown Raid Centennial, original manuscript in Boyd B. Stutler Collection, West Virginia State Archives, Ms78-1, www.wvculture.org/history/jbexhibit/bbsrp03-007.html.

"Oratory and old lace": *Washington Evening Star*, October 17, 1959, 24.

"Mrs. Cyrus Cavalier": A congressional receptionist on Capitol Hill, she had a degree in drama from the University of Washington, in Seattle, and also served as general chairman of the Centennial Committee. Two years earlier, she had been anointed National Apple Queen by the West Virginia State Society.

"an authentic chronicle": *New York Times*, October 19, 1959, 58.

"Everyone in the audience can decide": *Washington Evening Star*, September 7, 1959, 18.

"But the world is still filled": *Washington Sunday Star*, October 18, 1959, 17.

"Throngs, at least half": *Washington Sunday Star*, October 18, 1959, 18.

"the biggest splash of color": *Baltimore Sun*, October 18, 1959, 40; October 19, 1959, 30.

"To us, John Brown is a heroic figure": Greg Artzner, interview by author, June 10, 2017.

"Of course, we did not support": David Fox, interview by author, June 5, 2017.

"We wanted to try to not just": Todd Bolton, interview by author, June 7, 2017.

"That was very disappointing": Guinevere Roper, interview by author, June 9, 2016.

"It was like a celebration": Thomas J. Hopkins, interview by author, June 30, 2017.

"The family is extremely diverse": Brenda Pitts, interview by author, October 29, 2016.

"I was Caucasian my entire life": Donna Copeland Hill, interview by author, July 1, 2017.

"sixty-six relatives": Kim Fraser, interview by author, September 11, 2016.

"I was proud as shit": Dennis Howard, interview by author, March 15, 2016.

"It was just the whole thing": Sherrie Carter, interview by author, May 11, 2016.

"He has a great reputation": "New Superintendent Announced for Harpers Ferry National Historical Park," National Park Service press release, February 16, 2017, www.nps.gov/hafe/learn/news/new-superintendent.htm.

Epilogue

Ashton and I had spoken: Ashton M. Robinson III, interviews by author, March 17–21, 2017.

"the one-drop rule": The "one-drop rule," codified in Southern states from 1910 to 1931, classified any individual with "one drop" of African American ancestry or "blood" as black for purposes of racial classification in the segregation of schools, restaurants, and public facilities. Virginia's 1924 Racial Integrity Act stood until 1967, when the US Supreme Court declared the state's ban on

interracial marriage unconstitutional, in the case of *Loving v. Virginia.* The law had defined "a white person as one with no trace of the blood of another race, except that a person with one-sixteenth of the American Indian, if there is no other race mixture, may be classified as white." "The New Virginia Law to Preserve Race Integrity," *Virginia Health Bulletin* 16, extra no. 2 (March 1924).

Bibliography

Books

Anderson, Osborne Perry. *A Voice from Harpers Ferry: A Narrative of Events at Harper's Ferry.* Boston: self-published, 1861.

Aptheker, Herbert. *American Negro Slave Revolts.* New York: Columbia University Press, 1943. 50th anniversary ed. New York: International Publishers, 1993.

Ball, Edward. *Slaves in the Family.* New York: Farrar, Straus and Giroux, 1998. Paperback ed., 2014.

Bancroft, Frederic. *Slave Trading in the Old South.* J. H. Furst, 1941. Reprint with new introduction by Michael Tadman. Columbia: University of South Carolina Press, 1996.

Barfield, Rodney. *America's Forgotten Caste: Free Blacks in Antebellum Virginia and North Carolina.* Bloomington, IN: Xlibris, 2013.

Barnes, Gilbert Hobbs. *The Anti-Slavery Impulse: 1830–1844.* New York: Harbinger Books, 1964.

Barry, Joseph. *The Strange Story of Harper's Ferry: With Legends of the Surrounding Country.* Martinsburg, WV: Thompson Brothers, 1903. https://archive.org /details/strangestoryofha00barr.

Bigglestone, William E. *They Stopped in Oberlin: Black Residents and Visitors of the Nineteenth Century.* Oberlin, OH: Oberlin College, 2002.

Blockson, Charles L. *The Underground Railroad.* New York: Prentice Hall, 1987.

Bordewich, Fergus M. *Bound for Canaan: The Underground Railroad and the War for the Soul of America.* New York: Amistad, 2005.

Brandt, Nat. *The Town That Started the Civil War: The True Story of the Community That Stood Up to Slavery—and Changed a Nation Forever.* New York: Dell, 1981.

Bristow, Peggy, ed. *"We're Rooted Here and They Can't Pull Us Up": Essays in African Canadian Women's History*. Toronto: University of Toronto Press, 1994.

Brown, Thomas, and Leah Sims. *Fugitive Slave Advertisements in the "City Gazette": Charleston, South Carolina, 1787–1797*. Lanham, MD: Lexington Books, 2015.

Casper, Scott E. *Sarah Johnson's Mount Vernon: The Forgotten History of an American Shrine*. New York: Hill and Wang, 2008.

Cheek, William, and Aimee Lee Cheek. *John Mercer Langston and the Fight for Black Freedom, 1829–65*. Urbana: University of Illinois Press, 1984.

Clinton, Catherine. *Harriet Tubman: The Road to Freedom*. Boston: Little, Brown, 2004.

Cook, Robert J. *Troubled Commemoration: The American Civil War Centennial, 1961–1965*. Baton Rouge: Louisiana State University Press, 2007.

Crowe, Charles, ed. *The Age of Civil War and Reconstruction, 1830–1900*. Homewood, IL: Dorsey, 1975.

Dabney, Virginius. *Below the Potomac: A Book About the New South*. New York: D. Appleton-Century, 1941.

Dabney, Virginius. *Virginius Dabney's Virginia: Writings About the Old Dominion*. Garden City, NY: Doubleday, 1971.

Davis, James Andrew. *Music Along the Rapidan: Civil War Soldiers, Music, and Community During Winter Quarters, Virginia*. Lincoln: University of Nebraska Press, 2014.

DeCaro, Louis A., Jr. *John Brown: The Cost of Freedom*. New York: International Publishers, 2007.

Dohme, Alvin. *Shenandoah: The Valley Story*. Washington, DC: Potomac Books, 1972.

Donaldson, Alfred Lee. *A History of the Adirondacks*. Vol. 2. New York: Century, 1921. http://bit.ly/2tkYcWd.

Douglass, Frederick. *The Life and Times of Frederick Douglass: From 1817 to 1882*. London, 1882. http://lf-oll.s3.amazonaws.com/titles/2007/Douglass_1349_Bk.pdf.

Douglass, Frederick. *Narrative of the Life of Frederick Douglass, an American Slave*. New York: Bedford/St. Martin's, 2002.

Drew, Benjamin. *The Refugee: Or the Narrative of Fugitive Slaves in Canada*. Boston: John P. Jewett, 1856. https://archive.org/details/anorthsideviews00drewgoog.

Drew, Thomas. *The John Brown Invasion, an Authentic History of the Harpers Ferry Tragedy with Full Details of the Capture, Trial, and Execution of the Invaders, and of All the Incidents Connected Therewith*. Boston: James Campbell, 1860. https://archive.org/details/johnbrowninvasio00drew.

Drucker, Marcia J., ed. *A Bicentennial History: Jefferson County, West Virginia, 1801–2001*. Martinsburg, WV: Jefferson County Bicentennial Committee, 2001.

DuBois, W. E. B. *John Brown*. Philadelphia: George W. Jacobs, 1909. https://babel.hathitrust.org/cgi/pt?id=loc.ark:/13960/t7br8wc5j;view=1up;seq=11.

DuBois, W. E. B., ed. *The Negro Church*. Atlanta: Atlanta University, 1903. http://scua.library.umass.edu/digital/dubois/dubois8.pdf.

Earle, Jonathan. *John Brown's Raid on Harpers Ferry: A Brief History with Documents*. New York: Bedford/St. Martin's, 2008.

Ferguson, Moira, ed. *Nine Black Women: An Anthology of Nineteenth-Century Writers from the United States, Canada, Bermuda, and the Caribbean*. New York: Routledge, 1998.

Fletcher, Patsy Mose. *African American Leisure Destinations Around Washington, DC*. Charleston, SC: History Press, 2015.

Fletcher, Robert Samuel. *A History of Oberlin College from Its Foundation Through the Civil War*. Vol. 1. Oberlin, OH: Oberlin College, 1943. https://ia600802.us.archive.org/12/items/historyofoberlin01flet/historyofoberlin01flet_jpg.pdf.

Foner, Eric. *Gateway to Freedom: The Hidden History of the Underground Railroad*. New York: W.W. Norton, 2015.

Foner, Philip S. *History of Black Americans: From the Compromise of 1850 to the End of the Civil War*. Westport, CT: Greenwood, 1983.

Franklin, John Hope. *The Free Negro in North Carolina, 1790–1860*. Chapel Hill: University of North Carolina Press, 1995.

Frye, Dennis E. *Harpers Ferry Under Fire: A Border Town in the American Civil War*. Virginia Beach, VA: Donning, 2012.

Gilbert, David T. *A Walker's Guide to Harpers Ferry, West Virginia: Exploring a Place Where History Still Lives*. Harpers Ferry, WV: Harpers Ferry Historical Association, 1983.

Gozdzik, Gloria. *A Historic Resource Study for Storer College, Harpers Ferry, West Virginia*. Morgantown, WV: Horizon Research Consultants, 2002.

Greene, Robert Ewell. *The Leary-Evans, Ohio's Free People of Color*. Self-published, 1989.

Guild, June Purcell. *Black Laws of Virginia: A Summary of the Legislative Acts of Virginia Concerning Negroes from Earliest Times to the Present*. Richmond, VA: Whittet & Shepperson, 1936. Reprint compiled by Karen Hughes White and Joan Peters, Westminster, MD: Heritage Books, 2011.

Hendrick, George, and Willene Hendrick. *Black Refugees in Canada: Accounts of Escape During the Era of Slavery*. Jefferson, NC: McFarland, 2010.

Hickman, Jared. *Black Prometheus: Race and Radicalism in the Age of Atlantic Slavery*. New York: Oxford University Press, 2016.

Hinton, Richard J. *John Brown and His Men, with Some Account of the Roads They Traveled to Reach Harper's Ferry*. New York: Funk & Wagnalls, 1894. https://archive.org/details/johnbrownhismenw00hint.

Hollie, Donna Tyler, Brett M. Tyler, and Karen Hughes White. *African Americans of Fauquier County*. Charleston, SC: Arcadia, 2009.

Horwitz, Tony. *Midnight Rising: John Brown and the Raid That Sparked the Civil War*. New York: Henry Holt, 2011.

Hurmence, Belinda, ed. *Before Freedom: 48 Oral Histories of Former North and South Carolina Slaves*. Winston-Salem, NC: John F. Blair, 1989.

Ibrahim, Karen King, Karen Hughes White, and Courtney Gaskins. *Fauquier County, Virginia, Register of Free Negroes, 1817–1865*. The Plains: Afro-American Historical Society of Fauquier County, Virginia, 1993.

Jefferson County Black History Preservation Society. *African Americans of Jefferson County*. Charleston, SC: Arcadia, 2009.

Johnston, James Hugo. *Race Relations in Virginia and Miscegenation in the South, 1776–1860*. Amherst: University of Massachusetts Press, 1970.

Jones, Ray. *Harpers Ferry*. Gretna, LA: Pelican, 1992.

Kashatus, William C. *Just over the Line: Chester County and the Underground Railroad*. West Chester, PA: Chester County Historical Society, 2002.

Katz, Jonathan. *Resistance at Christiana: The Fugitive Slave Rebellion, Christiana, Pennsylvania, September 11, 1851—a Documentary Account*. New York: Thomas Y. Crowell, 1974.

Katz, William Loren. *The Black West: A Documentary and Pictorial History of the African American Role in the Westward Expansion of the United States*. 3rd ed. Seattle: Open Hand, 1987.

Langston, John Mercer. *From the Virginia Plantation to the Nation's Capital, or, the First and Only Negro Representative in Congress from the Old Dominion*. Hartford, CT: American Publishing, 1894. https://archive.org/details/fromvirginiaplan00langiala.

Laughlin-Schultz, Bonnie. *The Tie That Bound Us: The Women of John Brown's Family and the Legacy of Radical Abolitionism*. Ithaca, NY: Cornell University Press, 2013.

Lee, Deborah A. *Honoring Their Paths: African American Contributions Along the Journey Through Hallowed Ground*. Waterford, VA: Journey Through Hallowed Ground Partnership, 2009.

Leech, Samuel Vanderlip. *The Raid of John Brown at Harper's Ferry as I Saw It*. Washington, DC: self-published, 1909. https://archive.org/stream /raidofjohnbrowna02leec#page/n5/mode/2up.

Leonard, Elijah. *The Honorable Elijah Leonard: A Memoir*. London, ON: Advertiser Printing, 1894. https://ia902303.us.archive.org/35/items/cihm_08560 /cihm_08560.pdf.

Libby, Jean. *Black Voices from Harpers Ferry: Osborne Anderson and the John Brown Raid*. Berkeley: self-published, 1979.

Libby, Jean. *The John Brown Photo Chronology: Catalog of the Exhibit at Harpers Ferry 2009*. Palo Alto, CA: Allies for Freedom, 2009.

Libby, Jean, ed. and comp. *John Brown Mysteries*. Missoula, MT: Pictorial Histories, 1999.

Low, Denise, and T. F. Pecore Weso. *Langston Hughes in Lawrence: Photographs and Biographical Resources*. Lawrence, KS: Mammoth, 2004.

Lubet, Steven. *The "Colored Hero" of Harper's Ferry: John Anthony Copeland and the War Against Slavery*. New York: Cambridge University Press, 2015.

Lubet, Steven. *John Brown's Spy: The Adventurous Life and Tragic Confession of John E. Cook*. New Haven, CT: Yale University Press, 2012.

Maliskas, Ed. *John Brown to James Brown: The Little Farm Where Liberty Budded, Blossomed, and Boogied*. Hagerstown, MD: Hamilton Run, 2016.

Maris-Wolf, Ted. *Family Bonds: Free Blacks and the Re-enslavement Law in Antebellum Virginia*. Chapel Hill: University of North Carolina Press, 2015.

Marshall, Peter, and David Manuel. *Sounding Forth the Trumpet: 1837–1860*. Grand Rapids, MI: Revell, 1999.

McGinty, Brian. *John Brown's Trial*. Cambridge, MA: Harvard University Press, 2009.

Meier, August, and Elliott M. Rudwick, eds. *The Making of Black America*. New York: Atheneum, 1969.

Mitchell, William M. *The Underground Railroad*. London: William Tweedie, 1860. https://ia601404.us.archive.org/35/items/undergroundrail01mitcgoog/under groundrail01mitcgoog.pdf.

Monroe, James. *Oberlin Thursday Lectures, Addresses and Essays*. Oberlin, OH: Edward J. Goodrich, 1897. https://archive.org/details/oberlinthursdayl01monr.

Morris, J. Brent. *Oberlin, Hotbed of Abolitionism: College, Community, and the Fight for Freedom and Equality in Antebellum America*. Chapel Hill: University of North Carolina Press, 2014.

Moyer, Teresa S., and Paul A. Shackel. *The Making of Harpers Ferry National Historical Park: A Devil, Two Rivers, and a Dream*. Lanham, MD: AltaMira, 2008.

Mullin, Gerald W. *Flight and Rebellion: Slave Resistance in Eighteenth-Century Virginia*. New York: Oxford University Press, 1972.

Myrdal, Gunnar. *An American Dilemma: The Negro Problem and Modern Democracy*. New York: Harper & Row, 1944, 1962.

Nell, William Cooper. *William Cooper Nell: Nineteenth-Century African American Abolitionist, Historian, Integrationist, Selected Writings, 1832–1874*. Edited by Dorothy Porter Wesley and Constance Porter Uzelac. Baltimore: Black Classic, 2002.

Nelson, Truman. *The Old Man: John Brown at Harper's Ferry*. New York: Holt, Rinehart and Winston, 1973. Reprint, Chicago: Haymarket Books, 2009.

Newby, I. A. *The South: A History*. New York: Holt, Rinehart and Winston, 1978.

Oates, Stephen B. *To Purge This Land with Blood: A Biography of John Brown*. New York: Harper & Row, 1970.

Perdue, Charles L., Jr., Thomas E. Boren, and Robert K. Phillips, eds. *Weevils in the Wheat: Interviews with Virginia Ex-Slaves*. Bloomington: Indiana University Press, 1980.

Phillips, Wilbur H. *Oberlin Colony: The Story of a Century*. Oberlin, OH: Oberlin Printing, 1933.

Quarles, Benjamin. *Allies for Freedom: Blacks and John Brown*. New York: Oxford University Press, 1974. Paperback ed. with a new introduction. Cambridge, MA: Da Capo, 2001.

Quarles, Benjamin. *Black Abolitionists*. New York: Oxford University Press, 1969.

Quarles, Benjamin. *The Negro in the American Revolution*. Chapel Hill: University of North Carolina Press, 1961.

Quarles, Benjamin. *The Negro in the Civil War*. Boston: Little, Brown, 1953.

Redpath, James. *The Public Life of Captain John Brown: With an Autobiography of His Childhood and Youth*. Boston: Thayer and Eldridge, 1860.

Reynolds, David S. *John Brown, Abolitionist: The Man Who Killed Slavery, Sparked the Civil War, and Seeded Civil Rights*. New York: Alfred A. Knopf, 2005.

C. Ripley, Peter, ed. *The Black Abolitionist Papers*. Vol. 2, *Canada, 1830–1865*. Chapel Hill: University of North Carolina Press, 1986.

Robert, Joseph C. *The Road from Monticello: A Study of the Virginia Slavery Debate of 1832*. Durham, NC: Duke University Press, 1941. Reprint, Whitefish, MT: Kessinger Legacy, 2010.

Robertson, David. *Denmark Vesey: The Buried History of America's Largest Slave Rebellion and the Man Who Led It*. New York: Vintage Books, 2000.

Robinson, Gwendolyn, and John W. Robinson. *Seek the Truth: A Story of Chatham's Black Community*. Chatham, ON: self-published, 1989.

Root, Erik S. *Sons of the Fathers: The Virginia Slavery Debates of 1831–1832*. Lanham, MD, Lexington Books, 2010.

Russo, Peggy A., and Paul Finkelman, eds. *Terrible Swift Sword: The Legacy of John Brown*. Athens: Ohio University Press, 2005.

Sanborn, Franklin Benjamin. *Recollections of Seventy Years*. Vol. 1. Boston: Gorham Press, 1909. https://archive.org/details/recollectionsse01sanbgoog.

Sanborn, Franklin Benjamin, ed. *The Life and Letters of John Brown, Liberator of Kansas, and Martyr of Virginia*. Boston: Roberts Brothers, 1885. https://archive .org/stream/lifeandlettersof00sanbrich.

Scheel, Eugene M. *Culpeper: A Virginia County's History Through 1920*. Culpeper, VA: Culpeper Historical Society, 1982.

Schwarz, Philip J. *Migrants Against Slavery: Virginia and the Nation*. Charlottesville: University of Virginia Press, 2001.

Schwarz, Philip J. *Slave Laws in Virginia*. Athens: University of Georgia Press, 1996.

Shipherd, Jacob R. *The Oberlin-Wellington Rescue*. Boston: John P. Jewett, 1859. Reprint, Bedford, MA: Applewood Books, 2009. https://archive.org/details /historyofoberlin00ship.

Sinha, Manisha. *The Slave's Cause: A History of Abolition*. New Haven, CT: Yale University Press, 2016.

Sluby, Paul E., Sr. *Bury Me Deep: Burial Places Past and Present in and Nearby Washington, DC*. Self-published, 2009.

Smedley, R. C. *History of the Underground Railroad in Chester and the Neighboring Counties of Pennsylvania*. Lancaster, PA: Office of the Journal, 1883. Reprint, Mechanicsburg, PA: Stackpole Books, 2005. https://archive.org/details/histo-ryundergro00smedgoog.

Smith, Merritt Roe. *Harpers Ferry Armory and the New Technology: The Challenge of Change*. Ithaca, NY: Cornell University Press, 1977.

Smith, William Farrar. *From Chattanooga to Petersburg Under Generals Grant and Butler: A Contribution to the History of the War, and a Personal Vindication*. Boston: Houghton, Mifflin, 1893. https://archive.org/details/cu31924030905495.

Stamp, Kenneth M. *The Peculiar Institution: Slavery in the Ante-Bellum South*. New York: Vintage Books, 1989.

Still, William. *The Underground Railroad: A Record of Facts, Authentic Narratives, Letters, &c*. Philadelphia: Porter & Coates, 1872. https://archive.org/details /undergroundrai00stil

Stevens, William O. *The Shenandoah and Its Byways*. New York: Dodd, Mead, 1941.

Stewart, Alison. *First Class: The Legacy of Dunbar, America's First Black Public High School*. Chicago: Lawrence Hill Books, 2013.

Strain, Paula M. *The Blue Hills of Maryland: History Along the Appalachian Trail on South Mountain and the Catoctins*. Vienna, VA: Potomac Appalachian Trail Club, 1993.

Stutler, Boyd B. *West Virginia in the Civil War*. Charlestown, WV: Educational Foundation, 1963.

Taylor, Alan. *The Internal Enemy: Slavery and War in Virginia 1772–1832*. New York: W.W. Norton, 2013.

Taylor, Elizabeth Dowling. *The Original Black Elite: Daniel Murray and the Story of a Forgotten Era*. New York: Amistad/Harper Collins, 2017.

Villard, Oswald Garrison. *John Brown: A Biography 1800–1859*. Garden City, NY: Doubleday, Duran, 1929.

Walker, Barrington. *Race on Trial: Black Defendants in Ontario's Criminal Courts, 1858–1958*. Toronto: University of Toronto Press, 2010.

Webb, Richard D., ed. *The Life and Letters of Captain John Brown*. London: Smith, Elder, 1861. http://bit.ly/2rPzJJO.

Whitfield, Theodore M. *Slavery Agitation in Virginia 1829–1832*. Baltimore: Johns Hopkins Press, 1930.

Williams, William W. *History of Ashtabula County, Ohio*. Philadelphia: Williams Brothers, 1878. http://solomonspalding.com/SRP/saga2/1878Ast2.htm.

Wise, Barton H. *The Life of Henry A. Wise of Virginia, 1806–1876*. New York: Macmillan, 1899.

Writers Program of the Work Projects Administration in the State of Virginia, comps. *The Negro in Virginia*. New York: Hastings House, 1940. https://babel.hathitrust.org/cgi/pt?id=mdp.39015009063051;view=1up;seq=2.

Zittle, John H., comp. *A Correct History of the John Brown Invasion, at Harper's Ferry, W. Va, Oct 17, 1859*. Hagerstown, MD: Matt Publishing, 1906. http://www.libraryweb.org/~digitized/books/John_Brown_Invasion.pdf.

Newspapers and Periodicals

Afro-American

Baltimore Sun

Berkeley Journal

Confederate Veteran

Journal of Negro Education

Journal of Negro History

Magazine of the Jefferson County Historical Society
New York Times
Oberlin Evangelist
Provincial Freeman
Richmond Dispatch
Valley of the Shadow: Civil War Newspapers
Virginia Free Press
Washington Post

Articles and Reports

Annual Report of the Auxiliary Society of Frederick County, Va. for Colonizing the Free People of Colour in the United States. Winchester, VA: Auxiliary Society, 1820. https://archive.org/details/annualreportofau00auxi.

Berkeley Journal, no. 32, *Free Blacks in Berkeley County and the Black Community of Douglass Grove* (2006).

Eby, Carl D. "Escape from Harpers Ferry: The Personal Narrative of Owen Brown." *Magazine of the Jefferson County Historical Society*, 1998, 27–68.

Featherstonhaugh, Thomas. "The Final Burial of the Followers of John Brown." *New England Magazine*, April 1901. www.wvculture.org/history/jbexhibit/bbspr03-0015.html.

Givens, Thomas C. "Manumission of Slaves in Fauquier County, Virginia, 1830–1860." Honors thesis, University of Richmond, 1972. http://scholarship.richmond.edu/cgi/viewcontent.cgi?article=1301&context=honors-theses.

Glasgow, J. Ewing. *The Harpers Ferry Insurrection: Being an Account of the Outbreak in Virginia and of the Trial and Execution of Captain John Brown, Its Hero.* Edinburgh: Myles Macphail, 1860. http://historyonline.chadwyck.co.uk/getImage?productsuffix=_studyunits&action=printview&in=gif&out=pdf&src=/bap/bap00026/conv/bap00026.pdf&IE=.pdf.

"His Soul Goes Marching On": The Life and Legacy of John Brown. Online exhibit. West Virginia Archives and History. www.wvculture.org/history/jbexhibit/jbtoc.html.

Iseminger, Gordon L. "The Second Raid on Harper's Ferry, July 29, 1899: The Other Bodies That Lay A'mouldering in Their Graves." *Pennsylvania History: A Journal of Mid-Atlantic Studies* 71, no. 2 (2004): 129–163.

"John Brown's Raid at Harpers Ferry, an Eyewitness Account by Charles White." Edited by Rayburn S. Moore. *Virginia Magazine of History and Biography* 67, no. 4 (October 1959): 387–395.

Kahrl, Andrew W. "The Political Work of Leisure: Class, Recreation, and African American Commemoration at Harpers Ferry, West Virginia, 1881–1931." *Journal of Social History* 42, no. 1 (fall 2008): 57–77.

Krestsinger-Harries, Anne C. "Commemoration Controversy: The Harpers Ferry Raid Centennial as a Challenge to Dominant Public Memories of the U.S. Civil War." *Rhetoric and Public Affairs* 17, no. 1 (2014): 67–104.

Magazine of the Jefferson County Historical Society, 2009, *John Brown Raid Issue: 1859–2009*.

McClain, Mary Ellen. "Storer College: Harpers Ferry, West Virginia (1865–1897)." Honors thesis, Linfield College, 1974.

Moyer, Teresa S., Kim E. Wallace, and Paul A. Shackel. *"To Preserve the Evidences of a Noble Past": An Administrative History of Harpers Ferry National Historical Park.* Frederick, MD: Catoctin Center for Regional Studies; Frederick Community College; and Center for Heritage Resource Studies, Department of Anthology, University of Maryland, 2004.

Naton, Leslie. "John Brown's Grave." *North American Review* 287, no. 3/4 (May–August 2002): 74–77.

Ochiai, Akiko. "Continuing Skirmishes in Harpers Ferry: Entangled Memories of Hayward Shepherd and John Brown." *Japanese Journal of American Studies*, no. 23 (2012): 7–26.

Perks, P. Douglas. "'. . . How I Should Love to Know How My Own Dear Husband Is This Night': 1863 in Mr. Jefferson's County." *Magazine of the Jefferson County Historical Society*, 2013, 55–66.

Sanborn, Franklin. "John Brown and His Friends." *Atlantic Monthly*, July 1872, 50–61.

Schick, Kurt. "Slavery in Fauquier County." *News and Notes from the Fauquier Historical Society* 5, no. 4 (fall 1983): 1–2.

Simpson, Craig. "John Brown and Governor Wise: A New Perspective on Harpers Ferry." *Biography* 1, no. 4 (fall 1978): 15–36.

Stealey, John Edmund III. "The Freedmen's Bureau in West Virginia." *Magazine of the Jefferson County Historical Society*, December 2002, 19–73.

"Storer College: It Was Here a Century Ago That the NAACP Took Its First Steps." *Journal of Blacks in Higher Education*, no. 51 (spring 2006): 21–22.

Primary Documents

Boyd B. Stutler Database. West Virginia Memory Project. www.wvculture.org /history/wvmemory/imlsintro.html.

"Primary documents." In *"His Soul Goes Marching On": The Life and Legacy of John Brown.* Online exhibit. West Virginia Archives and History. www.wvculture .org/history/jbexhibit/jbprimarydocuments.html.

"Report of the Joint Committee on the Harpers Ferry Outrages, January 26, 1860." In *"His Soul Goes Marching On": The Life and Legacy of John Brown.* Online exhibit. West Virginia Archives and History. www.wvculture.org/history /jbexhibit/vajointcommitteereport.html.

Report [of] the Select Committee of the Senate Appointed to Inquire into the Late Invasion and Seizure of the Public Property at Harper's Ferry. June 15, 1860. https://archive.org/details/reportselectcommi00unit.

Collections

Afro-American Historical Association of Fauquier County, Virginia

Mary Ann Shadd Cary papers, Howard University, Washington, DC

Chatham-Kent Black Historical Society, Chatham, Ontario

Oberlin College archives, Oberlin, Ohio

Boyd B. Stutler database (see primary documents)

Henry A. Wise executive papers, Library of Virginia, Richmond

Index

Page numbers in italics refer to illustrations.

271